A GUIDE TO PRIVATE SCHOOLS

THE WASHINGTON, DC, NORTHERN VIRGINIA, AND MARYLAND EDITION

ANN DOLIN, M.ED.

iUniverse LLC
Bloomington

A Guide to Private Schools
The Washington, DC, Northern Virginia, and Maryland Edition

iUniverse books may be ordered through booksellers or by contacting:

iUniverse LLC
1663 Liberty Drive
Bloomington, IN 47403
www.iuniverse.com
1-800-Authors (1-800-288-4677)

ISBN: 978-1-4917-0651-0 (sc)
ISBN: 978-1-4917-0652-7 (ebk)

Printed in the United States of America

iUniverse rev. date: 10/24/2013

A GUIDE TO PRIVATE SCHOOLS

CONTENTS

To Alli and Nick –

A small return for all you've done

Preface

A PARENT ONCE SAID TO me, “Applying to a private school is a lot like dating. They check you out, you check them out, and then both sides decide if it’s a match.” How right this dad was! Just like a marriage, there’s a match to be made between your child and a prospective school. In fact, finding and ultimately committing to one school is one of the most important decisions you make as a parent. It can affect everything from your child’s eagerness to learn to his success in college. The process of finding this “soul mate” should be blissful, but that’s not usually the case. In fact, what should be a period of excitement can be wrought with sleepless nights, heart palpitations, and second guessing. What’s wrong with this picture? What’s causing such stress?

Let’s do the math. For the ninth grade, one prominent DC area school typically gets 200 applicants for about 30 spaces—15 boys and 15 girls. Another receives about 400 applications for 110 spots. This selectivity isn’t limited to high schools. Even in the primary grades, competition abounds. One local K-8 school reports receiving 63 applications for 16 kindergarten spots. Their figures aren’t unique. Simply put, many schools have more applicants than space available.

To top it off, we have many Type A parents in the Washington, DC area. I am one of them! Being a go-getter is generally a positive trait, especially in business, but it can be a problem when it comes to our kids. We have high expectations and want our kids to be successful as well, but sometimes our children aren’t wired the same way as we are. Differences in personalities can be intensified during the school search process. So often, the school a parent thinks is best might not be an ideal match for the child.

Even for the most prepared, the task of choosing a new school can seem overwhelming. How many schools should I visit? What distinguishes one school from the next? Which tests should my child take, and how do I prepare her? How much does a private school *really* cost? Is a co-ed or single-sex school best? And for some parents, the entire search starts with the most important question: Should I choose a private school or a public school? Using my years of experience in the education field as a teacher, tutor, consultant, and mother of two, I’ve written this book for every parent who wants to make the most informed decision possible.

My journey in education began in 1992 as an elementary teacher with Fairfax County Public Schools. Six years later, I made the difficult decision to leave my teaching position after the birth of my oldest son. Although I wanted to stay in education, I also wanted to be at home with my son. Part-time tutoring was a natural path. It was then that I started Educational Connections, Inc. In the beginning, I was my company's sole employee, tutoring one student at a time at my dining room table. Since then, the company has grown to employ over 200 instructors throughout the metropolitan Washington, DC area and our tutors have successfully worked with over 8,000 students, from kindergarten to college.

Lessons Learned

I learned a number of important lessons in Educational Connections' early years. First, even the brightest students sometimes need extra help as DC-area schools are competitive and school subjects can be challenging. We live in an area of the country that can be fast paced, stressful, and sometimes ruthless. On a daily basis, I taught children from various private schools and gained firsthand knowledge of each school's teaching methods and philosophies. I began to realize that what's contained in a brochure or on a website isn't necessarily indicative of what's taught in the classroom.

I've also learned valuable lessons from speaking to thousands of parents who have called our office to find the right tutor for their child. I noticed that a pattern emerged, especially for students in private school. Those with certain personality types and learning styles fit the mold of certain schools very well. Education consultants call this special match a "goodness of fit," meaning that the child really loved the school, was challenged academically, and developed meaningful friendships. In many instances, these students were also very involved within the school whether it was through sports, student government, or the drama program, for example.

On the other hand, some students were simply not a good fit for specific schools, and they struggled socially and academically (at times not challenged enough and sometimes challenged too much). In these cases, there was no goodness of fit. When this occurred, it wasn't problematic just for the child, but for the parents as well. I found that in many instances, parents desperately wanted their child to succeed at a particular school even though it wasn't truly the right place. This was particularly hard in families in which siblings went to the same school and the expectation was that all the kids would attend that school.

Finding a Fit

These days, I manage the day-to-day operations of Educational Connections, but perhaps my favorite part of my job is working directly with families who want help navigating the independent school world. As a consultant and professional member of the Independent Educational Consultants Association, I've had the opportunity to help many students and parents choose a school that will foster the child's academic, social, and emotional growth.

I've also visited about 70 schools in the Washington, DC area. Touring a variety of schools that serve different types of students is eye-opening. I've learned important information from each visit, especially when I've had the chance to speak directly to admission directors and current students. Students always give uncensored information that's impossible to get anywhere else. I appreciate and love their candor. And of course, the admission professional's honesty and unique perspective helps to paint a complete picture of the institution.

It didn't take long before I built a profile of a good fit for each school. This goodness of fit had very little to do with the things that we often think of when we hear the words "private school." It's not about the campus, the degrees teachers hold, the latest technology, or how many trophies the sports teams have won. It's more about students' personalities, interests, and work habits and how these factors gel with the mission of the school.

Over the years, this information has helped me assist many families looking for the right school match. The students with whom I've worked have been diverse in their ages, abilities, motivation levels, and personalities. Their parents have been very different as well. Many came to me with preconceived notions of schools they thought would be perfect for their child. In some cases, they were right on, but in other cases, they were completely off. Why? Because parents see their child subjectively, not objectively. They tend to have a narrow view of the schools they think would be appropriate for their child. Sometimes, having an outside person who does not have an emotional history with the child to provide feedback is highly beneficial. It allows parents to see their child in ways they wouldn't have before. When this occurs, parents are willing to look at schools they didn't previously consider.

The bottom line is that there really is a school in the DC area for every type of learner. It just might not be the school the parent initially considered and, quite frankly, it may not be a private (also called independent) school. There are many fantastic public schools in our area that have a culture of achievement and produce excellent, well-rounded students. For some families, their local public school is an ideal option.

As a former public school teacher, I am a firm believer in the public school system, but I am also well aware of its limitations. Some students are a natural fit for their local school, whereas others need more personalized attention. I've seen it firsthand on both a personal and professional level. My oldest son is thriving in an independent school and my youngest son is perfectly happy in his public school.

Whether looking at a public or independent school, parents should consider goodness of fit. Success is far more likely to occur when a child's temperament, motivation, and ability allow him to master demands and expectations. Simply put, when there's synergy between the child's personality and school environment, good things happen. The problem is that some well-meaning parents are often led by "name brand" recognition instead of by the school that will most thoroughly meet their child's needs. Finding the right place can be complicated and takes work, but my hope is that this book will make the process much easier for you.

A Toolkit at Your Fingertips

Inside this book you will find a complete toolkit to assist you with choosing the right school for your child. The following chapters tackle the most vital facets of private education, from applying to the right schools to actually getting accepted. You'll see the entire admission timeline from start to finish (and even what to do if you're late to the game) and the costs of private schooling, including financial aid options that were practically unheard of a generation ago. This guide will cover testing, interviews, and school visits, with professional advice on how to prepare for each. Lastly, you'll learn about the types of things school admission boards are looking for when they review your child's application.

The last section of this book contains in-depth profiles of almost 100 private schools in the DC metro area divided by region (Maryland, DC, and Virginia). It includes the entire range of educational experiences from competitive, nationally-recognized schools like Sidwell Friends to schools specifically designed to help those with learning disabilities, such as Oakwood. Each school's profile contains a look at its curriculum, fine arts programs, sports offerings, student life, campus, learning support, and schools attended by graduates.

There's no doubt that the school search process can seem tedious and draining at times, but I can promise you that it's worth it. There's no better feeling than seeing your child thrive in his or her new school environment.

Private vs. Independent Schools—What's the Difference?

To start, let's examine the terms "private" and "independent," which are often used interchangeably when we think of schools outside of the public realm. It's important to understand the difference. A private school refers to any learning institution that does not receive public funding from its state government. Independent schools are private schools that are overseen by a board of governors or trustees. In this book, we'll frequently use the term independent because it's the more commonly used term by the schools themselves. Although these two terms are similar, schools that fall into either or both categories are not all the same. Within the private school world, there are several subcategories:

Independent Private Schools: All independent schools are under the umbrella of private schools. They have a board of governors or trustees that is truly independent of any other organization, whereas a different private school can technically be governed by any outside entity, from nonprofit organizations to churches to for-profit corporations. The important distinction is that while both are non-public, independent schools have stricter rules for governance. Tuition is higher as well. Schools in this category have larger endowments and many have impressive facilities, from state-of-the-art science labs to stadium football fields. They may or may not have a religious affiliation. For a thorough list of 82 independent schools in the DC metro area that make up the association called Independent Education, visit www.independenteducation.org.

When you boil it down even more, there are many subcategories within independent schools.

Independent Catholic Holy Order Schools: These schools are also independent, but they are run by an order of the Catholic Church, such as Jesuits. They do not have to follow strict curriculum guidelines set forth by the Catholic Church. They have the highest level of autonomy. Because they do not receive funding from the local diocese, their tuition is higher than Catholic diocesan schools. Class sizes are smaller, too.

***Catholic Diocesan Schools*: These schools are linked directly to a Catholic diocese and can offer lower tuition for members of the diocese. Even without a reduced fee, these parochial schools have a much lower price tag than independent schools. One drawback is that the class sizes are typically larger. These schools are not governed by a board of directors—they follow regulations created by the diocese or bishop. Catholic diocesan schools are the most common type of Catholic school.

***Non-Catholic Religious Schools*:** There are other religious schools, ranging from Episcopalian to Jewish to non-denominational Christian, which are tied to their local church or other house of worship. These schools follow their own guidelines and some receive funding from their affiliated religious institution.

***All-Boys Schools*:** These are schools that serve only boys, typically beginning in the third or fourth grade. Most faculty and coaches are males as well.

***All-Girls Schools*:** Just as the name states, these schools serve only girls, also typically beginning in third or fourth grade.

***Learning Difference Schools*:** There are varying degrees of support services to serve a wide range of students, from those with severe learning disabilities to those with very mild issues who simply require a few accommodations. According to Rich Weinfeld and Jennifer Fisher of Weinfeld Education Group, schools can be categorized into distinct groups. "The first category of schools serves students with significant special needs. These schools are certified by the state and receive state funding. When the local school district is unable to educate the child, they may pay for an alternative placement. Many of these schools also have a good amount of private pay students. Schools such as Chelsea and Kingsbury are in this category. The second category of schools has chosen not to receive funding. As with the other schools, they too have small classes, trained staff, and learning specialists who work with students and consult with teachers. These schools serve bright students who need some remediation and accommodations. Siena, Commonwealth, and Nora School are examples within this group."

Finally, there are schools that support students with very mild learning issues, but the majority of their students do not have a learning disability or an ADHD diagnosis. These schools primarily serve the general student population; however, they employ learning specialists to work with those who need support. Nonetheless, students are expected to keep up with the general curriculum. This type of support is very typical in even the most exacting schools.

International Schools: These schools seek to provide students with an international experience and to prepare them for future schooling overseas. For younger students, these schools provide a global perspective and an emphasis on foreign language and cultures. Older students are prepared specifically for the option of attending a university outside of the United States by means of the International Baccalaureate program.

Boarding Schools: At boarding schools, students live on campus in dormitories, similar to college. Most faculty members also live on campus and there is a significant amount of structure in terms of oversight and planned activities. In our area, there are a handful of schools that have boarding options and one school, Episcopal, which serves only boarding students.

Certainly, there are a host of other categories, but this should give you a broad overview to get you started. It's my sincere hope that this guidebook will make your school search easier and enable your child to find the school of his or her dreams. I wish you all the best on your journey in education.

PART I

Is Private School Right For Your Family?

ARE INDEPENDENT SCHOOLS REALLY BETTER than public schools? That's a common question, especially in the suburbs of Washington, DC where the public school systems tend to be better than the national average. Many parents wonder, "Why choose independent when the school in my backyard is good and, better yet, free?" The answer is complicated. There is no one study that has found public to be better than independent or independent to be better than public, as a whole.

Education is complex and there are many variables to measure academic performance such as achievement in reading, writing, and math. There are other factors to consider such as SAT and ACT scores, college acceptances, personal well-being, and enthusiasm for learning. Additionally, independent schools do not gather the same data on student performance that public schools do and because they're not funded by a state or local government, they are not required to divulge any of their testing scores. In the end, comparing public schools to independent schools is tricky, sort of like comparing apples to oranges.

Furthermore, the debate is a contentious one. In our area with many educated professionals, it's hard to open up the dialogue without hearing strong and biased opinions one way or the other. As you may know, people aren't afraid to speak up on this topic. I had a client say to me, "I stopped telling people we're looking for a private school. The minute I mention a school's name, people have a story to tell. No one is shy about giving me their two cents. I feel like I have to defend my decision all the time, so now I say, 'We're exploring lots of options,' and leave it at that."

Perhaps one of the reasons residents of this area question whether an independent school is necessary is the cost—it's not cheap. Top day schools can run upwards of $30,000 per year, and that's for elementary school! Many high schools top off at $35,000. So essentially, without financial aid, a parent needs to earn $50,000 before taxes to privately educate just one child. The decision to go with the non-public option is a serious one that requires a tremendous amount of thought. In this section, you will find the reasons both for and against a private education. You'll also find details on the tuition costs involved and how financial aid plays a role in the decisions families make.

Chapter 1

Private vs. Public Schools

The debate over whether it's better to send a child to public or independent schools has been around for decades. Not surprisingly, public sentiment about both types of education runs deep. In a 2012 Gallup Work and Education Poll, 78% of Americans stated that children in independent schools receive an excellent or good education. Of those surveyed, 68% felt that students in parochial or church-related schools get a good or excellent education, but only 37% rated public schools in the same favorable manner. Interestingly, parents of school-aged children rate their own child's public school with a 75% satisfaction rate.

Those polled did not think highly of public schools as a whole but were quite happy with their own neighborhood school. Although there was a much higher rate of satisfaction with independent schools, it may also be the case that the media has a strong influence on public opinion. It is widely reported that American school children score significantly lower than those in other industrialized nations in basic academic skills. When parents hear those statistics over and over again in the news, their views can be influenced accordingly.

Nonetheless, I've found that parents living in areas with relatively good public school systems, especially those in Northern Virginia and Maryland, want to at least consider public education. In 2013, all ten of the top public high schools featured in the *U.S. News* ranking for the state of Virginia were located in Northern Virginia. At the top of the list were Thomas Jefferson High School for Science and Technology, Langley High School, and James Madison High School. In Maryland, seven of the top ten schools were located in Montgomery County. Leading the way was Winston Churchill High School followed by Walt Whitman and Poolesville. It's not just high schools that garner accolades. There are many high-performing elementary and middle schools in our area that produce highly educated students who feed into these secondary schools. With such impressive public options in the DC area, it is worth considering the public route.

For some students, charter schools are alternatives to traditional public schools. Within the Washington, DC city limits, approximately half of all public schools are charters. These institutions receive some public money, but usually less than the average public school. They generally have more flexibility with regard to teaching methodology and curriculum. Charter schools are free and attended by choice.

When a charter is at enrollment capacity, admission becomes lottery-based. Although the lottery system is open to all students, there is maneuvering that goes on behind the scenes when it comes to applying and getting into the best charter schools in the area. In recent years, some parents have opted to work with a consultant who specializes in navigating charter schools. Their goal is to better the likelihood of their students receiving a coveted spot in one of Washington's premier magnet or charter schools, such as DC Prep, Achievement Prep Academy, Thurgood Marshall Academy, or one of the KIPP academies.

Magnet schools are another type of public institution. These schools offer specialized instruction in an area such as mathematics, science, or applied technology. These schools are able to draw students from the surrounding area and have competitive entrance processes. Thomas Jefferson High School for Science and Technology (TJ) is a magnet school in Alexandria that consistently ranks first or second among public schools in the nation. Other magnet schools in the area include McKinley Technology High School in DC, and A. Mario Loiederman Middle School in Silver Spring.

Charter and magnet schools are an integral part of the education landscape in DC, but for the sake of brevity they are not included in this book.

The Matter of School and Class Size

About 10% of all students in America attend independent schools (about five million students in all). The main advantage of independent schools is that they consistently offer smaller class sizes. Public schools, on the other hand, in a crowded metro area like ours, can house classes of 30 or more. In the DC area, almost all of the independent schools we surveyed had class sizes of 8 to 22 students, with some going as low as 6 per class. In addition, it's not just small class size that's appealing, but also that there are more faculty members such as counselors, learning specialists, and college placement advisors.

Ultimately, class size does matter, and it matters a lot. Various research studies have shown that there is a positive correlation between a class size of fewer than 20 students and higher academic achievement. The effects are significant and long-lasting, especially when smaller class sizes are introduced in the earliest grades.

In general, an independent school also enrolls fewer students than a public school. According to the National Center for Education Statistics, independent schools are also less than half the overall size of public schools on average. At the elementary level, the difference may not be as pronounced. Most public elementary schools tend to house about 500 students, but as children grow older, their smaller, nurturing, neighborhood elementary schools feed into large middle and high schools. This is where the change in numbers occurs. At the high school level, some public schools top out at over 2,700 students, such as at Blair High School in Silver Spring, Maryland. Most high schools in the DC area have about 2,000 students in ninth through twelfth grade. There are outliers, however. George Mason High School in Falls Church only has 800 students and some alternative schools get as low as 600, such as H-B Woodlawn in Arlington, which covers grades six through twelve.

To many parents, the lure of an independent school goes far beyond academics. They see that their child has a greater opportunity to become a leader in a small environment. Whether it's starting a club or diving deeper into an academic subject, independent schools have more freedom to adapt their curriculum and allow students to drive their own studies. These leadership opportunities help students begin building college resumes early. Furthermore, opportunities for leadership can translate into confidence and real-world social and work experiences.

There is often more flexibility with extracurriculars and athletics in an independent school. With a smaller student pool, it's easier to make a sports team and still compete at a high level in independent and preparatory leagues. Most independent schools also have "no-cut" sports policies so that everyone is given the chance to play. Students who would not make their local public school team can enjoy the experience of competitive high school sports. Many have the chance to excel when they wouldn't make the cut in a pool of 2,000 students.

Advantages of Large Schools

Although a large school size may have drawbacks, it also has many advantages. A bigger student population supports more extracurriculars, from after-school clubs to sports. With more than twice as many students, it's much easier to start a computer club or field a hockey team.

Check out the after-school programs at any large high school and you'll find a plethora of opportunities.

A larger population means that students will almost always find a peer group that fits them. This is especially true for those who may not be part of a mainstream clique. These are the students who may feel more at ease in a larger school because they can make connections with others who are like them. When there are more kids to pick from, finding those with common beliefs and interests is easier.

In addition, there are often more academic offerings at larger schools, such as a greater number of college-level Advanced Placement (AP) or International Baccalaureate (IB) classes. For example, Bethesda-Chevy Chase High School (BCC) offers 20 AP courses, whereas some of the surrounding independents offer 10 AP classes. This is not to say that BCC is a better school; it is merely a reflection of the volume of students it serves.

As you're looking at schools, consider how easy it is for your student to get involved in clubs or academic programs. Will it be easy for your child to find an intimate group of friends? Will your child be challenged at the highest level if he's capable? And if he's struggling with a particular topic, will he get the extra help he needs? These are important questions. Parents want to ensure their child is more than just a number in a large class or school. Many feel that their child is less likely to get "lost in the shuffle" at an independent school.

A Distinct Culture and Focus for Each Family

Not only do schools offer different opportunities for activities in and outside the classroom, they also offer different cultures and values. Although there are variances in public schools, individuality is most pronounced in independent schools. Each independent school has its own set of guiding principles. For example, some schools highly value liberal, progressive education while others take a more conservative approach. You'll find some schools that value arts education almost as much as academics. While one path at an independent school is highly exacting, there are entire schools dedicated to helping students who need a lot of academic support along the way. Many independent schools have comprehensive programs committed to offering the right support structure for every kind of learner. These schools can offer everything from a demanding college prep curriculum to a more relaxed, stress-free approach, with a large safety net of academic support.

The variety of courses and extracurriculars offered by independent schools is significant. For instance, at The Barrie School, students can start taking equestrian at the age of four. At Washington Waldorf, handiwork like blacksmithing, woodworking, and bookbinding are offered as electives. At Ad Fontes Academy, students receive a traditional, "old school" Latin and classics-based education. Some schools shun technology, while at other schools every student receives an iPad or laptop. Families can pursue an International Baccalaureate education at the British School or Washington International, or they can get a straightforward, rigorous education at St. John's or Gonzaga.

There are also many non-traditional education models within the independent school world. At Emerson, for example, there are no extracurriculars offered at all. Students are given college-level instruction during block periods and are free to pursue athletics, the arts, and even lunch on their own time. The arts-focused education at The New School is so innovative, it may blaze the trail for arts education nationally. Further, there is a wealth of learning difference schools, from Commonwealth to Siena, which are specifically tailored to help students with various learning challenges.

In short, the variety of independent schools is seemingly limitless when you look at all of the options available. From traditional Catholic schools like Oakcrest and The Heights to schools that include gardening and farm work like Butler and Burgundy Farm, there is a fit for almost every student imaginable. As consumers, parents have the luxury of picking and choosing a school that aligns with their educational philosophy.

On the flip side, an independent school also has the luxury of being able to choose which families to bring in as part of its community. Families that are accepted generally value a strong education and are active in their children's lives. Since each school gets to handpick which families will be involved, you will generally find that students and parents are highly committed at an independent school. It's not to say that *all* students are buckled down and focused; it's just more likely to be the case when parents are investing a serious amount of money each year for their child's education.

Diversity

Nationally, public schools are generally more diverse (42% non-white), although independent schools are more diverse than you might think

(26% non-white). Independent schools have made an enormous effort to include students of different cultures, countries, and economic backgrounds. It's important to most schools to reflect the community in which they are located. Although independent schools have come a long way, there are parents who are concerned that these institutions are not a slice of America. They see value from a "real world" education where their child is working side-by-side with other students who come from many different backgrounds.

Diversity is an interesting topic when it comes to independent schools. Most schools strive to make their student body as diverse as possible. When visiting many of the schools listed in this book, I asked each admission representative the same question: "What sets your school apart?" The number one answer was "diversity."

School personnel are very cognizant of this issue and work diligently to include students of various backgrounds. Gone are the days of homogeneous classrooms with Caucasian children sitting at every desk. At some schools in our area, you'll find that 45% of the student body is of color, but typically, the number hovers around 25% at most schools. The crux of the issue is that diversity goes far beyond skin color or the child's country of origin. Schools are invested in teaching children to be accepting and tolerant of differing views. If diversity is important to you, look not only at the statistics, but at whether the school lives and breathes inclusiveness.

Similarly, parents often express concern about putting their child in what some may view as an "elitist" environment. I have several clients who worry that a sense of entitlement is part of the culture at many private day schools in the area. This may be the case at some schools, but, for example, 16-year-olds driving BMWs also exist at area public schools. A sense of entitlement is not unique to independent institutions. My observation has been that if the family is grounded, the kids tend not to be as influenced by materialism as their less-grounded peers.

Teachers Make All the Difference

One factor that makes a tremendous difference in a child's education is the quality of teaching. The National Center for Education Statistics highlights several advantages that public schools offer. For one, teachers are paid more and are more highly trained, on average. In 2011-2012, the average annual base salary of full-time public school teachers at $53,230 was higher than the average for full-time independent school teachers at $39,690. Teachers in the public sector are also more likely to have a master's degree and have pursued more in-service study hours prior to taking their teaching job. Thirty-eight percent of teachers have a master's degree or higher in independent schools, whereas 52% hold advanced degrees in public schools. Furthermore, public schools require teachers to be certified, which means that they must have a teacher's certification license. Independent schools are not bound by this regulation and are free to hire non-certified teachers.

Remember, there are many different types of private schools. Those that are governed by a board of directors tend to have high standards and their pay scale reflects these expectations. On average, these teachers make $52,779 per year. Although not quite as high as public school teachers, the pay is significantly greater than the pay of instructors at smaller schools or at those that are not overseen by a governing board. Keep in mind that some independents have endowments to pay teachers higher salaries while other schools may not have the funds to do so.

Another factor to consider is how red tape, district regulations, and teacher unions can impact the classroom. In the public school system, it's nearly impossible to fire a bad teacher. For example, in one local school district, only 0.03% of teachers were actually let go during the 2011-2012 school year. Quite often, the principal realizes the problem and wants the teacher gone but does not have the authority to get him or her out the door. This is not the case in an independent school where there is little red tape when a change needs to be made. Teachers can be asked to leave during or at the end of the school year. From time to time, every school is going to make hiring mistakes, but when incompetence affects children, poor teachers must be removed quickly.

While there are pros and cons to the staffing procedures at public and independent schools, ultimately, the quality of teachers must be looked at on a school-by-school basis.

The Importance of Academic Rigor and Safety Nets

One of the most common fears parents have is that their child is not being appropriately challenged or supported, and this can happen at any institution. Some parents feel that the academic bar is set too low in their child's current school. They are of the opinion that teachers "teach to the middle," meaning that they are providing instruction based on average ability. This approach allows teachers to reach the greatest number of students, but it leaves out those who are ready to excel. Parents of these students are sometimes concerned that their child isn't being pushed or challenged enough. Although some students have the drive to rise to the top of their class, others may become bored and aren't so inclined. These are the students who can get by with little effort and still earn top grades. If you're worried that your child is not being challenged even after you have addressed the situation with your child's current teacher and administration, it's probably the case that one of the more academically competitive schools in the area might be a better match.

There are other parents who have experienced the flip side of this coin. Although their children are very competent, they may need a little extra help in a particular subject area, such as math or writing. Still, other students don't necessarily need subject help, but they struggle to stay organized, plan ahead, and study effectively. They need a "safety net." In large schools with comparable class sizes, reaching various levels of student capability is tricky. Teachers report that they can't possibly meet the needs of every student in the class when there are thirty (or more) to educate.

With so many students to worry about in the public school system, learning differences can go unnoticed for many years, in some cases. Certainly, it's not that our area public school system isn't capable or doesn't care; it's simply that there are a tremendous number of students to educate. The system only helps the neediest even though many more are struggling. Most independent schools have greater staffing to provide a safety net. Not all students learn in the same way, and many independent schools understand and are committed to providing the right care for all different kinds of learners.

The academic safety nets at some independent schools are extensive. While not all are equipped to help students with specific learning needs, many have complete learning centers with full-time specialists on staff. Schools can assist with everything from specialized instruction for dyslexia and ADHD to just a little extra help in math or any other subject. Due to the close relationships between faculty and students in the independent school system, problems are often caught and diagnosed faster than in a public setting.

Learning support is one of the reasons many parents make the switch to an independent school. Parents who wouldn't have considered an independent school in the past now do because the public school system simply doesn't have the budget or the manpower to help every different kind of learner. For other students with a learning disability or ADHD, a specialized school can do even more than simply provide a safety net.

Schools like the Lab School and McLean School have stepped in to fill the gap by providing tailored approaches to students of all kinds.

Freedom from Outside Micromanagement

Another key difference is that most independent schools are free to develop their own programs of study, based on their own unique student population. In addition, they can measure students' growth and academic progress in their own way, not just by using standardized tests and scantron forms. Some schools use work samples they save into a portfolio to see how a student has improved throughout the school year. Others will create their own end-of-year tests; however, the majority of schools will also use some form of national standardized testing to compare their students to others.

The problem is that too much testing in the form of multiple choice tests is not good for kids. I am not aware of a single independent school that formally assesses students as much as our local public schools. While it's true that public school testing makes it easier to compare one school to another in the same district and state, any parent in the area can tell you that "teaching to the test" has squeezed a lot of creativity out of the classroom. In fact, the most common complaint received by the Fairfax County Public Schools school board over the last few years was about the amount of standardized testing. Parents have had enough and, quite frankly, teachers have as well. Teachers lament that students are primarily invested in learning material only because it's on a standardized test. When a student's first question is, "Will this be on the test?" we've got a problem.

In most districts, the last few months of the school year are dedicated to teaching students how to pass the Maryland School Assessments (MSA), Standards of Learning (SOL), or District of Columbia Comprehensive Assessment System (DC CAS). Simply put, students are reviewing material that will be found on the test and practicing multiple choice strategies. Furthermore, if a subject isn't tested as thoroughly as other areas, such as fourth-grade science, you'll see classes spending the minimum amount of time on it, even if the teacher is passionate about the subject or thinks it's meaningful to her group of students.

Current standardized testing is a result of the Bush-era No Child Left Behind Act. Although there were some good things to come out of the legislation, most educators and parents believe that the over-reliance on tests was certainly not one of them. It is my belief that too much teaching to the test leads to kids becoming disengaged in learning.

The Lowdown on Academic Achievement

One topic in the public vs. independent debate seems to draw the most concern from parents: academic achievement. You would think such an issue would be straightforward, but it isn't. The truth is education experts can't seem to agree on anything and the research generated about public vs. independent schools is contradictory at best. If you're looking for a study to concur with a particular view, I guarantee you can find it.

Looking at the statistics by simply comparing a national sample of students attending independent schools to those attending public schools, you'll find that those at independent institutions are performing at a higher academic level. A ten-year study by the National Assessment of Educational found that, in fourth grade, independent school students scored 14.8 points higher in reading and 7.8 points higher in math. In eighth grade, independent school students scored 18.1 points higher in reading and 12.3 points higher in math. However, when you consider socioeconomic factors such as ethnicity and income, these discrepancies become much less pronounced, to the point that in math, there is no significant difference between public and independent school achievement test scores.

The Center on Education Policy avows that independent school students do not outperform those in public school. Jack Jennings, the organization's president, stated that, "Contrary to popular belief, we can find no evidence that private schools actually increase student performance. Instead, it appears that private schools simply have higher percentages of students who would perform well in any environment based on their previous performance and background."

Opponents of the center's claim point out that the center does not acknowledge the findings related to the most widely used test of critical thinking and developed abilities—the SAT. The SAT is an aptitude test that assesses critical thinking and logical reasoning, whereas many achievement tests simply consist of contextual material students have covered and committed to memory in a particular year. Data from the study demonstrated that, while controlling for socioeconomic factors, students in independent schools outperform their public school peers on the SAT.

Furthermore, independent schools tend to do a better job at teaching writing, a skill that is difficult to objectively assess. Most independent schools incorporate a focus on writing across the curriculum, not just in English class. The lack of emphasis on state standardized testing allows independent schools to spend more time focusing on writing and critical thinking.

Comparing academic achievement at independent and public schools is a tricky task. Depending on the statistics and variables that you consider, you can find data to support many beliefs. Ultimately, whether you choose public or independent, the decision should be a unique one based on the personality and abilities of your child.

College Counseling

In many public schools, counselors are responsible for overseeing 300 students. They help with everything from scheduling classes, to mediating peer conflicts, to writing college recommendations. It's a lot to handle for any one person and virtually impossible for them to provide teens with enough advice in choosing the right school. In fact, many public school parents pay out-of-pocket for a college counselor in private practice. This is a growing industry, and for good reason.

In independent schools, college counseling is its own unique department. The attention each individual student receives is significant. Most counselors manage between 30 and 50 students. The counselor is with the student through the entire college application process, sometimes beginning with course selection in ninth grade. These rich relationships between students, families, faculty, and staff lead to a more personalized education and often more thoughtful and convincing recommendations when it's time to graduate.

For some parents, such as Michelle Rice, it is the college advisory program that sealed the deal. As she searched for an independent high school for her rising freshman, Lily, and a sixth-grade slot for her younger daughter, Olivia, there were many factors that helped her to make the decision to move from their public schools. "The whole college advisory program is really phenomenal. We are grateful to have professionals looking out for her every step of the way."

College Acceptances

While college counseling can make a difference in a student's acceptance to his or her top-choice university, the student's experience over all four high school years has a greater impact. Peter Sturtevant is the director of the School Counseling Group in Washington, DC. Over the years, he and his staff have counseled thousands of families searching for day and boarding schools and colleges. According to Peter, "It is true that most independent schools offer comprehensive college admissions counseling as part of the educational package, a service not available at most public schools, where guidance offices are overburdened with multiple tasks beyond supporting seniors in the college process. But the college process at independent schools is most influenced by the highly supportive academic culture and relative intimacy. Because of smaller student-teacher ratios, many students thrive in ways not possible for them in larger, more impersonal settings. The extra contact and encouragement allows students to develop more skills, more confidence, and to take more risks, which pays off during college admissions."

Competition is Intense Everywhere

Certainly, there are many highly qualified candidates coming out of the top independent schools in the area, and they are all vying for a spot in the college of their choice. Some parents believe that this puts students at a disadvantage because colleges may only take a certain number of students from a given high school. With many impressive students to choose from, it's difficult for even the most talented students to stand out.

In reality, competition is fierce wherever you go, whether it is an independent or public school. Although parents feel that their child has a better chance to rise to the top of their local public school, this isn't necessarily the case. Consider the fact that at James Madison High School in Vienna, which is similar to many high-performing public schools in Virginia and Maryland, 25% of seniors graduate with at least a 4.0 GPA. In fact, individual names of top performers are no longer called out at the commencement ceremony; there are simply too many to read aloud.

Perhaps one of the most common questions on parents' minds is, "Will an independent school education get my child into a better college?" The answer is, "It depends." Schools with a proven track record of academic excellence and the reputation to go with it can have exceptional results. Colleges and universities (colleges are typically smaller and serve undergraduates while universities tend to be larger and have extensive post-graduate programs) are well aware of the top schools' academic programs and they understand that a B at a school well known for challenging academics may be similar to an A elsewhere. Colleges will pull from elite schools because they have a history of sending well-prepared students.

Only Thomas Jefferson High School for Science and Technology (TJ) competes with the top independent schools in the area when it comes to acceptances into the Ivy League. By far the strongest public school in the area, TJ graduates regularly attend MIT, Carnegie Mellon, and the Ivies.

Within independent schools, you will find that some have a synergy with certain colleges and universities. For example, Georgetown Prep in Potomac regularly sends more young men to Georgetown University than any other independent school in the United States. And in Virginia, Potomac School's graduates matriculate heavily to the University of Virginia.

Although independent schools send more students to highly selective colleges and universities, most professionals will tell you that the school doesn't have nearly as much impact on admission as does the candidate. In the end, it all comes down to the student's academic ability, work ethic, and outside interests.

The Connection Between School Choice and College Admissions

Although students at independent schools are more likely to attend a top-tier college, the truth is that the school may not be a differentiating factor. Luke Chung is a local entrepreneur who owns a well-established software company. He volunteers his time by serving on the Business and Community Advisory Council to the Fairfax County Superintendent, and he represents the School Board on the county's IT Policy Advisory Committee. He is also an interviewer for students in the area applying to his alma mater, Harvard. Many highly selective universities have similar programs, since it's virtually impossible for the admission team located on campus to meet with each applicant.

Over the years, Luke has interviewed hundreds of students and understands which qualities are important for acceptance. "Harvard admits about 2,000 students a year. There are more than 2,000 high schools in the country, which means they can't accept every valedictorian. The self-selected candidate pool is extremely strong and the admission office says more than 90% of the candidates are academically qualified, meaning they could be admitted and graduate.

"It's important for students to differentiate themselves beyond great grades, coursework, and test scores. Successful applicants have credentials way beyond academics. Harvard seeks distinction at regional, state, and ideally national levels, whether it's sports, music, science, math, chess, art, writing, performing, business, community service, etc. Awesome teacher recommendations are also important. Students essentially need 'best ever taught' recommendations. Harvard wants to see achievement with passion, while doing great academically. They want students who are not only educated but able to change the world after they graduate.

"What's important when I talk to kids and parents is that they understand it's of no benefit to get into a school that's too difficult for them. No student will do well when they are stuck in the bottom 10%. That's terrible for morale and self-esteem, and probably leads to worse post-graduation outcomes than if they attended a better-suited school for them." Although Luke is referring to a good college match, the same is certainly true for K-12 schools. When considering a school for your child, be sure it's one in which your child will thrive, not one where he will struggle to keep up day in and day out.

The list of schools attended by graduates should not be the primary factor influencing your decision, whether you're deciding between independent and public school or simply which independent school is best for your child. There are too many other important variables, and one of them is quality of life. Ask yourself, "Will my child be successful?" and just as important, "Will she be happy at this school? Will my child have a balanced life or will the academics be all-consuming? Are tutors and other professionals going to have to support her just to maintain average grades?" If the answer to the last question is "yes," it's best to sit back and rethink things. The process of a good education is more important than the product it achieves. If school feels arduous, your child will not be happy and probably won't perform at her best. When this occurs, it won't matter how prestigious the school, she will not stand out among other applicants.

Location Matters When It Comes to Public Schools

Another important consideration that influences a parent's decision to stay with their public school is the district in which the family lives. Location matters when choosing between public and independent. In Maryland, schools in the Chevy Chase area, for example, boast higher scores than in Rockville. In DC, schools in the Northwest area of the District are stronger than in Southwest. In Virginia, public schools in the Arlington area have higher test scores than schools in Alexandria. Where your home is located is going to be a significant deciding factor in whether to choose independent or public.

How do you know if your local base school is a good option or not? One way to make this determination is to look at the data. The easiest marker is test scores. Look at average SAT scores, MSA scores (Maryland), SOL scores (Virginia), and Advanced Placement (AP) offerings as a starting point. I especially like the *Washington Post*'s education columnist Jay Matthews's Challenge Index. It's a yearly ranking of the top public high schools in the United States determined by the availability of AP and IB classes and the number of graduating students. You can find more information on the Challenge Index on the *Washington Post*'s website.

For websites that allow you to compare local schools, try www.greatschools.org or www.schooldigger.com. You can sort by grade, type of test, and subject scores. Standardized tests are the easiest way to compare public schools to each other, and any extra time you spend on research will pay off in your search.

Closer to home, the Maryland Department of Education has an outstanding website to help parents review its 24 school systems. Here you'll find information on the Maryland School Assessment (MSA), High School Assessment (HSA), and demographic and enrollment facts. By far, this website is the easiest to use when considering public schools in the close-in suburbs of Montgomery County. Visit www.marylandpublicschools.org/MSDE/schoolsystems.

If you live in or around Fairfax County, Virginia, check out Marina Brito's website, www.homebyschool.com. Although it's primarily focused on helping families choose a public school when they are moving to the area, I've found great value in using it to gather data on various schools. The Northern Virginia school systems, especially Fairfax County (the nation's 11th largest), do not do a good job of putting all their data (state test scores, ACT and SAT scores) into one place. Instead, parents are left to sift through individual school websites. Although other websites are a good resource, Marina's site is unbiased and relies on the data.

Beyond the Data

Although numbers are helpful, take them with a grain of salt. Too many parents make the mistake of deciding on a school based on test scores alone, but data doesn't tell the whole story. You will want to get feedback from those in the trenches. You will want to talk to your friends and neighbors about local public schools. Open up the dialogue with many people with different types of children. Seek out a family with a high achieving child, one that might have a child with special needs, or another with a fairly average student—although many won't admit to that! Get many viewpoints from different types of parents. At the same time, understand that when it comes to education, people have very strong opinions and aren't afraid to voice them. It may be that their experience is an outlier and is not indicative of what life is really like at that particular place. That's why it's important to hear from lots of people to understand the overarching opinion.

I also recommend that parents visit their local school. Arrange for a meeting or tour while the students are in session. Don't be quick to rule out the public school option; many offer programs that might be a match for your child.

Beyond academics is your child's social and emotional well-being. When considering a public school, realize that your child may have connections to his or her community that go far beyond academics. It's important to listen to your child, especially if he or she is older. I've worked with many parents who feel a change is necessary, especially in the high school years, yet their child doesn't buy into the move. These are the kids who sit across from me in my office with tears flowing down their cheeks, upset because they don't think their parents listen to them. When the move from public to independent is thrust upon a child, most students end up enjoying their new school, but some are resentful. When considering a switch, have a heart-to-heart discussion with your child so that he or she is a part of the decision-making process.

An Independent School is Not Right for Everyone

Keep in mind that there are many students who thrive in a large school environment. They love the big sports programs and don't feel lost in the crowd. These are the kids who will ask their teachers for help if they need it. They are the ones who are self-motivated and can easily navigate a large school. When students are doing well academically and socially, they are good candidates to stay put.

If finances are an issue and you find yourself scraping together funds to afford a particular school, consider sticking with the public system and supporting your child with tutors, other professionals, or local activities. Sometimes parents find that they are better off hiring tutors for enrichment to get ahead or remediation to catch up, rather than paying a tuition bill they really cannot afford. Others have found that they can get a similar experience of a special art program at an independent school by paying for outside sculpting, drama, or painting lessons.

The public option also allows kids to stay with other neighborhood students. For some, the socialization aspect of riding the bus and hanging out with friends in the neighborhood who all attend the same school is attractive.

There are many outstanding offerings in the public school system. For example, Fairfax County has a fantastic Advanced Academics Program (AAP), which was formerly called the Gifted and Talented Program. Children in elementary school and middle school receive accelerated instruction by highly qualified teachers. It's hard to go wrong in this program. There are also some students who don't qualify for AAP, but are highly motivated and will advocate for themselves. If their teacher assigns a two-paragraph essay, these are the kids who will write three paragraphs. These are the students who will raise their hands to ask questions or meet with their teacher after school to get extra help. In other words, they take advantage of every learning opportunity and tend to do well in the public system.

But how about the child who is very bright yet bored in class because the general education material isn't interesting or challenging enough? Or what about the student who is content doing a minimal amount of work? When asked to write two paragraphs, that's exactly what he'll do and no more. These are the students who are perfectly fine sitting in the back of the room, not engaging in instruction unless called upon. They need a push to get engaged and produce high-quality work. Frankly, this is not likely to happen in a class of 25 or 30 kids. It's very hard for a teacher to meet every student's specific learning style and needs in a large classroom. Individualization and engagement is far more likely to happen in a smaller classroom. I do believe that students are more likely to realize their potential in smaller schools with low student-to-teacher ratios and various opportunities for leadership.

Certainly there is evidence for and against an independent school education. My personal opinion is that there is no right answer as a whole. The decision must be made with the individual child's personality and needs in mind. I live in Fairfax County where the public schools are arguably some of the best in the nation, yet I made the decision to send my oldest son to an independent school. It took time to sort out the pros and cons, but it ultimately came down to engagement. Where would he be inspired most? Once he, my husband, and I answered that question, the decision was easy.

The Greatest Predictors of College Success (Hint: They Are Not GPA or SAT Scores)

In the end, it's important to remember that there are factors other than scores on a report card or on the SAT or ACT that best predict college success. In fact, these predictors are things that are usually not discussed, but they're essential for all parents to know. Even if you have a young child and you're simply searching for a preschool, don't skip this section. Here's what parents should know and how this information came about:

In 2009, Gallup, Inc. launched the Gallup Student Poll based on their research into three factors shown to correlate with student outcomes. These factors were also shown to be malleable, meaning that given the right environment, such as school setting, outcomes could change for the better or worse. What are these powerful keys to success? They are hope for the future, engagement in the classroom, and general well-being.

You may be wondering, "What in the world does this have to do with selecting an independent school?" Plenty! The issue of school engagement, which accounts for one-third of a student's success, is a huge factor. Engagement, which is defined by "involvement in and enthusiasm for school," can make or break a student.

Gallup's groundbreaking 2012 poll of over 500,000 public school students found that with every year of schooling, engagement drops. In elementary school, eight out of ten students are considered engaged. By middle school, the number drops to six in ten, and alarmingly, by the freshman year in high school, it's four in ten. According to Gallup Education Executive Director Brandon Busteed, "The drop in student engagement for each year students are in school is our monumental, collective national failure. Imagine what our economy would look like today if nearly eight in ten high school graduates were engaged." He cites two possible reasons for poor engagement, including "our overzealous focus on standardized testing and our lack of experiential and project-based learning pathways." Simply put, when teachers must teach to the test, students become disengaged. Furthermore, when learning is monotonous and lecture-based, students pull back even more.

In visiting many schools throughout the area, I've found that some schools do a better job of engaging kids in learning than others. When you tour schools, be sure to observe classes in action. If you find that students are engaged in discussion with their peers, working in groups, and attentive to their teacher, that's a good thing. If you walk from class to class and find that students are sitting in rows and the teacher is lecturing as the sole distributor of information, that environment may not be rewarding for your child. Later in the book, you will find specific engagement criteria to watch for when you visit schools.

CHAPTER 2

The Cost of a Private Education

FOR MANY FAMILIES, INDEPENDENT SCHOOLS seem financially unreachable. However, there are more aid structures in place than ever before to help pay for a student's education. In fact, the 82 schools that are a part of the Independent Education Association awarded over $116 million in aid during the 2012-2013 school year. That's not a small number. The bottom line is that aid is available for financially deserving families. In this section, I will cover what to expect when looking at independent school tuition as well as how to navigate the waters of financial aid and scholarships.

Tuition

The national median twelfth-grade tuition at independent schools is $16,970 per year, but locally, the average independent school runs $24,167. It's typically lower for church-based schools ($13,316). But unless the school can offer full tuition assistance (and a few can), public school can't be beat for cost.

In general, the least expensive options are religious schools, but by no means do these schools offer a poor education. Many small Christian schools make it their mission to offer tuition as low as possible so that no one is deprived of the religious education they desire. Some schools offer tuition as low as $10,400 (Trinity Christian School) before financial aid is factored in.

By far the least expensive option is available for members of a Catholic diocese. The Catholic Church will help pay for tuition with its regional funds. The rates are higher for those who are non-Catholic or not a member of a parish, similar to how state universities treat out-of-state students. Average tuition for diocese members is a low $6,668 in elementary school, and $13,448 for secondary school.

The more expensive independent schools can reach upwards of $35,000 or higher, with extra fees for those with a boarding option. Most yearly tuition payments fall into the $20,000 range. Even the priciest of schools do not want to preclude students based on finances alone, and they boast large financial aid budgets to help those in need.

The reality is that since independent schools do not receive state funding from taxes, they have to rely on tuition, private grants, and fundraising as sources of income. Some schools will offer multi-sibling discounts and most give the option of a payment plan so that a lump sum does not have to be paid all at once. Schools are very willing to have honest conversations about finances and, when possible, arrangements can be made to best suit your needs.

With the exception of a few for-profit schools, independent institutions are not run like businesses. "Profits" are usually invested directly into the student body, the faculty, and the development of new facilities. Well-established schools will use surplus funds to bolster the endowment, but for the most part, independent schools are focused on providing the best education they possibly can and serving their families faithfully.

Other Fees

Some common questions parents ask are the following: does tuition include hot lunch, books, uniforms, fees for extracurriculars, fees for technology (laptops, iPads), transportation? Transportation in particular can run a few thousand dollars, so make sure you know up front what the school expects of its families. Some schools, such as Nysmith, offer their tuition at face value with no other costs added, but others will require you to pay out of pocket for additional services.

Beyond these fees is the unwritten expectation that every family will contribute to the school's annual fund. A contribution is the norm, not the exception. I remember my first exposure to this unwritten rule when my youngest son attended preschool at Green Hedges School in Vienna, Virginia. On top of the annual tuition, which at the time was in the low teens, we were expected to give to the school's building fund, silent auction, and a number of other fundraisers. In total, we contributed almost $2,000 in donations by the end of the year.

Many parents are turned off by this expected contribution, but they shouldn't be. There's a reason schools request donations from their current families and alumni. It takes a serious amount of money to run a school and independents are not supported by tax dollars or religious organizations. Tuition covers approximately 75% of the funds needed to operate a school; the rest is generated through fundraising, an annual appeal, and interest earned from the money set aside in the endowment fund. Schools are in the business of educating students to the best of their ability and to do so, money is needed for cutting-edge technology, teachers' salaries, and building renovations. Discerning parents want and expect great teachers and state-of-the-art facilities.

Financial Aid by the Numbers

Financial aid has also grown tremendously in the past decade. On average, independent schools dedicate 12% of their overall budget to supporting families through financial aid. With more assistance available than ever before, it's important to understand the process if aid is a necessary component of your school search. Not all schools are able to offer it, but those that do are very upfront about what they can realistically provide. Some schools offer a greater amount of money, such as $10,000 per year. Others will grant smaller awards, such as $2,000 per year, but give them out to a greater number of students. It's appropriate to ask schools about their average package amount, but a student's specific allotment of aid will not be known until decision letters are sent out in March.

Most financial aid is needs-based, which usually means the tuition cost is looked at as a percentage of your total income. Certainly, families with lower means will be the first priority, but more and more schools across the country are reporting a huge increase in financial aid requests from parents earning more than $150,000 per year. Overall, tuition costs went up 4% in 2012 over 2011, and since 1998 tuition at most private schools has increased 5% to 8% annually. Families that could have afforded a $25,000 school a few years ago now need aid to keep their child there.

How Financial Aid Works

Be aware that most financial aid is awarded on a year-to-year basis, and there may be no guarantee of assistance down the line. Any concerns should be worked out before enrollment, and schools will appreciate your open communication and professionalism.

The good news is that the need for financial aid is not taken into consideration during the admission process. Students are accepted, waitlisted, or denied based on the strength of their application. Financial aid is a separate consideration. A student is not denied admittance because he or she needs help with the costs; however, it is common for students to decline enrollment if the aid package isn't significant enough or within the family's means.

Financial aid is expected and normal for many independent school students. Even in the top schools in the DC metro area, normally 20-25% of the student body receives aid of some kind. Nationally, the average financial award, according to the National Association of Independent Schools (NAIS), is $2,772 for day school and $7,744 for boarding school. There are also merit scholarships available at some schools. This kind of assistance depends on achieving high grades or possessing a particular talent. Always ask if there are additional scholarships available in addition to traditional financial aid awards. Bank loans are also possible under the right circumstances, but if your finances are tight, don't give up until you've exhausted your options within the financial aid system—you'll be surprised at how much a school is willing to help.

Financial Aid Forms

The financial aid application itself is almost always submitted at the same time as the application for enrollment. The most popular financial aid form used by schools is the School and Student Services (SSS) form provided through the NAIS, which has over 1,400 member schools. Some schools use other processes and other forms, such as the Private School Aid Service (PSAS), Financial Aid for School Tuition (FAST), and Tuition Aid Data Services (TADS), but all follow a similar format and will ask for the same financial information.

The core of the SSS form is a Parent Financial Statement (PFS) that is submitted electronically. The PFS is considered the "common application" for financial aid since it's used by so many schools, similar to the common application for undergraduate study, which covers nearly 500 universities and colleges. The PFS gathers in one place relevant financial information regarding income, expenses, family size, tax and business information, and assets. Once the PFS is completed, the form is sent only to the schools that you have selected. Schools use your PFS as a starting point in calculating financial aid awards. Many schools will want additional forms filled out to support their decision.

Apply Early

Financial aid directors at schools around the area encourage parents to be well aware of deadlines. Some families are not conscious of cut-off dates or don't adhere to them. Schools try to give away their available aid to those who have filled out the forms on time, so if a great student comes along after the deadline and needs financial assistance, usually none is available. The most successful families build relationships with the financial aid office early on. Honesty and open communication are essential.

Monetary awards are not negotiable, but if there is new information after the application is submitted, such as a death in the family, sudden health issue, or job loss, the school is able to reevaluate the situation. Although aid is reassessed on a year-to-year basis, schools will not abandon a student once they've agreed to provide financial support. The calculation is very specific, and the school will not expect you to pay what it knows you cannot afford once it has seen your PFS. Financial aid directors want to help parents navigate the waters and remind families that there is absolutely nothing wrong with asking for help. If a parent feels overwhelmed, most schools are happy to work through the first form together with parents.

PART II

The Application Process: A Toolkit at Your Fingertips

IN THIS SECTION, YOU'LL LEARN a system of organizing, completing, and submitting applications that gives your child the best shot of getting into the school of his or her choice. From creating a preliminary list to making a final decision, Part II has everything you'll need to successfully navigate the application process. This section includes the following chapters:

CHAPTER 3

Getting Started: Cast a Wide Net

WHEN IT COMES TO THE application process, there are deadlines to meet, papers to file, and details to juggle. But perhaps one of the biggest surprises for families is how early they need to start the school search process. Some parents start looking for schools in the same calendar year they want their child to begin, only to find out that they are too late. For example, if you want your child to begin in the fall of 2015, you must start the process by the fall of 2014 if you want to maximize your chances of finding the right school. This is true for all schools that have a traditional application deadline on or around January 15.

Despite great intentions, deadlines can be missed. Sometimes, life gets in the way and you may not realize that your child's current school isn't the best match until late in the year, well past the deadline. That's what happened to me with my older son. He was doing okay as a freshman in our local public high school, but it was a very large school and he was simply one of many. In a nutshell, he wasn't engaged. I kept thinking things would get better, but that never really happened. It wasn't until the beginning of March that we realized that a smaller school might be a better match. I panicked because we were so late in the process, but I decided to call a few schools to see if they happened to have openings for tenth grade. Luckily, a few did and we rushed to finish the applications, submit the transcript forms, and request teacher recommendations. He also had to cram for the SSAT and complete the student questionnaires. It was hectic to say the least.

It worked out in the end, and now my son is happy and thriving in his new school, but I share this story with you because sometimes you simply can't predict what will happen in the future. The fact is, I was caught off guard, and I work in the field of education for a living! So don't fret if you are late to the game. You can still find a great school for your child.

In this chapter, you'll learn about the application timeline from the initial steps of creating a list of potential schools to questions to ask when you visit each one. You'll also find specific information for parents of young children applying to preschools. Whether your child is four or fourteen, this section will help you get started on your school search the right way.

Understanding the Application Timeline

In finding the best match for your child, it's important to understand the timing of the school application process. Although the timeline varies a bit from school to school, the following schedule is a good overview of what to expect and when to expect it. Here's what you'll need to know and do, and when:

Spring – Late Summer

- ✓ Begin to compile a list of schools that meet your criteria. Request catalogs from selected schools and peruse their websites.
- ✓ Record preliminary information on the AppList form on page 33.
- ✓ If permitted, tour the school. If the school will not accommodate a tour, drive to the school to get a feeling for the campus and to make sure that the commute is realistic.
- ✓ In late summer, take an SSAT diagnostic test.

September

- ✓ Fill out online applications for the schools you are considering. Begin the financial aid process.
- ✓ If you haven't already done so, attend an open house or go on a tour. (Note: Some schools require an application to be submitted prior to touring the school.)
- ✓ Update your AppList worksheet to reflect schools you're considering.
- ✓ Schedule interviews and shadow days.
- ✓ Schedule SSAT test prep tutoring.

October

- ✓ Practice interview skills.
- ✓ Request transcripts from your child's current school.
- ✓ Complete the AppAssist tracking form for each school.
- ✓ Request letters of recommendations.

- ✓ Register for the SSAT or any other necessary testing to be completed in December. If you need accommodations, plan about a month ahead to make sure you have all the necessary documentation.
- ✓ Submit the candidate questionnaire (usually for grades 7-12).

November

- ✓ Complete the interviews and shadow visits. Send thank-you notes afterwards.
- ✓ Complete financial aid forms.

December

- ✓ Take the SSAT and make sure that schools of interest are listed as score recipients.
- ✓ Submit applications and send in all supporting documents for schools with December deadlines.

January

- ✓ Be sure all applications, testing, and supporting documents have been submitted. Beat deadlines by a week or more.
- ✓ If necessary, follow up with admissions to ensure documents have been received.

February

- ✓ Stack rank your schools.

March

- ✓ Watch for decision letters, which usually arrive via email early to mid-month.
- ✓ Plan revisit days to the schools to which your child was accepted.

April

- ✓ Make a final decision.
- ✓ Inform the schools that your child won't be attending of your decision.

Getting Organized . . . An Easy Way

Even though you're just getting started, it pays off in the long run to keep track of details from the beginning. I suggest you use two forms to stay organized. The first is my AppList worksheet, which will help you maintain a broad, general list of the schools you're considering. The full form can also be downloaded from my website at www.ectutoring.com/privateschools. An abbreviated version is on the following page. You'll want to keep a record of every school that you consider, even if it doesn't result in an application. There will be many schools to evaluate and if you don't feel one is a match for whatever reason, it is helpful to document why it's not a fit. I've found that without these notes, it's easy to forget why the school was taken off the list in the first place. This form provides an easy reference.

Here you will record the good and the not-so-good qualities of each school. Be as specific as possible. For example, if the science program was compelling, write "Biology lab facility" instead of "great science program." These notes will help you to better remember what stands out about each school.

Before you get started, purchase an accordion file (or a similar system), label each tab with the name of the school, and place a manila folder into each. That way, you'll have a section for each school. Bring the manila folder with you on visits so that you can keep the school's information in one place. At the front of the accordion file, label the first tab with "AppList." Again, use this form as your main, comprehensive list. Alternatively, you can keep electronic files, but either way, be sure to have some system in place.

The AppList School Tracking Form

School	Pros	Cons
Maple	- Great location - STEM program - 1:1 laptops - Top tennis team	- Class size - Limited learning support - Homework load
Evergreen	- Community service program - Ranked football - Feel at home - Metro accessible	- Far from home - Limited extracurriculars -Formal dress code
Oakview	- Lots of technology - Strong arts - IB program - Up to Latin 5	- Hard to get into - Long class periods - Limited athletic facilities

To record information about individual schools, use the AppAssist form. On this sheet, you'll list important dates and deadlines. Staple the form onto the left side of each manila folder or save it electronically.

AppAssist
Individual School Tracking Form

Name of School: Maple School
Contact Person: Joe Smith
E-Mail: jsmith@maple.edu
Application Deadline: Jan. 15
Online Application Submitted: Sept. 30
Financial Aid Deadline: Jan. 15
Date & Time of Open House/Tour: Oct. 13 at 7 pm

Testing:
Name of Required Test(s): SSAT
Date & Time of Test: Nov. 14
Test Site: Educational Connections (0211)

Supplemental Information:
Date Transcript Requested: Oct. 16
Date Received: Oct. 30
Candidate Questionnaire: Completed Oct. 22

Recommendation Forms:
Date Given: (English) Nov. 8 to Mrs. Bailey
Date Given: (Math) Nov. 9 to Mr. Patrick
Date Given: (Optional) Nov. 8 to Coach Sylvester

Interviews:
Student Interview: Oct. 13 with Joe Smith
Parent Interview: Oct. 14 with Peter Parker

Admission Notification:
Date that School Notifies of Decision: March 1
Enrollment Contract is Due: April 15

Casting a Wide Net: Creating a Preliminary List of Schools

The start of the school year (or even a bit earlier in the late spring or summer) is the best time to take the first step: compiling a list of potential schools. You'll want to create an initial list that is fairly long, anywhere from five to fifteen schools. The list can always be narrowed down later. How do you know which schools to consider at first? Speak to your friends, acquaintances, and teachers in your child's current school to get an idea. Use the profiles section in the latter half of this book to help you. You want to utilize as many resources as possible.

The next step is to visit the schools' websites and request an information packet to be mailed to you. Many parents find that they can quickly eliminate a few schools based on the website and print information they gather.

Consider having a seasoned consultant review your list. Did you include every appropriate school? Is there a great potential match that may have been left out? Is your list reasonable or do you have too many highly competitive schools with low rates of admission? On page 60, you can find more information on finding a consultant who will be a good match for your family.

Expect Pushback

Also consider that while you're just starting to explore schools, your child may not be completely onboard with the idea. As I gathered information for this book and spoke to many admission directors, parents, and students, I found that parents primarily care about academics; they want a school that will provide the very best education for their child. Kids, on the other hand, are far more concerned about friends, including the ones they will leave behind and the new ones they'll meet. Because of the friendship issue, some children are very reluctant to move schools, even when it may be the best thing for them. It's a tightrope that parents must walk.

Dr. Pat Quinn is a nationally-known developmental pediatrician and author. She has worked with hundreds of families that have successfully navigated the transition from one school to the next. "Over the years, I have found that most children do not want to leave their current school or friends, but that the majority adjust quite well after only a few weeks and that the success these children ultimately achieve is well worth initial discomfort. Parents of elementary and middle school-aged children should expect to encounter some pushback from their kids when suggesting a school change, but resolve to hold firm to their decision to send their child to a carefully chosen, well-matched, supportive environment where he or she will thrive. Children do not possess the cognitive skills to make such an important decision until well into adolescence and it's a parent's role to make it for them."

Considering Crucial Factors

As you compile a preliminary list of schools, you'll want to consider certain factors. Here's a list to get you started:

Location

Is the school close by or logistically feasible? Many students travel great distances to find a goodness of fit. Consider that your child will likely stay after school for clubs or sports and that rush hour in this area can be miserable. More importantly, if a school is too far from where you live, your child may miss out on social opportunities on the weekends. This is something that parents overlook in search of a good education, but for most kids, a social life is equally as important. When friends are too far away, weekend get-togethers and even midweek study groups are tricky. As far as daily transportation, ask the school about bus service (many provide it) or possible carpool arrangements. Most admission directors will give you a list of families in your area who are willing to carpool.

Single Sex vs. Co-Ed

Preschools and primary schools (up to third grade) are almost always co-ed, but single-sex schools become an option starting in the fourth grade. Some students and their parents will quickly rule out a single-sex education, but that can be a mistake. There are many beneficial aspects of a single-sex school. For example, staff members at all-boys schools understand that boys learn best with movement and hands-on activities. They are able to capitalize on boys' high energy and learning style. The curriculum has been designed around the way boys learn best.

Studies have shown that girls are more open to taking risks in math and science in single-sex environments. While girls are fully capable of conquering any subject, they often feel more comfortable doing so in an all-female classroom. Many of the all-girls schools in the area have strong STEM (science, technology, engineering, and mathematics) programs that allow students to explore subjects that have been traditionally viewed as male-oriented.

In 2005, the U.S. Department of Education published a study on single-sex public education that concluded, "There is some support for the premise that single-sex schooling can be helpful, especially for certain outcomes related to academic achievement and more positive academic aspirations, however for many outcomes, there is no evidence of either benefit or harm." While the findings were inconclusive about the academic impacts of single-sex education on students, it did reflect a link between single-sex education and positive student interactions.

Some parents question whether a co-ed school will prepare their child better for college, which will likely be co-ed, and work life in which individuals are required to get along with both sexes. On the whole, the research is ambiguous. There is no doubt that students benefit from interactions with both boys and girls at some point; therefore, if you're looking for a same-sex school, be sure that you ask about opportunities for ample socialization. For example, most boys' schools have mixers and dances with girls' schools and in many high schools, opportunities are available to take co-ed classes on or off campus. Pros and cons can be made for both single-sex and co-ed, but ultimately, parents must make the decision based on what's best for their child's particular learning style and needs.

Academic Challenge, Safety Net, or a Balance of Both

Are you looking for all-out rigor and accelerated academics or would your child benefit more from a balanced, less intensive approach? If your child is highly motivated, has a natural desire for learning, and is academically advanced, a school with a reputation for challenging academics might be ideal. In contrast, some students need a school that can provide significant scholastic support, while others would do well at a school with an in-between, balanced approach.

Instructional Method

In the DC area, there is no shortage of diverse teaching methodologies. Some schools pride themselves on a "progressive model." This approach focuses on hands-on projects and critical thinking. Instruction goes beyond rote learning to focus on analyzing information and solving problems. Classroom lessons often involve group work and the teacher is seen as a collaborator in education, not as the all-knowing purveyor of information. Teachers are often called by their first names. The goal of progressive education is to develop lifelong learners and for students to have the flexibility to learn about what interests them.

The "traditional model" is a back-to-basics approach to ensure that students have strong foundational knowledge in many content areas. Although this approach may involve group work, it also involves seatwork and individual assignments. The teacher is the head of the class and he or she is called by her last name. Instruction is often delivered through lecture and textbooks (hard copy or online). Children are taught primarily using one unified curriculum, even though they may be on different levels.

Most schools, including public schools, take a balanced approach. They appreciate individual differences and are willing to differentiate education when possible. They believe in a combination of individual assignments, lecturing, collaborative groups, and discussion. As you tour schools, ask what model they tend to use and don't be afraid of asking why they subscribe to the theory. Most administrators feel passionately about their school's methodology and will tell you why they feel it works for their students.

Traditional Model	Progressive Model
Instruction: Teacher-centered; the teacher is the authority figure and the disseminator of most information. Students may sit at individual desks in rows. Textbooks are used frequently. Instruction is mostly lecture-based.	Instruction: Student-centered; students learn from each other in small groups and independently through self-study and projects. Discussion-based learning. Teacher is the facilitator and may be called by first name.
Beginning reading: Phonics-based approach	Beginning reading: Sight word approach
Math: Focus on basic skills and computation	Math: Focus on problem solving
Grading: Traditional letter grades on the report card to measure performance	Grading: Some letter grades are used, but teacher comments are more common
Progress: Monitored through frequent quizzes and tests	Progress: Monitored by some testing, but also by portfolios of work samples
Curriculum: Focus on reading, writing, math, history, geography, and science	Curriculum: Focus on reading, writing, and math. Social sciences emphasize diversity and social consciousness
Curriculum: Units are compartmentalized. Each subject has its specific units, which are not typically connected across the content areas	Curriculum: Units are taught across different subjects. For example, the topic of "rivers" may be studied in language arts, social studies, and science
Technology: Used at times, but students also learn to take notes by hand	Technology: Used frequently - laptops/iPads brought to class
Overall focus: Building academic skills in core areas	Overall focus: Academic skills and social/emotional growth

Athletics

Are sports important to your child? If so, this factor may make a school more or less attractive. Although academics are of the utmost importance in most families, sports often run a close second and for good reason. Not only do sports give kids an outlet for their energy, studies show that students who participate have a higher grade point average and a stronger commitment to the school than those who don't. Take notice that some schools require students to play a sport in middle and high school every semester and every year. Other schools require only periodic participation. When visiting schools, be sure to ask about the sports program that interests your child and request a meeting with the coach.

K-8 or K-12

Some parents prefer a larger K-12 school where their child can stay put for the long haul, while others are more comfortable with a school that caters to just young children or one that runs from kindergarten through eighth grade. Proponents of K-8 schools consider them a great option because, quite frankly, you don't know what kind of student your child will turn out to be. A school ending in eighth grade gives you flexibility to move schools for high school, and while that's also an option for K-12 schools, it is far less likely. It's also an opportunity for a child to reinvent herself in later years. A fresh start is a good thing for some students. Others desire a K-12 school where their child can stay grounded for their entire school career and the teachers and administrators know their child at a deep level. It also means that you only need to go through the application process once.

Chance of Acceptance

Is the school known to be highly competitive, meaning that only a small percentage of students gain acceptance each year? Is the school looking for very high test scores and top grades? These are the schools that might be hard to get into. Be sure your list contains some of these "reach" schools, but also others that may provide a better chance of acceptance. For more on this, see Chapter 5.

As you consider these crucial factors, don't be afraid to start with a long list including schools you may be hesitant about at first. You may be pleasantly surprised on your tour. The same works for schools considered by others to be "the best." It could be that a particular school does live up to your expectations.

Four Mistakes Parents Make

When you're thinking about schools for your child, beware of a few common obstacles that seem to trip up even the most seasoned parents.

1. **Putting all your eggs in one basket:** Sometimes parents will have one school in mind that they view as "perfect" and all their energy goes into getting their child into that single place. Don't let unbridled optimism get the best of you—otherwise, you and your child will be disappointed if that top school doesn't work out. Focusing on one school, even though there may be others that are just as good or even better, is never a good thing. This doesn't mean you shouldn't have a top choice, just that you should always have a backup plan.

2. **Equating low acceptance rates with superior quality:** It's easy to assume that the harder the school is to get into, the better the education, but that simply isn't true. Don't make the mistake of putting a highly competitive school with very low acceptance rates a rung above another school that may not be quite as tough to get into. There are many academically challenging schools in our area that provide just as good of an education as their counterparts without the same exclusivity. Look beyond acceptance rate data to the mission of the school and strength of its academic program.

3. **Having too many "reach" schools on the list:** This is the biggest mistake parents make and it's explained in detail in Chapter 5. Last year, I had a mom come to me in March after her daughter had received denial letters to all three schools to which she applied. Upon examining her grades (which were excellent) and her SSAT scores, which weren't so good, I would have encouraged her to apply to one or two less competitive schools, but at that point it was too late. She had no option but to enroll her daughter in the local public school.

4. **Ruling schools in or out based on their matriculation list:** I've seen too many parents add or subtract a school from consideration based on the school's matriculation list. This is a big mistake. Although the school your child might attend next is always a factor, it should

never be the deciding factor in where to go right now. When too much emphasis is placed on getting into a competitive high school or top-tier college, it sends the message to kids that school is all about grades and test scores, and that a person's self-worth is defined by where they attend school. Far more important is the process or the journey. Developing socially and emotionally is just as important as developing academically. Be sure that your judgment is not clouded by factors that are only a small part of the equation.

Late Birthdays and Retention

The concept of repeating a grade or skipping one entirely is an important topic and one that warrants more discussion than it frequently gets. It's especially important when parents are making their list of schools and touring various campuses. Ultimately, your child must apply to the right grade.

It's common for parents of young children to wonder if their child would benefit from another year of preschool before moving on to kindergarten. Some call this the "gift of another year." It's typically the case that parents ponder the question of retention, but don't act on it. I've worked with many families over the years who have considered holding their child back in preschool or early elementary school, but decided not to do so for one reason or another. The question often lingers in the back of their minds for many years if they see their child struggle to fit in socially or to keep up academically. They wonder, "Should I have kept my child back after all?" or "Is it too late now?"

Hundreds of studies have shown that retention early on (kindergarten through third grade) and in later years (fourth through eighth grades) is not beneficial. The National Association of School Psychologists reviewed the research and published its "Position Statement on Student Grade Retention." In it, the organization reports that academic achievement of students who were retained is actually poorer than that of others with similar skill sets who were promoted to the next grade. Although some gains can be seen immediately following retention, they fade after two or three years. In addition, holding a student back *after* preschool has a negative effect on peer relationships and self-esteem and increases problem behaviors. The only time when retention is more likely to have a neutral or positive impact for a struggling student is when intensive remediation is provided to address skill deficits or behavioral problems.

Retaining a child for academic reasons in fourth grade, for example, is far different from a youngster staying in preschool for an extra year. At a very young age, little stigma is attached to completing another year in preschool. In the affluent areas surrounding DC, giving children with late birthdays (June through September) an extra year in preschool or kindergarten is the norm. This trend is especially true of boys who develop slower than girls. If you're considering keeping your child in preschool for an extra year and he or she has a summer or early fall birthday, you are not alone. Think twice about making this move if he or she is advanced academically and socially. Sometimes, children become bored when they are working beyond others their age.

A more recent trend is retention for older students when catch-up is needed. Some parents will hold back an older child when he or she is switching schools. The data cited earlier is clear that repeating a grade in the *same* school is not beneficial; however, the data isn't clear with regard to retention when switching schools. My experience has been that if you have a child with a late birthday who is behind academically or socially and could use an extra year, it should be considered only if the child is on board and if he or she will be attending a *new* school. Keep in mind that if you have an older child who is disengaged in school, adding an extra year is probably not a good idea. Even in a great school, adding one more year could prolong an arduous experience. Some students who underperform in middle and high school go on to do great things in college once entrenched in their major.

While the research does not support retention, I've had a number of positive experiences over the years with families that have retained their children with good results. The decision is a complicated one that can be life-changing. Before considering retention, always consult with a professional who specializes in this area.

Skipping Grades

Although not nearly as common, I've also had parents ask me if I think their child is a good candidate for grade acceleration. I almost never recommend it. If the child is old for his grade, has been tested well above grade level, and is very mature, he may be a candidate. Even then, it might only be workable if the student is switching schools.

These days, grade acceleration is very rare. Schools are not proponents because, as with retention, the research simply does not support it. Furthermore, instructional practices in today's classrooms are different from the practices of 30 years ago, when skipping a grade was not unusual. Teachers regularly differentiate instruction and are typically able to challenge a student who is well above grade level. If you have an exceptionally bright child who is ready to go ahead, consider the level of differentiation available as you search for schools. The right school will be able to meet your child's needs without moving him to the next grade level.

Chapter 4

Visiting Schools: What to Look For

Once you have a preliminary list together, it's time to see these places up close and in person. Glossy brochures and interactive websites are great, but the only way to get a flavor for the school is to actually visit. This is initially done through an open house or small group tour. Check the schools' websites for dates or call to arrange a tour. At many schools, open houses are well-publicized and represent a good way to get to know the school.

Be aware that some competitive schools that receive many applications without much publicity will not have open houses or frequent tour dates. Be sure to contact these schools early on since popular dates for tours can fill up months in advance. Do your research beforehand and don't procrastinate so that you can hit the ground running the first of September. Some schools will not allow visits prior to the application year. So if your child is applying to ninth grade and you want to get a jump start in the late spring of the seventh grade year, it may be impossible to arrange a visit. You may need to wait until the fall.

Think Ahead Before You Go

Parents who cast a wide net will sometimes visit the school first without their child in order to whittle down a long list. This is a good approach, since you'll want to weed out any schools that are not a good fit academically, financially, or logistically. I've seen many students visit a school and fall in love with it, only to later find out that it's too expensive, too far to drive, or the admission standards are too lofty. Be sure to do your homework before bringing your child along.

Another factor to remember is that the school starts a file on your child on day one. They want to work with families that are friendly, caring, and polite. If a family is rude or demanding on the tour, you can be sure that the school is taking note. Be respectful and considerate so that you can show the school that you belong in their community and will contribute to their educational mission.

Notice the Little Things

What should you look for on the tour? As soon as you walk in the door, take note of the general atmosphere. Are staffers friendly and welcoming or dour and matter-of-fact? I've found more often than not the employee who greets you at the entrance is indicative of the school atmosphere as a whole. After all, this person was hired by the administration and, to some degree, reflects the culture of the school.

As you walk the halls, note the tone the school is trying to set. If there is a lot of student art on the walls, that's a sign that the school values the arts and is trying to build an environment that encourages creativity. Are the halls clean, orderly, and undecorated? The school may have a strict atmosphere that emphasizes respect and structure. At every turn, take note of the facilities, and try to picture whether your child would be happy and eager to learn in the environment.

Check out Teaching Styles

Take a peek into each classroom. Is the teacher lecturing or are students engaged in discussion? Are students sitting individually at their desks or are they working in small groups? Do they seem attentive and inspired? I've observed many classroom lessons displaying a range of teaching methods and various levels of student engagement. I've seen some students at highly respected schools with their heads down on their desk while the teacher lectures on. These instances may be unusual, but when you notice a general culture of disengagement and your gut tells you the school isn't an inspiring place, pay attention.

Similarly, I've walked from room to room in other schools to see incredibly enthusiastic teachers and fully engrossed students. Students learn best when they are in an environment in which they are engaged and the instruction piques their interest. It's no longer acceptable for students to simply endure school, especially at the high school level. If you're paying good money for an independent school education, it's imperative to find a place where your child will feel invigorated, not one where he simply goes through the motions.

The school's teaching philosophy is incredibly important to your child's success. Make note of these teaching styles because they should factor significantly into your decision.

Look Beyond Academics

In addition, pay special attention to how students behave in class and how they treat each other. To a large extent, children reflect the behavior of those around them. Unless your child is highly self-motivated, sticking him in a group of inattentive kids will not help him academically.

Furthermore, friendship is an important aspect of a child's social life at school, so ask yourself whether your child would fit in with these students. Are students interacting with their teachers and peers in the classroom? Do they genuinely seem happy to be there? That's a great sign that the school is doing a good job of creating a friendly learning environment.

Factor in Emotional Well-Being

One of the most overlooked, yet most important parts of a child's school experience is their emotional well-being. Annie Farquhar, Director of Admission at Maret School in Washington, DC, says that parents often do not necessarily regard these "soft skills" as valuable aspects of their child's education, but she encourages parents to consider this viewpoint when evaluating schools. "We care about addressing the 'whole student,' and so we expend the effort to ensure the students are not only being educated, but are also becoming socially and emotionally healthy human beings."

Though many schools claim to subscribe to the "whole-child approach" to education, which focuses on physical, emotional, and intellectual development, it is important to ask schools what they do to promote your child's emotional well-being. For example, at Maret, Annie states that the school has "teams consisting of the school nurse, counselors, teachers, athletic directors, and others that meet regularly to discuss how the students are doing socially and emotionally." Annie elaborates that these meetings are "in addition to regular meetings between faculty and directors to discuss curriculum issues, school plans, and so on." As you tour schools, it may be apparent how teachers stimulate children intellectually, but also ask specific questions about physical and emotional well-being.

Record Your Impressions

During your quest to find the right match for your child, you will visit many schools and will learn valuable information that can later influence your final decision. You will be given facts and data. Although important, your intuitive reaction to each school is probably even more telling.

To make the most out of your visits, it is imperative that you take note of the facts but also record your feelings. The tour reaction form is an easy way to quickly remember the details when it comes time to make a decision about the school in the future. You can find this blank form at www.ectutoring.com/privateschools.

Tour Reaction Form

School: Maple School
Visit Date: October 13

Rank from 1 (terrible) to 3 (great):
Campus: 3 Teachers: 2 Students: 3
Classrooms: 1 Technology: 3 Academics: 3
Athletic Fields: 3 Art Studios: 1 Other: ___

The Kids Seemed	Yes	No
To be working hard	X	
Friendly	X	
Like Me	X	
Happy	X	
Bored		X

The Teachers Seemed	Yes	No
Friendly	X	
That they liked their students	X	
Easy to talk to	X	

The Work Seemed	Yes	No
Like my current schoolwork		X
Harder	X	
Easier		X
More Interesting	X	

Two things I liked: Tennis team record, 1:1 laptop program

Two things I didn't like: class sizes, lots of homework

Can I see myself at this school? Yes!

The Balance between Process and Product

As you visit, pay attention to what schools claim versus what you observe. A lot of schools are claiming the same thing: small class sizes, more personal attention, highly trained faculty, etc. If you look closer, however, not every school has the same approach to education. For many, the differences are obvious (traditional versus nontraditional teaching methods), but keep your eyes open for what are typically referred to as "process" schools and "product" schools. Few schools will strictly be a process or product-driven school; however, most schools will value one approach slightly more than the other.

Process schools go to great lengths to instill community service, character building, and social responsibility in addition to academic readiness. The emphasis is on the entire educational process, not just where the student ends up in college. This approach is common for many K-12 schools in the area because they are able to manage a student's entire academic upbringing.

Product schools, on the other hand, offer an education that is rigorous, with a main goal of matriculating into a highly selective four-year college or university. This is not to say that they do not focus on developing well-rounded students. Neither approach is necessarily right or wrong; it all depends on the best fit for your family. Keep this distinction in mind when looking at schools and you'll be able to find the right fit for your child faster.

Questions to Ask

Prior to the tour, peruse the school's website to develop a set of questions that are unanswered for you. You may want to ask some of the same questions at each school so that you can compare apples to apples. You'll want to ask questions that you think are most important to your child's educational experience, but here are some good examples of general questions to get you started:

For Elementary School

- How do you teach reading? Phonics, whole language, or a bit of both?
- How much do students write on a daily basis?
- How much homework do students typically receive?

- How do teachers communicate with parents?
- How is technology used throughout the day?

For Middle and High School

- What is a day like during the week? Are there any built-in study halls or teacher assistance periods?
- How would you describe the students who attend this school?
- How frequently are grades reported, and what is the usual level of communication with parents?
- How does your college planning program work?
- Do students bring laptops to class? How is technology utilized?
- What freedoms do the students have, and what is prohibited?
- Are athletics required?

Questions to Avoid

Sometimes, a parent's innocuous questions can seem off-putting to school staff. It's best not to ask questions that may be taken the wrong way. Here are a few that will ruffle feathers:

- What makes your school worth such a high tuition?
- What colleges will my child get into if he goes here?
- What will it take to get my child into this school?
- Why don't you focus on math the same way the school down the street does?

If you have a question that needs clarification or is highly specific to your child, ask it during the interview, not during a group tour. This way, the staff can respond to you personally and you won't take up others' time.

After a few tours, you'll have a good idea of where your child might fit in and this information will enable you to refine your list. If there are a couple of schools that you've fallen in love with, be sure to send a thank-you note or email. Schools take notice and it will go into your file.

Applying to and Visiting Private Schools

DC is no different from most other metropolitan areas throughout the nation—competition for a good preschool is fierce. It doesn't need to be that way because there are many outstanding preschools in our area that turn out very prepared kindergarteners. Admission to one of the more recognized schools may not give your child a lofty advantage. Step back and think to yourself, "What are the values of my family? Where will my child be happiest?" For some families, entrance into a top primary, K-8, or K-12 school is highly important. If that is your preference, call the schools that interest you to ask which preschools they think create the best prepared students.

Perhaps you're the type of parent who wants to consider many options—from your small local church school with a low price tag, to a competitive independent school. The process of applying to preschool is obviously different than applying to upper grades. Parents determine the schools of interest, get their child tested (the WPPSI is the test of choice for young children), submit the application, and schedule a visit. Teachers rate students by their readiness for learning, propensity to get along with others, and ability to follow directions. Students are considered on the strength of their applications, primarily based on testing and the visit. Although siblings and children of alumni are given preference, they are not a sure thing.

CHAPTER 5

Reach, Target, and Safety Schools

THIS CHAPTER IS DEDICATED TO increasing your child's odds of getting into a school that will be a great fit. By organizing schools into reach, target, and safety categories, you can feel confident that your child is applying to an assortment of schools.

Narrow Your List One School at a Time

In the early fall, you should have visited every school you're considering, usually in the form of a group tour. These visits will give you a good idea of which schools feel right. Parents and students often say that after ten minutes or so on a school's campus, they have a feeling about whether it's a fit or not. It's been my experience that your gut instinct is usually right. Based on your intuition, tour of the campus, and conversations with your child (if he or she is old enough), you should be able to weigh the pros and cons of each school. If you're on the fence about a particular school, leave it on the list for now. If you know it is definitely not a match, remove it.

There really is no hard-and-fast rule about how many schools you should have on your list, except that you do want enough so that your child has an excellent shot at a few schools loved by the whole family. In order to optimize your chances, you'll need to sort the schools on your list into specific categories based on his or her chances of getting in.

Determining Reach, Target, and Safety Schools

You may remember applying to college many years ago or you may have an older child who has gone through the process. Most college counselors encourage students to apply to schools that might be very hard to get into, some that they have a good chance of getting into, and ones that would very likely offer acceptance. The same strategy works with independent schools. Unless your child is an outstanding student in every possible way, she will likely not get into every school to which she applies.

A good approach is to put the schools on your list into one of three groups.

Categorizing Your Schools

Reach – These are the highly competitive schools that are academically challenging. Reach schools are those that are highly selective and have low enrollment rates compared to the number of applications they receive. These schools may be long shots depending on the strength of your child's application.

Target – Target schools are realistic options. They provide an excellent education and their curriculum may be just as challenging as reach schools. You have a good sense that admittance is likely, but is definitely not a sure thing.

Safety – Your child has a high probability of being accepted to these schools. This isn't to say their academics aren't as strong; it's just that their admissions aren't as selective.

How do you know which category each school fits into? It depends on the strength of your child's application. A reach school for one student may not be for another; however, there are simple considerations that apply to all applicants.

Compare Grades

Right off the bat, one of the most important factors is grades. This is the easiest way to distinguish students from one another and to weed out anyone who's unqualified. If a student has not succeeded previously in school, it's hard to argue that he or she should get a spot over someone who has demonstrated academic success. This is an easy way for schools to make the first cut when looking at a pool of applicants. Be aware that different schools have different standards; strong arts schools may value musical ability as much as grades for some students, but in general, grades and test scores are the first factor in an admission board's decision.

As you tour schools, it's okay to ask about grades. You may not get a specific answer such as, "Students need to have a 3.8 GPA," but you may learn that they are looking for students with a solid A/B average. If they are, and your child earns Bs and Cs, then this school could be considered a reach.

Parents often ask how admission committees compare one student to another when the schools in which they're currently enrolled have different standards for report card grades. They wonder if an A from one school equates to an A at another. The answer is that it's hard to make an exact comparison, but admission officials are savvy and are well aware of the differences among the various schools. When students have unusually high marks from a school known for giving lots of As, test scores are even more important because they may more accurately demonstrate a student's abilities compared to others applying to the same school.

Test Scores Matter

In order to get a general idea of how your child might score, a practice test is necessary. If your student is applying to fifth grade or higher and the school requires the SSAT, have him take a diagnostic test to see where his score falls. A practice test can be done early in the season before your child takes the actual test in December. These scores will not be reported to schools; they are merely a way for parents to gauge how their child will score. My company, Educational Connections, proctors practice SSATs at our Fairfax location on a regular basis. Your child can also take one online at www.ssat.org. If your child's scores aren't what you anticipated, bring in a tutor. Though there is no magic number, a good rule of thumb is to apply to anywhere between two to five schools.

Determine the Number of Spaces the Class Has Available

It is important to know what your child's chances of acceptance are. Sometimes, it comes down to how many slots a school has available and how many children apply. For example, if the school typically gets 100 applications for 10 slots, five of them for boys and five for girls, you may be looking at a reach school solely based on numbers. In cases like this, don't panic because the number of students accepted is always much higher. Regardless, be cognizant that schools with low enrollment rates are inherently harder to get into. Even students with straight As, very high test scores, great recommendations, and expertise in a sport to boot, can get waitlisted. That's why having a target school or two on your list is very important.

Acceptance vs. Enrollment

Take note that there is a big difference between acceptance and enrollment. Acceptance refers to the number of students who have been sent an acceptance letter; however, not all of these students will actually choose to attend that school. Those who do agree to attend count as enrollment. For example, one local school has space for about 110 boys in the ninth grade. They receive over 400 applications. They accept about 200 students and enroll 110. Often times, parents become fixated on the enrollment number. They may fret, "My son will probably not get in! He only has a 25% chance." Not so fast. In reality, his chances are closer to 50 percent. Schools will reveal the number of spaces they have available for each particular grade level and will typically tell you how many applications they receive, but not all will give out their acceptance rate. In any case, it doesn't hurt to ask. This information will help you better understand your child's chances of getting in.

In the end, categorizing schools is certainly more of an art than a science. Parents may not know their child's chances of gaining acceptance to any one particular school. It's been my experience that families have too many reach schools on their list and not enough target schools. There needs to be a balance to ensure a successful application process. I encourage families to have two reaches, two targets, and a safety school. In fact, you may not need a safety school if you have a larger number of target schools, but be sure not to overestimate your child's chances. Remember, a safety school is one that you still feel would be a great match for your child. Do not apply just to have an extra option as a "backup" if you don't honestly see your child attending that school.

When considering reach schools, it's one thing to have on your list schools that might be a challenge to get into, but in which your child will thrive. It's another thing to include places where your child may struggle academically to keep up. That's not fun for anyone. Be realistic and thoughtful when it comes to reach schools

Here's a hypothetical example of how the reach, target, safety strategy works:

Using the Strategy

Lauren Smith, an academically motivated, thoughtful, and athletic girl, is applying to sixth grade. Although she's performed well in her public elementary school, her parents worry about the size of their local middle and high schools. They think she'll have a greater opportunity to shine in a smaller, independent school environment. Lauren and her parents initially considered eight schools, but upon perusing websites and considering the logistics of travel, they narrowed the list to six. In the fall of her fifth grade year, they visited each school and found that they didn't feel strongly about one place, so now their list has whittled to five. Lauren took a practice SSAT and scored in the 50th percentile on all three sections (reading comprehension, verbal, and math). Her report card grades are typically As and Bs. Mrs. Smith filled out the online applications for all five schools. Although the schools were very different, there were qualities about each one that the family loved.

Here's how Lauren's breakdown of schools was made:

Reach: Maple School and Elm School

Both Maple and Elm schools are reaches for Lauren because they generally admit students with As and very high test scores. Admission to these schools might be a stretch, especially given that they only accept six to seven girls for the sixth grade and tend to pull many students from local independent feeder schools.

Target: Evergreen School and Dogwood School

Evergreen and Dogwood like to see As and Bs and solid SSAT scores, which Lauren will likely receive based on her practice test. Lauren is also very personable and her parents feel that she will do well during the interview and shadow visits. Although Mrs. Smith feels good about these schools, her friend's daughters were waitlisted last year, so she doesn't feel they are a sure thing.

Safety: Oak View School

Oak View is a safety school mainly because it begins in sixth grade and has a large number of openings. In addition, Lauren's older sister Jenny attended Oak View and Mrs. Smith believes that her relationship with the school and Jenny's solid grades and test scores will almost certainly produce acceptance. Although Oak View is a safety school, Mr. and Mrs. Smith feel it would be a fantastic fit for Lauren. Lauren likes it as well, but she would like to step out of the shadow of her sister.

The family's strategy worked for Lauren. Although she was waitlisted at Maple and Elm, she did get into the three other schools, which gave the family many fantastic options.

Other Things to Consider

Outside of grades, test scores, and the number of openings a school has available, there are other factors that can make your child's application more or less attractive. The grade for which your student applies can make a big difference and so can familial or personal contacts within the school. And of course, the school from which the child is applying is important. Although a stellar academic record brings the applicant to the forefront, other factors can push him or her further to the front of the pack.

Entry Years

In general, "entry years" are the easiest grades to get into. These are the grades at the beginning of each major school division (kindergarten, fifth, and ninth, although this varies by school). In ninth grade, for instance, schools accept a lot of new students in order to form a high school class, so there are many openings, especially if the school does not maintain a middle school. By tenth grade, however, the class has already been formed and most students will be there until graduation. There may be only a few openings, if any, and these may be by attrition, such as a family moving out of town.

The Applicant Pool

In any given year a school may have a high volume of applicants from legacy families, a large influx of international students, or a disproportionate amount of male or female applicants. The boy/girl ratio is particularly hard to predict, and in one year the acceptance rate for girls may be half of the acceptance rate for boys. Unforeseen factors can vary from year to year and from school to school. These things are out of a parent's control.

Feeder Schools

A feeder school is one that "feeds" into a larger school as students graduate. For instance, in the District, Beauvoir, The National Cathedral Elementary School, which ends in third grade, is a feeder to St. Albans and National Cathedral School. Another example is Sheridan School, which feeds into Georgetown Day and Sidwell Friends, among others. In the public sector, over 47% of TJ's incoming freshman class comes from three middle schools: Carson Middle School in Oakton, Longfellow Middle School in McLean, and Rocky Run Middle School in Chantilly.

Of course, attending a feeder school is no guarantee of admission, but it can help. Independent middle and high schools that pull from feeder schools know that they are getting qualified applicants. They are fully aware of the school's academic track record and that the school has a history of sending well-prepared kids. Positive experience most definitely helps, which is why feeder schools, such as Norwood, have excellent results at placing students at top high schools in the area.

Legacies, Siblings, and Special Contacts

Do legacies get preference? The answer is a resounding "yes." Schools have an interest in keeping families involved in the school, not only for fundraising purposes but also because they want to sustain the school's mission and vision. That's easy to do with families that are already part of the system and passionate about the school. Being a son or daughter of an alumnus is a commonly-known advantage. In fact, even being the grandchild of someone who has graduated from the school can provide a leg up.

Another significant factor is whether the student has a sibling at the school. I've consistently found that children with siblings at the school have an advantage in the admission process. In many instances, these students would have probably been waitlisted without a familial link. Their applications were simply not strong enough on their own. This is not to say they wouldn't be successful at the school—after all, no admission committee wants to knowingly admit a student who will likely struggle—but it's the case that the family connection makes a difference.

Parents also ask, "What if I know somebody at the school? Will that help my child's chances?" Knowing the parents of a currently enrolled student or a member of the board, or having a consultant lobby for you can be helpful, but it's no guarantee of a spot. These things can improve your child's chances, but only on the margin. In addition, the contact must know the child well and not be just a family acquaintance that the student has merely met once or twice. If you have a connection at the school, you can certainly ask him or her to write a letter on your child's behalf and you may include the letter as part of your application packet. In the end, factors such as grades and test scores are far more important and play a much greater role in the admission board's decision.

Should I Use a Consultant?

Every parent feels a different level of stress when it comes to searching for and applying to schools. A certified educational consultant can provide clarity and an objective opinion. He or she will meet with you and review prior records such as report cards and test scores and will meet with your child to get a sense of his or her personality and to perform a brief skill-based assessment. Many parents value an objective point of view about which schools would be a good match for their child and which ones they have a chance of getting into.

According to Mark Sklarow, CEO of the Independent Educational Consultants Association (IECA), there needs to be a connection between the family and the consultant. "In seeking a qualified independent educational consultant (IEC), one criterion often overlooked is the chemistry between the child and the IEC. Just as you would with a therapist, doctor, or realtor, an honest, open, sharing relationship is critical. Some kids need someone who can deliver a quick kick in the pants to get a teenager off square one, while others need someone warm, caring, and encouraging. Beyond this, look for specific knowledge related to the type and location of schools you're looking for. Legitimate questions to ask include:

✓ What is your background, experience, training, education?
✓ How do you stay current on changes at schools (regular and repeated campus visits is ideal)?
✓ What services do I get for my fees? What won't you do?

Finally, avoid anyone who promises to use their influence or says their role is 'to get you in' to a particular school." For more information, visit www.iecaonline.com.

CHAPTER 6

Completing the Application

NOW THAT YOU'VE NARROWED YOUR list, it's time to complete the paperwork. Application packages can be due as early as December or as late as February, but for most schools the deadline falls in mid-January. Above all, the most important thing to remember is to submit the application on time. In fact, aim to beat the deadline by two weeks. If the legwork is done before Christmas, the holiday break will be much more relaxing. Missing the deadline makes getting in more difficult and sometimes impossible. Competitive schools have long waitlists with many qualified students clamoring for a few spots.

Regardless of good intentions, deadlines can be missed. If you're late to the game, don't panic; you're far from alone. If you're just a little late, by a few weeks or so, call the school to see if they have space available. If they do, move as quickly as possible to complete applications. Most schools will fill their classes from "round one" (those who have submitted applications on time), but if they have a slot or two open, they will look at latecomers in "round two" or on a space-available basis. The most competitive schools, however, will remove their application forms from the website to discourage late applicants. These are the schools that do not typically have a round two because they have such a great depth of qualified students who applied on time.

Even if you're more than a month late, call the admission offices to see if there is any space available. Although there's a far greater chance of being waitlisted or even denied acceptance if you're behind schedule, you never know until you ask. This is especially true of non-entry years, which generate fewer applicants. I had a colleague contact a prominent K-12 school at the end of August to inquire about a space. She came to the realization at the eleventh hour that her local middle school would not be challenging enough for her son. She never expected that such a competitive school would have an opening, but as luck had it, it did. Someone had moved out of the area at the last moment. She jumped on the opportunity and hasn't looked back since.

Many of the schools profiled in this book have a mid-January deadline, although not all do. There are a number of outstanding schools on a rolling admission system such as French International, Congressional, Loudoun Country Day, and St. Anselm's Abbey. They will accept applications at any time of year, given space is available.

Filling Out the Paperwork: Crossing Your T's and Dotting Your I's

As you start to sift through each school's application, you'll find that each one is just a little bit different. The good news is that there are some commonalities. Here are the ins and outs of what you need to know about each part of the application.

Online Application

These days, most every institution begins the process by asking the parent to complete a brief online application. This is a preliminary first step required by some schools to even take a tour. Schools want to know that you're interested in applying before they take their time to meet with you and your child. Do this sooner rather than later, preferably around Labor Day. Be prepared to provide basic information including your contact information, child's school background, and a photo of your child. Choose a school picture or a snapshot of your smiling child, but don't submit a silly photo. You may also be asked to respond to a few open-ended questions. Remember, completing the online application does not mean you're committed to submitting all your documentation and formally applying to the school; it merely means that you're interested. In some cases, parents fill out the required online form, visit the school, realize it's not a match, and stop there. They will not submit the essay, test scores, and supporting documents such as a student's transcript. Other parents will want to apply in full.

Parent Responses

In order to obtain insight into a family's educational goals and values, most schools ask for parents to answer questions like, "What are your child's strengths and weaknesses?" Some schools require this information as part of the online application, but others have supplemental forms for answers. Let's take a look at both an over-the-top and an appropriate response when the hypothetical question asked is, "What is unique about your child?"

> **Try This:** *Jenny is one of those kids who is quick to smile and laugh, but what most delights us is her compassion for others who may not be as fortunate. Jenny is an avid lacrosse player and has been since she was six years old. This spring, there were three girls on her team who couldn't afford new equipment. Without guidance from anyone, Jenny decided to get her teammates together to have a carwash at the local gas station. They raised $295, which they all agreed would go toward buying new sticks for the three girls and a new net for team practice. As her parents, we were proud that she took the initiative to make a difference in her teammate's life.*

> **Not This:** *Jenny is perhaps one of the brightest girls in her eighth grade. Not only is she academically gifted and scores off the charts on standardized tests, but she's a very hard worker. Her fourth grade teacher once told me that she wishes she had an entire room of Jennys! Rick and I are incredibly proud of our daughter and the grades she receives. Her last report card showed straight As! I feel that she will be very successful at Maple School if accepted, and that her education will allow her access to some of the top colleges in the country.*

Although it's our natural instinct to describe the wonderful qualities in our child, lists of accomplishments can be off-putting. Instead of placing your child on a pedestal, take time to think of other ways he or she is special, perhaps through a story or a specific event. It's perfectly fine to share the good news of a special award, but be sure not to paint an unrealistic picture. A little self-deprecation is a good thing.

Student Essays

Students applying to middle or high school will be expected to answer questions as well. These questions can be quite probing and may require serious thought. It's a good idea to talk through some ways to respond. In order to get your child started and to reduce procrastination, discuss possible responses or encourage your child to jot some simple thoughts down on paper. Once your child has a good sense of her answer, have her start writing. Whatever you do, do not excessively coach. When parents do the writing, it's abundantly clear to school personnel. They've read thousands of applications over the years and have a keen sense of what looks more like a parent's essay than a child's.

Teacher Recommendations

Strong teacher recommendations are essential. Educators tend to trust other educators, and the recommendations give school personnel a chance to hear how well the student learns from the people teaching him. A glowing review can go a long way to impress an admission director. Schools want students who will add to the community and work well with others in the classroom. Teacher recommendations offer valuable insight into whether the student will fit in the environment.

At a minimum, your child's current teacher or principal/head of school will need to submit a recommendation. For students applying to middle or high school, the current English and math teacher will need to evaluate the student. Because most teachers don't yet know their new students well enough at the beginning of the year, most schools will not accept recommendations prior to mid-November. By waiting a few months, teachers have more time to gain a greater understanding of the child's personality, work ethic, and academic ability.

Given that positive recommendations are vital, it's important that your child get off to a good start with her English and math teachers. If the school accepts an additional recommendation, and you have a reference in mind who can write a shining review, go for it. This doesn't necessarily need to be written by a teacher. Think about a coach or perhaps a Boy Scout or Girl Scout leader who may know other special, non-academic qualities about your child that will make him or her stand out. Schools look for leadership qualities in students. A good recommendation will highlight these characteristics.

Most recommendation forms are automated these days. As you fill out the online request form, you will be asked for the teachers' email addresses. The system will send an email asking the teacher if he or she is willing to complete the form. Once they respond positively, the link is sent to them. Upon completion, you will receive an email verifying the status. If you don't receive a confirmation close to the deadline, personally reach out to the teacher (or have your child do so) to make sure the recommendation gets submitted.

It's a good idea for your child to ask their teachers for a recommendation before an automated request is sent. Some students are very apprehensive about approaching their teachers. If you have a reserved child, role-play the appropriate ways to ask. Older students can ask in person or by email. Either way, I always feel that connecting personally with the teacher, counselor, or administrator is best.

Extracurriculars and Outside Pursuits

Admission panels also want to know what your child will contribute to the school. They want students to get involved, not just attend for the academics and leave the minute the school bell rings. As part of the application, you will be asked to list your child's involvement in outside activities. For an older student's application (those applying to middle and high school), activities like sports, leadership roles, and unique experience in the arts make a difference. Special accolades or awards in a musical instrument, drama, or visual art can set a student apart and make her very appealing to the school. If your child is gifted athletically, make it very clear to the school that he or she can add value to the athletic program. For some schools this can be a major factor, so don't be shy about highlighting athletic experience or artistic prowess.

Unique pursuits can stretch further than you think. Has your child done any charity work through a church or after-school program? Does he have unique hobbies that translate into anything academic? Even something like placing second in a Lego robotics competition looks great to a school looking for talented engineering prospects. Just as important as sports, music, and the like is community involvement. Having a strong moral compass and social conscience is highly valued at every school. In addition, be sure to mention any unique travel experiences if it adds to a student's hobbies or passions. This paints a picture of an interesting, diverse student who is ready and willing to learn and add to others' experiences. Schools want to diversify their population and bring in a variety of students with talents and passions. Even if your child is in elementary or middle school, be sure to include special activities or accolades.

Transcripts

A transcript is a copy of your child's permanent academic record. This document is the most important part of the application because it contains the *final* report card grades (not quarterly marks) earned over the years. You must ask the registrar at your current school to send transcripts directly to the schools to which you're applying.

Standardized Testing

Test scores are another part of the application. They are sent directly to the school from the SSAT, ISEE, or the private psychologist who has administered the WISC or WPPSI. For those applying to a Catholic school, HSPT results will also be sent to the schools that you request.

Other Testing to Submit

If you've had your child tested for ADHD or learning difficulties, you are obligated to submit the report to the school if the question, "Has your child ever been tested?" is on the application. There are three reasons to be forthcoming. The first is that admission directors know the type of student they can and cannot support. They are the professionals, and from past experience they know if your child will be a good fit. I've found that parents often underestimate the amount of support their child will need. Be up front and leave that decision to the school.

Secondly, if the school finds out that a parent has withheld testing, the relationship is inevitably damaged. No one wants to work with someone they perceive to be dishonest. Although you are not required by law to turn over private documentation, it's the right thing to do when your child's academic future is at stake.

Lastly, and most importantly, it's during the review process that the admission department will determine whether your child qualifies for extra help. By submitting your child's latest testing, he or she can be appropriately evaluated for learning center services.

The Standard Application Online: Streamlining the Process

As you can see there are many parts of an application, and completing just one can be time consuming. The good news is that there is a common app for independent schools but for various reasons not every school uses it. The SSATB, the organization that publishes the SSAT, also produces the Standard Application Online 2.0 (SAO). For those of you who have gone through the Common Application in your college search process for an older child, this is very similar. Instead of completing a separate form for each school, you can fill out one primary application and financial aid form (if needed) and apply to multiple schools at once. This application includes essay questions for students; but be aware that many schools will ask for a supplemental form specific to their school. Nonetheless, the

SAO streamlines the process for families and can save you a lot of time and headaches if the majority of schools you're applying to accept it. Of the schools we list in this book, many accept the SAO through the SSAT's new service. These include Alexandria Country Day School, Browne Academy, Bullis, Capitol Hill Day School, Congressional Schools of Virginia, Foxcroft, Grace Episcopal Day School, Holton-Arms, Landon, Langley, Loudoun Country Day School, Madeira, McLean School of Maryland, Middleburg Academy, National Presbyterian, Norwood, Oakcrest, Sandy Spring Friends, Sheridan, Stone Ridge, St. Andrew's, St. Stephen's & St. Agnes, and Washington Episcopal School. To fill out an SAO, register at www.ssat.org and follow their step-by-step instructions.

Scheduling a Shadow Visit

After you've completed the online application and have attended an open house or tour, the next step is to schedule a shadow visit. This step should only be taken if the school is a serious contender. During a shadow visit, your child spends a full or half day following a current student through his classes. Your child will be matched with a student with similar interests. For example, if your daughter is passionate about lacrosse, she might be matched up with another girl who is on the team.

A shadow visit is a great opportunity to get an idea of the school's routine and whether she will fit in socially. Because shadow visits require time away from your child's current school, be selective. I don't recommend partaking in one of these long appointments unless the school is one you can definitely see your child attending.

Shadow visits are as important to the admission committee as they are to the student who is applying. Be aware that your child is being observed, and faculty will talk to admission officers afterwards about their impressions.

For preschoolers, kindergarteners, and first graders, the shadow visit is more like a play date. Although it should be a relaxed and happy experience, be sure to let your child know that he is expected to follow the rules of the classroom and not simply to show up to play. Teachers want to see a child who can follow directions, get along with others, and display age-appropriate, pre-academic skills.

Regardless of age, most schools have teachers complete a rating form (this document is unique to each school), which provides the admission department information about the child's visit. This feedback is taken into account later when the child's application is reviewed for admission. Schools want to be sure the child had a successful visit and will be able to assimilate well if chosen to attend.

CHAPTER 7

Acing the Interviews

PARENT AND STUDENT INTERVIEWS ARE an important part of the process. This section will cover what to expect and how to prepare. Remember, school personnel aren't just looking at the child; they're looking at the whole family.

The Student Meeting

School personnel want to get to know your child, so the interview is a crucial step in the application process. Many directors of admission report that this is the favorite part of their job because they enjoy getting to know the students on a deeper level. Some schools will start interviews as soon as September.

Interviews are generally conducted for older elementary, middle, and high school students with the headmaster, director of admission, or another staff member. To make younger students feel more at ease, the interview is often informal—sometimes consisting of a conversation during the tour or shadow day.

Regardless of who conducts the interview and how it's done, the standards are the same; honesty and open communication are essential. Be sure your child knows what to expect beforehand so that he or she feels comfortable with the process. There's a distinct difference between helping your child feel comfortable and overly preparing her. The last thing a parent wants to do is pressure or coach excessively. Admission personnel can see through a child who has been overly coached and doesn't seem genuine. Kids should be encouraged to be themselves; they should not deliver memorized lines or canned responses.

Sometimes, students will be asked a question and their answer will consist of a word or simple phrase because they are nervous. It's appropriate to encourage your child to highlight a couple of successes that she may be especially proud of. For example, if your daughter is asked about her favorite subject, this would be a good time for her to talk about why she loves math and her experience with the *Math Counts* competition.

Here are some, but certainly not all, questions that may be asked of students:

- Why do you want to attend this school?
- How would your teachers describe you?
- Tell me about a challenge you've encountered and how you overcame it.
- What are your favorite subjects?
- What's your favorite book? Do you read outside of school?
- Who is the most important person in your life?
- What do you like to do for fun outside of school?
- Where else are you applying?
- Which three adjectives best describe you?
- Do you have any questions about our school?

Students should have a few questions of their own prepared. This shows effort and interest on the student's part. A few generic questions to consider are:

- How will I get to know new people?
- What will my daily schedule be like?
- Is there a study hall built into each day?

Students will also want to have questions specific to their own interests. Some examples include:

- I love debate, but I noticed that you don't have a debate club. If I found some other students who are interested, could I start my own after-school club?
- How many AP classes do you recommend that juniors take?
- I'd love to try out for the basketball team. How competitive is it?

Prior to the interview, be sure that your child has perused the school's website and is knowledgeable about the basics of the school. You don't want him asking obvious questions that show he knows very little about the school.

Practice Introductions

One overlooked part of the interview is the initial introduction. With your child, practice the proper way to shake hands and make eye contact. It's surprising how many kids don't have experience with this life skill. Students should be able to shake hands firmly and say, "Hi Ms. Carlson! It's so nice to meet you. Thank you for inviting me to your school today." Sometimes kids feel overwhelmed when greeting an adult in a leadership position. Practicing this skill actually makes the whole interview go much smoother because the student has started off on the right foot. Old-fashioned manners are also a must. It goes without saying that students should exhibit common courtesy by using "please," "thank you," and other niceties.

Dressing appropriately also shows respect for the school's culture. One of the most common questions I receive from parents is about what to wear for the interview. Students should adhere to the school's dress code. If the environment is formal, such as a jacket and tie or skirt and button down, then be sure your child dresses along those lines. Even at schools with no dress code or a relaxed one, it's better to be overdressed than underdressed. The same goes for the parent interview. Business casual is a good rule of thumb to follow.

The Parent Interview

Just as school personnel want to accept kids who are going to be a match at their school, they also want to engage like-minded parents. Administrators realize that parental support is vital, especially since moms and dads are involved in things like volunteering in the classroom, helping their children with homework, and going on fieldtrips, especially in the lower grades.

The importance of positive parent-school interactions cannot be overstated. An overly anxious or difficult parent may not be best for a particular school culture and admission personnel know it. I've seen students denied admission because of their parent's brusque behavior. Although cases like these are rare, keep in mind that a parent's actions can impact a child's chance of admission.

As for your interview, prepare as you would for any other important meeting. Dress professionally, have some questions prepared, and make sure you know as much as possible about the school. Lastly, be certain you and your spouse are on the same page about your child—you don't want to have a disagreement during the interview. You certainly don't need to have scripted answers, but it's a good idea to discuss beforehand possible questions you may be asked. Expect to talk about your child's strengths and weaknesses and why he or she wants to attend the school. Don't be afraid to ask questions in response. The best parent interviews flow smoothly and are not one-sided.

What Questions Can You Expect?

Aside from the initial prompt, "So, tell me a little bit about your child," there are specific questions that may be asked. Here's a list of common questions for you to think about:

- Why do you want your son or daughter to attend this school?
- What is the most important thing you would like us to know about your child?
- (If transferring schools) What prompted you to change schools?
- What are your child's strengths?
- Where does your child need improvement?
- How would teachers describe your child?
- What excites your child (specific interests, extracurriculars, etc.)?
- Tell me about a challenge your child has encountered. How did he or she overcome it?
- What does your son or daughter like to do for fun?

You will probably be asked if you have any questions about the school. Be prepared, as your inquiries show interest in the school. Consider asking some of the same questions at each school so that you can compare apples to apples. Here are a few to get started:

- Is there a particular type of child who excels at this school?
- What is the normal homework load?
- How involved are parents?
- (For primary and elementary) What is the school's approach to reading?
- Are elementary or middle school students automatically admitted to the high school?
- Does the school have any plans for expanding its facilities?
- How are grades and progress reported?
- Can you tell me about the opportunities for leadership?

If your student is pursuing athletics, consider arranging a visit beforehand with one of the coaches. This meeting will give you a good sense of the school's athletic program. Afterwards, be sure to send a thank-you note or email to the admission director and anyone else you met with.

Student Interest Can Be Compelling

Student interest is important because schools are more inclined to accept those who are highly committed and will attend if offered a slot. Admission panels do consider a student's level of interest when they evaluate applications.

If the school is truly your child's first choice, let the admission team know during the interview. However, honesty is incredibly important. It is unethical to mislead an admission associate into believing that your child will attend the school when selected if this isn't completely accurate. Many admission directors have mentioned to me that they've had parents purposefully make misleading statements about interest in order to improve their child's chances. A handful of directors mentioned that the problem has gotten worse in recent years because parents realize that interest is factored into the equation. For everyone involved, honesty is definitely the best policy when it comes to student interest.

CHAPTER 8

Getting Ready for Testing

THE EARLY FALL IS THE best time to prepare for and schedule testing. Most schools will require some type of standardized assessment to determine academic potential or current ability. Scores are an easy way to compare one student to another. But more importantly, this data is used to determine if the child is a good fit for the school. Although testing data is helpful, admission committees also realize that the numbers don't fully predict a student's level of success. That's why grades, the interview, recommendations, and extracurriculars are important. Testing is just one part of the equation.

Nonetheless, standardized tests are an important element and it's helpful to know what to expect. Most independent schools will require those applying to third grade through eleventh grade to take the Secondary School Admissions Test (SSAT) or the Independent School Entrance Examination (ISEE). Catholic schools will require the High School Placement Test (HSPT) for incoming ninth graders and many schools administer special in-house testing as well. There are also cognitive evaluations for younger students, such as the Wechsler Intelligence Scale for Children (WISC-IV) and the Wechsler Preschool and Primary Scale of Intelligence (WPPSI). In this section, you'll find information on these tests and how to help your child prepare.

The SSAT

In the DC area, the SSAT is the most widely used assessment for independent school admission. For the last nine years my company has administered the SSAT to hundreds of students throughout the Mid-Atlantic region. There's no doubt that this assessment produces a tremendous amount of anxiety. Kids place a lot of pressure on themselves. They are well aware that the most competitive schools want to see strong scores. But in some cases, the adage "a parent's stress is a child's stress" is true. Although this test and other assessments play a role in acceptance, it's vital to keep testing in perspective. There are many other factors that are more important.

The SSAT offers a national test once a month at local independent schools and testing centers from September through June. Parents can expect to pay $80 for the lower level test and $120 for the middle and upper level test. It's also possible to schedule a Flex test with a certified testing center for an additional fee. A Flex test is scored the same as the nationally administered SSAT, but it's given at a private testing location at the convenience of your schedule. The problem is that due to a new policy, there are very few Flex centers available, so finding a location to administer the test can be difficult. I now encourage parents to schedule a Flex or national test date a few months out because the centers get booked quickly. Although the national test can be taken as many times as the student wishes, the Flex test can only be administered to a student once per school year.

The most popular test date is in December, but students can actually take the test as late as early January and still be on time with their applications. Scores are sent directly from the SSAT and do not accompany the student's application. Parents can designate schools for their student's scores to be sent to during the registration process. Be sure to check the website (www.ssat.org) and sign up just as soon as registration opens.

The Nuts and Bolts of the SSAT

The upper and middle-level SSAT is a long test. It's a three-hour-and-15-minute academic assessment that begins with a 25-minute essay. Although the essay isn't graded, it is reviewed by the admission team so that they can get a sense of the child's writing ability. The writing sample is followed by five multiple choice sections. In order, the five sections are Quantitative, Critical Reading, Vocabulary, a second Quantitative portion, and an Experimental section (not graded). Critical Reading is 40 minutes, the Verbal section and each Quantitative section are 30 minutes, and the Experimental section is 15 minutes. There is a 5-minute break after the essay and a 10-minute break after the Critical Reading section.

There are three levels of the test: elementary for third and fourth grade, middle for fifth through seventh grade, and upper for eighth through eleventh grade. Students with special needs who normally have accommodations through their school, such as extra time on tests, can apply for accommodations on the SSAT. These requests must be made ahead of time through the SSAT website and proper documentation is required. This typically takes two to three weeks, so be sure to plan ahead.

How It Is Scored

The SSAT is a strategy-based test, which is often very different from what a student is used to in the classroom. For correct answers, students gain one point. For incorrect answers, students lose one-fourth of a point. For answers left blank, there is no positive or negative effect, simply a zero towards the raw score. The fact that students are penalized for wrong answers greatly affects test-taking strategy on the SSAT. Students are not necessarily expected to answer every question, and many sink their score by rushing to finish questions they may not answer correctly.

The educated guessing strategy is a best practice for students. Here's how it works: if you know the answer, fill it in and move on. If you don't know the answer, but can eliminate two of the answer choices, take a guess. This puts your odds of getting the question right at one-out-of-three (five possible answers with two eliminated). A one-out-of-three chance is worth risking one fourth of a point since, statistically, you will gain points in the long run. If you do not know the answer to the question and cannot eliminate any choices, leave the answer blank. The ultimate goal of the guessing strategy is to answer all of the questions that you have the best chance at getting right while avoiding the questions that are likely to drag your score down. It takes some practice, but if a student can master this scoring strategy, she will maximize her score on the SSAT.

The total amount of points gained and lost creates a raw score for the test, which is then converted to a range between 200 and 800 points (similar to how the SAT is scored). When you receive the score report, you will see an SSAT percentile that tells you how well your student fared against the other test takers in the *same grade* and of the *same gender*. Scoring in the 80th percentile means that the student was in the top 20 percent of his or her demographic.

In addition to the SSAT percentile, students in fifth through ninth grade receive an estimated *national* percentile, which is a comparison to other students across the country, not just to those applying to an independent school. As you can imagine, the national percentile score is higher than the SSAT percentile score, since test takers are compared to a wider pool of students from varying backgrounds. For example, a student can have a verbal score in the 53rd percentile on the SSAT scale and in the 87th percentile on the national scale. This creates a lot of confusion. Parents panic when they see that their child, who earns mostly As and Bs as report card grades, scores at a level not consistent with their classroom performance. Take these SSAT scores with a grain of salt; your child is compared *only* to others taking the SSAT. By nature, students applying to a private school are going to be academically advanced when compared to a national sample of students coming from different upbringings. Although schools only look at the SSAT score, as a parent, consider both scores to get a better indicator of your child's ability.

What Schools Are Looking For

Schools will accept a wide range of scores, with the most selective schools looking for SSAT percentile scores in the 80th or 90th percentile. Many top-flight schools, however, will accept students in the 50th to 60th percentile range on any one subtest if they think the student is a good fit due to other strengths of the application. I've had many students earn fantastic verbal and reading scores and average math scores. I've seen others score well on the math and reading, but much lower on the verbal section. As schools review paperwork and notice a difference in scores, they may dig a little deeper. For example, the student with high reading and math abilities, but substantially weaker verbal skills, may not speak English at home. Committees consider the reasons behind scores and take them into account.

Although you would expect that highly selective schools would consider only those with off-the-chart scores in each domain, that's not the case. They may select a student who has outstanding grades and only mediocre math scores because she is an exceptional writer and musician. There's no doubt that strong test scores open the door, but they do not entirely define the student.

Parents often ask, "How many times should the test be taken?" Once is usually sufficient, but if your child believes she can do better another time around, it's worth a shot. Schools will see both sets of scores unless you do not report them. Scores are only sent to the schools that are listed on the form when you register through the SSAT and are not made public. Some savvy parents will have their child take the test in October or November. If they aren't satisfied with the scores, the student can prepare some more and take it again in December or early January at the latest. Remember that the national date tests can be taken an unlimited number of times, but a Flex test can only be taken once.

The ISEE

The Independent School Entrance Examination (ISEE) is not as popular as the SSAT among independent schools in this area, but most will accept an ISEE score in its place. The cost to take the test begins at $98 for online registration. The ISEE has three levels: lower (fifth and sixth grade), middle (seventh and eighth grade), and upper (ninth through eleventh grade). For each level, the test consists of five sections: Verbal Reasoning, Quantitative Reasoning, Reading Comprehension, Mathematics Achievement, and a 30-minute essay.

Students are given 20 minutes to complete the Verbal Reasoning section, which covers synonyms and sentence completions. The Quantitative Reasoning section is a 35-minute math segment that covers algebra, geometry, number operations, problem solving, data analysis, and probability. The Reading Comprehension section is 25 minutes at the lower level and 35 minutes at the middle and upper levels. It contains short reading passages (from literature to history to science) followed by comprehension questions. The Mathematics Achievement section is 30 minutes at the lower level and 40 minutes at the middle and upper levels, and covers questions similar to the Quantitative Reasoning portion. The 30-minute essay is based on a random prompt and is not graded; however, like the SSAT, the essay is sent to schools as a writing sample.

The HSPT

The High School Placement Test (HSPT) is the main entrance test used by schools tied to a Catholic diocese. The cost is typically rolled into the school's application fee. It is a two-and-a-half-hour, multiple choice test divided into five sections: Verbal, Quantitative Skills, Reading, Math, and Language. Test takers are not penalized for wrong answers, meaning that even if time is running low, every answer should be filled in to have a chance at more points. The HSPT mainly consists of math problems, reading passages followed by questions, and vocabulary. Test scores range from 200 to 800, and standards vary from school to school.

Some schools will have a minimum score requirement while others are flexible. Since the scoring is more straightforward than the SSAT, students don't have to master a complex guessing strategy, but it's a challenging test nonetheless.

It's important to know that a student currently enrolled in a diocesan Catholic school can apply only to two schools in the state or district in which he or she takes the test. For example, if your son attends St. Mark

Catholic School in Vienna and wishes to apply to Paul VI and Bishop O'Connell, it's not a problem. He can also apply to one other school in Maryland or DC, such as Gonzaga, but he is not permitted to apply for additional schools in Virginia, Maryland, or DC. Catholic schools have this policy to prevent students from applying to too many schools in which they're not fully invested. It forces students to research and tour schools of interest in order to narrow down the list to serious contenders. Boys and girls applying from independent or public schools are not limited by this policy.

The WISC-IV

The Wechsler Intelligence Scale for Children (WISC-IV) is an intelligence test that can be given to children ages 6-16, and it does not require any reading or writing. The test is administered by an examiner, typically a psychologist, for 65-80 minutes. After the test, an IQ score is generated, which is used as a broad representation of a child's cognitive ability. The WISC-IV is divided into fifteen subtests, but it tests four core abilities: Verbal Comprehension, Perceptual Reasoning, Processing Speed, and Working Memory.

The format of the test includes everything from asking direct questions ("Define this word") to questions about visual stimuli ("Which pictures go together?"). Children are asked to describe how two things are similar, answer general knowledge questions, use clues to discover a word, complete missing pictures, and provide letters and numbers in particular orders. The result is an IQ score that schools can use as a marker for general cognitive ability.

Costs vary and can range from $350 to $450. The school to which your child is applying can provide you with a list of experienced local testers.

The WPPSI-IV

The Wechsler Preschool and Primary Scale of Intelligence (WPPSI-IV) is similar to the WISC-IV, but intended for children between two-and-a-half years old and seven years and three months old. Like the WISC-IV, the test assesses developmentally appropriate skills and results in a Full Scale IQ score as well as an evaluation of five core abilities: Verbal Comprehension, Visual Spatial, Working Memory, Fluid Reasoning, and Processing Speed. It typically takes 60-75 minutes to complete. Children are asked to recreate color patterns, match symbols, solve matrices, put puzzle pieces together, and answer general knowledge questions.

As with the WISC-IV, fees for administration also vary but may be slightly lower because of the shorter duration of the test. Parents can expect to pay between $325 and $425. Ask the school for recommendations in your area.

Preparing for the WISC-IV and WPPSI-IV

According to Diana Dahlgren, Ph.D., a licensed clinical psychologist who specializes in testing and evaluations, IQ preparation is not advisable. "Unlike group standardized tests such as the SSAT, there is no preparation for an individually administered IQ test such as the WISC-IV or WPPSI-IV. It is helpful for parents to tell a child one or two days before the appointment that he will be meeting with a person who is similar to a teacher who will have him do puzzles, look at pictures, and answer questions. By definition, an IQ test consists of questions and tasks a child has not seen or practiced before. The WISC-IV and WPPSI-IV materials are copyrighted to protect the validity of the test results and are not available for review either before or after the test. Details about a child's intellectual skills, strengths and weaknesses, and learning style are given to parents in a feedback session, but the specific questions are not released. Parents should know that experienced psychologists help a child feel at ease during a warm-up session and give all of the proper directions to a child during the test with the goal of getting an accurate assessment of a child's cognitive abilities. Thus, there is no preparation for an IQ test except the classic admonition that a child should get a good night's sleep and have a good breakfast before taking any test."

In-House Testing

Some schools will require special in-house testing in addition to (or in place of) a standardized test. By giving candidates their own test while they're on campus, usually during the shadow visit, admission personnel can quickly compare potential new students to their current students who may have already taken the same test. They can see where the child might fit in the school. In-house testing is also beneficial because the test's questions and problems are in line with what the school believes students should know at any given grade. It's hard to prepare for these tests since there are no study guides or tips, but the good news is that every other student is in the same boat. Besides good test-taking strategies (get plenty of sleep, eat breakfast, cross off bad answers), there's often not much more you can do, and that's okay.

Other Testing

There are other tests that a student can take, and if a student is past his freshman year in high school, schools will often take his PSAT score in lieu of other testing. When in doubt, feel free to ask the school. There is more flexibility in testing than you would think, so don't assume that your student's ERB or other test scores won't count. Ultimately, all of these tests are examining the same thing—general subject knowledge (math, reading comprehension, and writing).

Would My Child Benefit from Test Prep?

Students need to be prepared for what they will encounter on test day on the SSAT, ISEE, and HSPT. At a minimum, your child should know the types of questions he will see, the correct test-taking strategies to use, how the test is scored, and how to pace himself throughout the test. You can order a prep manual for your child to work through, but most students do not have the discipline to study independently. A tutor experienced with the ins and outs of standardized testing can help students perform up to their potential. According to Dr. Diana Dahlgren, "The SSAT is similar to a mini-SAT so it is good practice for the tests students will take in high school, and very few students walk in and take the SAT or ACT without practice."

Most students perform best when preparation is threefold and includes: content review, strategy practice, and simulated practice tests. A good tutor will review your child's practice test scores to see where he can improve and structure sessions to maximize gains.

CHAPTER 9

Making the *Right* Decision

BY MID-JANUARY, ALL THE HEAVY lifting should be complete. Applications, transcripts, recommendations, essays, and standardized testing should be behind you. Now it's time to think ahead.

Stack Ranking Your Schools

In late February, sit down with your child and significant other to create a game plan for dealing with the admission letters you will receive in another week or so. Start by writing down the top three choices. In a perfect world, Plan A would have your son or daughter being accepted to choice number one, but the reality is that you need Plan B, Plan C, and probably Plan D, too. Basically, by the time decision letters come out, your child should have a good idea of where she'll attend even if her first few options aren't realized. Ask yourself questions like: "If she doesn't get into #1, is #2 just as good?" and "If her first two choices don't work out, is #3 a good option?"

Planning for Possible Outcomes: Denial, Waitlist, Acceptance

Just the other day I had a parent tell me, "Waiting two months to hear is the hardest part of the whole thing!" By mid-January you will have submitted every last piece of paperwork, but not knowing the outcome is stress-inducing even for the calmest parent. For schools with a January deadline, admission decisions are typically mailed (usually emailed these days) in early March. Your child will either be accepted, waitlisted, or denied.

If your child has been waitlisted or denied, it's not the end of the world, and it doesn't necessarily mean that you did anything wrong. Competitive schools have so many qualified applicants that they can fill their class twice over and still have to say no to many. In fact, one admission director mentioned that he could fill each grade level with siblings of current students and still have a waitlist after that. At the most selective schools, acceptance is a numbers game.

Competition can also vary greatly year to year, and it can be harder for boys than girls and vice versa in a given year depending on the applicant pool. In certain years, I've had students accepted into highly competitive schools and waitlisted at less competitive schools. There was almost always a reason behind these outcomes. For example, in one student's case, the school we thought she'd be accepted to had many daughters of alumni apply that particular year. Factors like these are out of parents' control and there's no sense staying awake at night worrying about it. Here's what you can do if your child has been waitlisted or denied admission.

The Denial Letter

Receiving a denial letter is tough to take because it feels like a personal rejection. The first thoughts that crop up in a parent's mind are, "Why didn't the admission committee like my daughter?" It's easy to go on the defensive, but you shouldn't go in that direction. Admission departments review applications for a living and these folks know which types of students will do well at their school and which ones will not. Their experience allows them to accept students who are best suited for the school. Sometimes a denial is a blessing in disguise because it's likely that the student would not have had a positive experience at that school.

If you submitted an application to a handful of schools, then you can take a denial letter in stride. The problem occurs if your child applied to only a few schools and was denied acceptance into all of them. At that point, you have three choices:

1. **Apply late to less competitive schools.** Some of the most engaging and compelling schools in our area accept a range of students with varying abilities and many of these schools are on rolling admission. It's not unusual for students to apply in late spring or early summer if the school has fall openings. Make some phone calls right away to determine which schools have space.

2. **Put off the decision to the following year.** If you have flexibility, consider keeping your child in his current school and applying the following year. If the rejection came down to academic deficiencies, you can spend the next year building your child's skills for a better

shot in the future. Most admission departments will be fairly honest with you about the reason behind your child's denial.

3. **Consider the public option.** Independent schools aren't the only option. Assess the viability of your public school. Things can change from year to year, so even if it wasn't a possibility earlier, a new administrator, new teachers, or additional programs could make it a worthwhile choice.

If you ultimately decide to hold off and apply again the following year, it's important to know that some schools will roll the application over to the following year so you won't need to start from scratch. That means that you may not need new recommendation forms and standardized test scores. If you're still interested in the school for the following year, let the admission office know right away.

How Do I Break the News to My Child?

Many parents often ask, "How do I tell my son he was not accepted?" or "What if my daughter breaks down in tears because she's so upset?" The best way to handle the situation is with honesty. I've found that it's best not to withhold the truth because the child may find out later on his own. You can explain that many students apply and that the school only has room for a few students. Let your child know that it isn't a personal decision as to whether or not the school likes him. In many cases, it simply comes down to the numbers. Schools can take only a certain number of students, so they will naturally choose those with top grades, top test scores, and other accomplishments.

The Waitlist Letter

Receiving a letter notifying you that your child has been waitlisted can be confusing. What exactly is a waitlist? The waitlist is actually a pool of all applicants who are waiting to gain admission to the school. Students are not ranked in any particular order on the waitlist because the school may not know yet what type of student they'll need to round out the class. For example, a school may accept 40 students for 20 available openings, hoping to enroll 10 boys and 10 girls. If 15 students accept enrollment and 10 of these students are boys, the admission team is going to pick mostly girls from the waitlist to create a balanced class. Sometimes there are other factors at play, from academic interest to athletic ability to cultural diversity. Ultimately, the decision of who is taken off the waitlist comes down to what type of student is needed to complete the student body that year.

Moving Off the Waitlist

When do schools take students off the waitlist? There are a few time frames that this is likely to happen. The first is just after new student contracts are due, which is typically around mid-April. At this time, all students who were offered admission and plan on attending must officially enroll and put down a deposit. If there are still openings, students on the waitlist will be contacted. Soon thereafter, on or around June 1, accepted students who were waiting on additional financial aid must let the school know if they will be attending. If the student's aid package isn't large enough and additional money is not available from the school, the student may decide not to accept enrollment because he or she cannot afford to attend. That may result in open spaces becoming available as well.

Throughout the summer, some students who may have initially accepted may choose not to attend, for a variety of reasons, thereby opening up additional slots. As Ann Miller at Madeira School points out, "We take people off the waitlist throughout the summer because there are so many factors to be considered. For some students, financial aid issues are at hand." She states that it's always a good idea for parents to call the school directly for more information on their child's status.

According to consultant Clare Anderson of Bethesda, Maryland, the chances of getting off the waitlist "can vary significantly from school to school. A waitlist status means that your child meets criteria for admission to the particular school, but for one reason or another, space is at issue. Keep in mind that should a space surface, the admission committee will meet to review the entire wait pool. That is, your child, along with the other students on the waitlist, will be discussed to determine who is the best fit, always considering the make-up of the class and how successful your child might be in this group."

Clare also understands that parents want to know where their child stands in the mix. "Parents need to contact the school directly to emphasize their child's continued strong interest in the school. Always call and ask about the possibility of being accepted from the waitlist. Prepare yourself for what you may not want to hear. Admission officers tell it like it is when it comes to the waitlist. Do keep in mind that the name says it all." In other words, the more selective the school, the harder it may be to get off the waitlist. Furthermore, some schools tend to waitlist the majority of students they do not accept and some maintain a very small waitlist. That's why contacting the school to get a sense of where your child stands is helpful.

Interest is a big factor, according to Clare. "Schools want to enroll students who want to attend their school. Timing is everything when it comes to a waitlist. It is a win-win for an admission committee to be able to select a student from their waitlist who they are almost 100% certain will accept their offer. Sometimes it simply means waiting if you are able and willing to stay in the running."

The question is, "Are you willing to wait it out?" If you have other solid options, then giving up your slot at another terrific school on a hope and a prayer that your child will get into the school that has waitlisted her is probably not a good idea. Some parents will hold off on sending in the contract to the second-choice school until the very last minute to see if their child makes it off the list, but the chances of that happening are usually slim.

The Acceptance Letter

If your child is accepted, congratulations! All of your hard work has paid off. Now the exciting part begins of deciding between schools that have accepted your child. If you went through the process of stack ranking schools earlier, you probably have a good sense of the best choice, but opinions can be swayed in those final weeks leading up to an ultimate decision.

What Should Influence Your Decision and What Should Not

Receiving acceptance letters from multiple schools is a good thing, but for some families, having lots of options can lead to more anxiety. Thankfully, there are "revisit days," which are pre-arranged days of festivities for parents *and* students. Schools go all out to make a great impression because they want their accepted students to commit and enroll in their school. Although a revisit day isn't mandatory, your child should absolutely attend if the school is at the top of the list. I love it when my clients go to revisit days, for two reasons. The first is that they are completely energized if they have a great day, and most do. Students often tell me that they've fallen in love with the school all over again (especially when it's their first choice) and can't wait to attend in the fall. But even more importantly, the revisit days provide clarity to the whole family. If the student attends three revisit days at equally qualified schools, he will typically get a clear sense of which school he feels most drawn to. Parents will have a feeling one way or another as well. For most families, revisit days are all it takes to make a final decision.

But for others, multiple acceptance letters and revisit days lead to second-guessing, mainly because parents and students have competing interests. Parents may be gung-ho about one school, while their child may be most excited about another. If you get down to brass tacks, the question may be, "Whose opinion matters most?" Is it the child's or the parent's? And if both sides have varying views, how do they come together to make the *right* decision?

I asked directors of admission this very question. The consensus is that the older and more mature the student is, the greater say he should have, but the ultimate decision should be one that the parents make. Many stated that they've seen more and more parents in recent years put the decision in the hands of their adolescent, which isn't necessarily the right thing to do. They feel that students, most of whom are rising middle and high schoolers, are given too much power without enough parental direction. Even in the teenage years, students still need guidance that only an adult can provide in order to settle on a school for the right reasons.

In Tucker's case, the decision was a family consensus guided by him. Tucker, a rising freshman from Great Falls, Virginia, and his brother Wyatt, a rising seventh grader, considered five different schools. After touring each one, he and Wyatt knew that two schools stood out among the rest. "We really liked Bullis, and my dad especially liked Bullis, but he didn't tell me that right away." Instead, Tucker's father, Conrad, encouraged his sons to think more about each school without revealing his opinion.

Tucker said, "Bullis is pretty big, I was intrigued by that, but I've been in a large public school for a long time. At Landon, everybody was one big family and everyone knew each other and had connections with each other. Not only does Landon have great academics, they have a phenomenal sports side to the school."

Conrad reserved his judgment until his sons mulled over their options. As a family, they talked about it and ultimately came down to Landon as their first choice. "Collaborating about it felt good," said Tucker. "I had a sigh of relief that we got in and everything was done. As the year has gone by, my parents have given me a lot of leeway with big decisions. My family is a little bit different from others, but all in all it came down to what I said and what I wanted to do. We narrowed it down and the final decision was pretty much mine."

Other Factors Can Be at Play

As a consultant, I've noticed that many students are influenced by factors that are not highly meaningful. I recently asked one eighth grader about the compelling reasons for each of the top schools on his list. He mentioned that he loved the two-week golf trip that one school offered over Spring Break and he thought that receiving a MacBook Air at another school was "really cool." As adults, we understand that these factors are not significant when making a life-changing decision, but to adolescents, they are influential.

Students can give superficial reasons for liking a school merely because they can't put their finger on what it is that resonates with them. I've found that sometimes students will focus on non-important information when asked why they liked a school. They may say, "The lunch was great!" or "The history teacher remembered my name from when I met him on the tour," or "I loved the girl who was with me on the shadow visit!" or "They have a 3-D printer!" I always try to dig a little deeper because, in some cases, students are really pointing to a general feeling of inclusiveness and warmth that they felt.

If this is the case with your child, try asking specific questions in response to his statements. If your child mentions the delicious cafeteria food, you might say, "Did you meet a lot of kids in the lunchroom that seemed a lot like you? Do you think you'll fit in well there?" In response to the history teacher comment, try asking, "Was there something about his teaching style that you liked? How did he make the topic seem exciting? Did you notice that other teachers were inspiring, too?"

It's not uncommon for kids to become fixated on a school with exceptional sports facilities or state-of-the-art technology. You may ask, "How does the 3-D printer help learning? Do you see yourself becoming involved in the school's robotics program?" In other words, don't just brush off your child's seemingly superficial comments. Try to see if there's a deeper sentiment. For some there is, and for some there isn't. And for those students who are influenced by factors that shouldn't be important, it's your role as a parent to guide them properly.

Friends Matter More Than You Think

Keep in mind that your child's desires will probably be based on things outside of academics. Parents, on the other hand, are most influenced by the academic reputation of the school. It really takes a marrying of the minds to come to a consensus.

The driving influence for most students is whether the school feels like a fit socially. It's not surprising that when decision letters come out, students are often eager to go where their friends might be going. For instance, if your son realizes that the majority of his friends will be attending a school that wasn't at the top of his own list, he can become conflicted. Don't be surprised if he suddenly announces that he's changed his mind. It's always a good idea to reaffirm why your child wanted to go to his top choice in the first place. Instead of overreacting, sit down and calmly discuss the pros and cons of both schools. Sometimes, kids need a calming influence in order to think rationally so that they don't get caught up in a purely emotional approach to selecting a school. Often, these reactions are fueled by anxiety and a simple case of nerves. Last-minute decisions solely based on who is attending which school are never a good thing.

Prioritize the Most Important Criteria

If you're in turmoil about the decision and seem to be at an impasse, try this technique: Take a piece of paper and pencil and jot down what's important to your family. I do this activity with the families at the end of the process when there's a decision to be made quickly, but it also helps parents at the beginning when they are first putting together their list of schools. This type of data-driven activity eliminates preconceived ideas that can sometimes influence decisions. If you're considering a move from public school in the first place, it's well worth the time. Here's how it works:

First, with your child, jot down as many factors as you think are important in a school. Some ideas include: strength of academic program, sports, social life, opportunities for leadership, single-sex or co-ed, location, specialty programs that interest your child, quality of teachers, low cost, study abroad, etc. Your list should be long—be creative and let the ideas flow. Next, choose the top three that are most important and then select three to five secondary factors that are also important.

Now, pop each school into a simple spreadsheet. Here's an easy example to get you started:

Criteria	Maple	Everwood
Strength of Academic Program	1	1
Competitive Soccer Team	1	1
Kids are Like Me	1	0
Top Categories – Add and Multiply by Two	3x2=6	2x2=4
Robotics Program	1	1
Good Location	1	0
Matriculation List	0	1
Grand Totals	6+2=8	4+2=6

For the three most important factors, rate the school as a "1" if it's highly likely to meet the criteria or a "0" if it's not likely to meet the criteria. Add up the total in each column and multiply by two. You will doubly weight these three factors because you have deemed them to be highly important.

In the second section (criteria that are important but not as vital as those in the first section), rate each factor with a "1" or a "0." Similarly, a "1" means the school is highly likely to meet the criteria and "0" means it's not likely to meet it. Add these numbers to the result in the first section. You should now have a total tally for each school. In the example above, Maple School might be a better option when evaluating the facts and taking emotion out of the decision.

You only need to go to these lengths if you're truly stuck and need objectivity to help make your decision. It's far more likely that your intuition will guide you in making the right decision, but don't be afraid to apply a little mathematical impartiality when needed.

Making the Right Decision

As you will hear from parents interviewed in the following chapter, gut instinct matters a lot and it almost always puts you on the right path. Once you've listened to your intuition, collaborated with your child, and weighed the objective information you have, the *right* decision will have been made. In the end, the decision is not about "the best" school or where *you* may have liked to have gone yourself when you were a child. The decision must be about goodness of fit.

PART III

Advice from the Experts

THE FOLLOWING SECTION IS ONE of my favorite parts of this book. It's enlightening to hear others' points of view. It may be your first inclination to read only the chapter with hints and tips from the admission directors themselves, but I encourage you to learn from other parents and students, too.

I want to sincerely thank all the individuals who contributed their personal stories to this section. The admission personnel took precious time out of their day in the middle of admission season to speak to me. Many of the parents shared heartfelt information that they feel may help others. And the voices of the children are especially precious.

Some parents and students felt their experiences were a bit too revealing and asked to have their names withheld. Their requests were, of course, granted. In a few cases, the child's name was changed completely and in all cases only first names were used.

I hope that this section, filled with advice and experiences, will be helpful to you during your school search.

CHAPTER 10

Interviews with Local Admission Professionals

JUST WHAT EXACTLY ARE ADMISSION boards looking for in the first place? Is it the same at every school? What should I emphasize on the application? These seemingly simple questions are on every parent's mind, but the answers are more complicated. What one admission committee values in an applicant may not be important to another school's committee. On the following pages, you will find inside information from some of the well-respected professionals in the area. I'm confident that their experience and words of wisdom will help guide your search and final selection.

Choosing the Right Students Is More a Work of Art than a Science

Brian Gilbert, Dean of Admission at Georgetown Preparatory School in North Bethesda, relies on his school's mission statement to guide decisions his office makes. "Our mission is really central to everything we do here. We are trying to form men of confidence, compassion, competence, and courage. Academically, they have to be really driven young men that have shown academic success." As you can see from Prep's mission statement, it is not just about academics: "Along with this, we're looking for contributors. We want young men who will contribute in athletics, extracurriculars, and as leaders. At the end of the day, they have to be interested in our Catholic mission. We are the oldest Catholic school in the nation for boys. Students here don't have to be Catholic, but they do have to be open to being involved in what that mission entails—going to mass with us, being in service to others, joining in on the retreat." Outside of the mission, Brian says that it's important that potential students fit into the school's culture.

Brian is quick to point out that "Test scores and grades get you in the conversation," but that there are many other factors they consider.

"Someone who has done really great service work always stands out. We get the typical student who has worked through their church or has done a canned food drive, but something that is above and beyond always makes a student stand out. So does a student who is multi-talented in terms of athletics and music or the arts."

At Georgetown Prep, a student's essays and interview are vitally important. "If you can make your essay or your interview stand out, that certainly helps push some over the top. For the interviews, you have to have done some research on the school and certainly show a desire to want to attend the school and enroll if you're accepted. We're really looking for honesty. The canned responses don't really fly that well. I think that being prepared, in that you know the school and you know yourself, can help you do well."

According to Brian and other admission directors, positive teacher recommendations are a must. "Teacher recommendations play a big part. It's always difficult when a great student has rough recommendations because, from a confidentiality standpoint, it isn't something that we can share with families."

There are many different types of students who do well at Prep. "If there were just one type of student, we wouldn't really be true to our mission. Consistently, the students who are driven and hardworking do really well. We do work our guys. We often hear when students return from college that college is easier than our high school. This is not a school where the kids leave at 2:45. Many of them are here for 12 hours and many live here (the school has a small boarding population). It's kind of a second home for many of our students."

Brian has some good advice for parents who are new to the admission process. "I think you need to start a little early. By seventh grade you should have gone to some open houses and narrowed down your list. I think the most important thing is that you want to be at the point where, by the time acceptance letters come out, you know where you want to go. It saves families a lot of headaches. In addition, financial aid can be pretty daunting to families, so you want to make sure that you get all your information and documentation in early."

He also recommends that parents visit schools outside of planned tours and other events. "Go to the schools when they're not expecting you. Go to sporting events, go to plays, and try to get a sense of the students and the environment at each school. You want to see what the students are like when they don't know you're watching. I think that can reveal a lot about a school."

Although Brian feels that students should be part of the decision-making process, he believes that parents need to take the lead. "A kid has to be happy, but at the same time, parents have to help the student decide what is best and guide him through the process. It can't just be about where a young man's friends are going or how happy they were at lunch and how good the food was, which is often what drives a 14-year-old boy.

"Parents can help their student learn to make a wise decision. Parents are often surprised to find that their son's decision may be driven by social media such as Facebook and Twitter. Suddenly, the boy sees on a posting that 15 of his friends are going to one school and his natural reaction is to jump on the bandwagon. I think that parents need to be involved in the whole process with their sons and daughters as they make these decisions."

Brian points out that there are many great options in our area and in some ways you can't lose. "So many families think these decisions are the be-all-end-all. I think that taking a step back and realizing that, at the end of the day, these kids are going to be okay is important. Just having a little bit of perspective about this process is a good thing—staying off the blogs, not listening to what the neighbors are saying or the chatter about who got in where or what this young man's SSAT scores are. Comparing your child to other children just drives everyone insane."

Keep an Open Mind

Scott Conklin is the director of admission at Episcopal High School on a 130-acre campus in the heart of Alexandria. Episcopal is a unique place because it's the only all-boarding school inside the Beltway where students live on campus, as does most of the faculty.

The college prep curriculum is a rigorous one; therefore, strong report card grades and standardized test scores are essential. "The first thing we look for is academic readiness. To evaluate that, we look at a student's transcripts from the past few years. We also require standardized testing. The average GPA for an incoming freshman student is a 3.5, so we're looking for A/B students. The average standardized testing is around the 70th percentile. We want to be sure that students can handle the work load academically."

At Episcopal, there's more to an applicant than grades and test scores. "We're also looking for really good kids with character and integrity. In a 100% boarding environment, we need kids who can get along with each other and who will also be engaged in the community.

To assess that, we look at their recommendations from their school principal or counselor and English and math teachers. We look for work ethic but also for character and integrity. We evaluate that through the interview, which is a required part of the application process. Because we ask our students to participate in afternoon options such as athletics, the arts, or community service, we're really looking for kids with either special talents or the desire to try different things."

The most successful students have to be able to be hardworking and willing to advocate for themselves. "At Episcopal, 90% of the faculty lives on campus, so there are many opportunities to find time to meet with your teachers. Kids are successful here if they recognize that they need help and take advantage of the opportunities available to them."

Scott encourages parents to be proactive and visit all types of different schools. "There is so much to a school that you can discover on your visit. Our tours are student led, so you really get to engage the students, talk to them about their experiences, see classrooms in action, and observe the teachers teaching. Go visit campuses, meet the people, see the school in action—I think that's critical.

"Look at various types of schools. See what feels right. Early in the process you can narrow down your list to schools that you feel are appropriate fits. I think that looking in the spring of seventh grade or early eighth is helpful. Start the process early, identify which schools you're really passionate about, and tour the campus and meet the people. If you complete those by Thanksgiving break, that puts you in a great position to avoid some of the stressors when you're trying to complete applications in December or January, when the deadline is right around the corner."

Ninety-Six on the Waiting List . . . And It's Only Preschool

Tania Ryan is an expert in the field of early childhood education. For the last 12 years, she's been the director at the highly sought-after Meeting House Cooperative Preschool in Old Towne Alexandria. "When I started here 12 years ago, 90% of the kids went on to kindergarten at independent schools. Then I saw a shift as the public schools started getting better and better and the economy started getting worse. Parents were entertaining the thought of going to their public school. Now, more than half go to public and the remaining go to independent schools. Of those, some travel as far as Beauvoir, Maret, and St. Patrick's. Some go to St. Stephen's & St. Agnes, St. Mary's, Potomac, and Burgundy Farm Country Day."

Tania says that choosing a school after preschool is a very difficult decision for most parents. Some will choose their local public school, but others are committed to an independent education. "What I like to say to them is, 'Forget about what your neighbor is doing. Forget about what your mother-in-law is saying to you. Sit down and think about the core of your own family, what you believe in, and what your goals for your child are. And then think about the reality of what an independent school will cost you. Will that tax you in a way that will create such a strain on your family and ultimately your marriage?' Get a hold of that first, and then understand where you land. Explore independent schools with open eyes."

She encourages parents to look at many options, including their local elementary school. "Go to PTA meetings at your public school. The funny thing is that people don't realize that they can learn so much about the local public school just by attending PTA meetings. You get to know about the issues bubbling up at any school. You get to hear from the principal, from the PTA president, from the active parent population. It's an hour and a half well spent."

Although Meeting House does not require the WPPSI IQ test for young children, Tania recommends it to all parents, whether their child is headed to an independent or public school. "This information starts your benchmark of understanding where your child is cognitively, without being something that you have to share with everyone outside your family. It can serve as a good guide for understanding your child's ability now and as he or she gets older."

Getting in Early is Key

St. Patrick's Episcopal Day School in Northwest DC enrolls approximately 500 students from nursery school to eighth grade. Once students come to St. Pat's they typically stay through middle school, so applying and getting in early is key. In fact, the school's largest entry points are at ages three and four. Jennifer Danish, the assistant head of school for enrollment, communications, and marketing, states that St. Pat's looks for several criteria. "We're looking for general school readiness in very young children. We have students come to our campus for play dates and oftentimes these play dates can be stressful, particularly for parents. We work very hard to make it a warm and accommodating process for a young child."

For some youngsters, separating from their parents when they arrive at St. Patrick's can be a scary experience since they're going to a new place filled with many new faces. So often, when children become visibly upset, their parents worry that their behavior will negatively impact their child's chances of getting into the school. Fortunately, that's not the case. "We make it clear to parents that the separation moment is not a make-or-break moment for us as a school and our decision making. It's important for parents to stay calm and be themselves, to be as forthcoming and honest as they can about their child and what kind of fit they're looking for."

Beyond preschool, St. Patrick's has some available slots. "We often have more than a few spots available for fourth grade and sometimes seventh grade, usually due to attrition. And when we do, we're looking for kids who can fit into our program and successfully make a transition into a new school setting."

Jennifer recommends being geographically flexible. "If you live in Virginia, don't rule out schools in DC; if you live in DC, same thing. Give yourself a pretty broad reach. Look at the websites, look at the educational philosophy. Is there a plan that the school employs to teach? Be a savvy consumer; use some of that internet research and get an initial feel. In the end, you've got to go on school tours. You've got to be in the school, in the buildings. If you can get a chance to hear from the head of the school, that's a really important part because he or she can speak to the strengths of the program. Make sure you plan for fall open houses or individual tours that the school offers."

Although Jennifer encourages parents to consider many different schools, she doesn't believe that parents need to apply to more than a few. "Parents have gotten to the point where they are applying to six, seven, eight schools and I think that's a little too much. Internet research and touring can help pare down a really good list for families. Parents know their children and they have to trust their instincts about what is needed in a school setting."

Intuitive Factors Are Just as Important as Tangible Data

As director of admission at St. Stephen's & St. Agnes (SSSAS) in Alexandria, Diane Dunning has worked with hundreds of families throughout the years. She believes that one unexpected factor is equally important for admission personnel and parents alike—intuition.

When Diane and her committee review an applicant's file, they consider the expected criteria such as test scores, grades, teacher recommendations, and outside interests, but they look for something more than that. "There are intangibles that we look at. We want students who are intellectually curious, who are excited about learning. What often sets a child apart is that intellectual spark. That's the only way I can describe it, since it's intangible. You see it in a shy child as much as you see it in a highly extroverted one."

Another factor that can make or break an applicant's chances is the way the student interacts with others. "We want to see that children will get along with each other and that they are respectful of their peers as well as adults." Diane said that they look for children who can be kind to other people, not because they feel the microscope is on them but because it is in their innate personality. Diane elaborated, "Sometimes I am working with a family with a child who has extraordinary test scores across the various disciplines, and they are surprised if the student isn't accepted. But it may be that the other area, the character area, was a challenge for that child. Both areas are important to us."

Diane did not wish to downplay the role of tangible data. "I'd be dishonest if I said test scores weren't important, but we also know that character and intuitive factors allow students to have success both morally and academically."

This expectation is directly in line with SSSAS's mission statement. "It is vital that families understand and agree with a school's mission statement. The mission is more than just words on the school's website. It's something you feel the moment you step foot on the campus." This mission statement should be reflected in everything the school does, and "once you get the whole tour [of the school], you will probably have this emotional connection or disconnect with that particular school. I think what you're feeling is the reflection of the mission. So as much as you need a lot of data, I think you need to combine your data with your parental instinct."

Ultimately, Diane believes that if both the family and the school present themselves honestly and both parties trust their instincts, the child will be placed in the best environment. "I wish I could provide families with an exact algorithm on how to figure all of this out, but the truth is there is no proven formula in choosing the right school for your child. It's not an exact science, it's more like an art. The decision doesn't lie in the prestige that you hear about the school, or standardized test results, but again back to that right match, between the child's strengths and needs and the school's expectations and offerings. It's important to never make a child feel that only one school is successful because if it's not the right match, the child is going to pay the price both academically and emotionally. We know that parents see us [the admission department] as gatekeepers, but we really want to be the people who open doors to as many families as we can."

Every Parent's List Should Contain at Least One Same-Sex School

Madeira School is an independent all-girls boarding and day school in McLean. The school serves approximately 320 students from 20 different states. About half of the students live on campus and the other half are day students. For the last nine years, Ann Miller has been the director of admission at Madeira and, as you can imagine, she is passionate about all-girls education. "Every parent who is looking for an independent school for their child should have at least one single-sex school on their list. I don't think parents are doing due diligence in a search without that. These schools are such unique institutions."

Over the years, Ann has found that parents and their children will rule out single-sex schools without even visiting them. "You owe it to your child to understand this concept better and the best way to understand is to visit. Girls have preconceived notions about what single-sex schools will be like and they are not anything like that. Our current students tell us that all the time. There are many girls here who say, 'Never in a million years did I think I'd end up at an all-girls school. But when I came to Madeira and saw the opportunities available here, it overruled my concerns about the single-sex piece. I realized I really liked it.' If you don't consider a single-sex school because of preconceived notions, you're cutting out important schools."

Ann states that a girl's success after high school and college begins in the classroom. "We know that when teenage girls are upset, stressed, or socially self-conscious, the ability to learn diminishes. The concept is that if you have all this social stimuli you're processing while you're also trying to study chemistry, for example, it's very difficult to accomplish both. We know that experientially and from what has been published in the research. When you put girls in a single-sex academic setting, the social pressure is so low that they can learn freely in an unfettered way. I can recommend a great book by JoAnn Deak called *How Girls Thrive*, which explores the science behind girls' learning."

When Ann and her admission team review applications, they look for specific elements that help determine a girl's readiness. "We at

Madeira are very concerned about an academic fit because the program is a challenging one. We are providing a rigorous academic program in four days with the fifth day dedicated to the internship program where girls are off campus. Our goal is to make sure the girl coming in can be successful in our academic program. We want her to be able to thrive here in the classroom, on the stage, on the athletic fields, in making friendships, and in taking leadership roles.

"We have a fairly narrow set of assessments. One is the SSAT test. But for girls coming from the Washington, DC area, we actually pay more attention to the transcript and teacher recommendations. We know these schools and we know these teachers. For example, for a girl coming from the DC area, we're looking for As and Bs on her report card, and an English and a math teacher recommendation that speaks about her resiliency and her ability to work hard and be prepared in class. At the next level, we look at SSAT scores. We also factor in the interview and other pieces of information we've gathered."

When asked about how she compares applicants' grades, especially when an A from one school may be a B at another school, Ann said, "All of what we gather serves as information—none of it is in a vacuum. If a girl has a B from school X, but has very strong verbal and reading SSAT scores, and if the teacher talks about her ability to dissect complicated text, that girl is a very strong candidate for us. Similarly, a girl with an A from another school, but with moderate SSAT scores and an English teacher recommendation that's not extraordinary, is not somebody who's going to go to the top of our list. There is no hard-and-fast rule. We have about 400 applications that we read every year and we admit about half of those girls."

Like other upper schools in our region, Madeira serves high school students in grades nine to twelve. As can be expected, ninth grade is the largest entry year at Madeira, but interestingly, Ann and her staff receive many applications for tenth grade. "The sophomore year is a big entry year for us now. There's a whole group of families in Fairfax County who say, 'Let's give the ninth grade a try in our public high school,' and then come spring, they get the report card and realize that the school didn't meet their goal." In the end, Ann encourages parents to broaden their horizons to consider an all-girls school, whether it's for the freshman or sophomore year.

Finding a School You Can Buy Into

Burgundy Farm Country Day School educates almost 300 children from junior kindergarten through eighth grade. The school's primary 25-acre

Alexandria campus is complemented by a 500-acre site in West Virginia. For the past two years, Lori Adams has served as director of admission. Because of the uniqueness of Burgundy, she feels that it's important that parents appreciate the school's philosophy. "We want parents who understand our mission and have complete buy-in to our program. For instance, we send our children to our West Virginia campus, starting in the first grade, on an overnight trip and subsequently twice a year from second grade on. We want parents to know in advance the kind of experience their kids will have."

Lori and her team are looking for students who are inquisitive and have a love for nature. "We are looking for bright children who are creative and enthusiastic about learning. Burgundy provides a very collaborative learning experience, very hands-on, and project-oriented. We want kids who aren't afraid to get their hands dirty since they go outdoors a lot. Our campus includes a barnyard and barnyard animals, a pond, and a garden area. In addition, the students take a number of 'specials' classes, including music, art, drama, P.E., library, and computer. We expose them to French and Spanish from the very beginning, when they're four years old. We're looking for the families who want this very enriched experience for their children."

Burgundy is in demand. Lori receives hundreds of applications each year, but there are things families can do to stand out. "I know a family is really excited about what we have to offer if they make an effort not only to come to an open house, which many families do, but also do an independent tour with me as well. That really shows me that they feel a connection. I know many people are applying to a number of schools, but I can see from the schools to which they're applying whether we are the kind of environment that they believe would best serve them. Let's say we are the only progressive school they're considering and they're looking at five other schools that are very traditional in nature. I will ask a lot of questions to get a sense of their comfort level with our progressive program."

Independent schools can come with a steep price tag, but that should not be a limiting factor. "Don't assume that independent schools aren't possible because of tuition costs. There are many schools that can help support a child's enrollment with financial assistance. I am not saying every school can enroll every child or will be able to provide all the financial aid it takes, but many do provide assistance to enroll a socioeconomically and multiculturally diverse student population and students who will contribute to their schools' communities.

"When considering schools, it's important to be introspective. Do parents want their children to go to the most competitive high schools and, subsequently, colleges and universities in the country? Do they want their children to come out of the learning experience with a natural curiosity that's been nurtured so that they can continue to be lifelong learners? What kind of learning environment is the best match for my child? Those are the kind of questions parents should think about as they explore school options.

"And if the parent feels stressed and outwardly shows stress about the child's required visits to schools to which they're applying, that might rub off on the child. So make the visit a fun experience for a child to see what another school is like. How a child responds can be modeled by a parent. It's better when a parent says, 'This is going to be fun; we are going to let you visit this school to see what it's like,' rather than, 'You will be going to this school and you're not going to be seeing your friends anymore.' Let the children explore the possibilities for their own education. Make it fun and exciting as opposed to scary and difficult."

Rank Your Priorities

Nora Webb is the middle school director at Nysmith School for the Gifted, located in Herndon. The school, which specializes in providing an education to the gifted population of Northern Virginia, has students taking classes up to four years above grade level. For example, some eighth-grade students with a propensity for math can take pre-calculus, which is way beyond the traditional eighth-grade math course.

The school is highly regarded in the area for having a very advanced math and science program, though Nora states that only about one-third of the Nysmith student body would identify themselves as being oriented towards math, science, and technology over liberal arts. Additionally, many parents seek enrollment at Nysmith due to its high TJ acceptance rate. More than 50% of all eighth-grade students from Nysmith are accepted to the nationally-recognized, public magnet school.

In the classroom, instruction is accelerated, but to different degrees. According to Nora, "The most obvious differentiation will be math. All of our fifth and sixth graders have math at the same hour and each child goes to whatever math course they need. Most of our students are one to four grade levels above in math. Within the classroom, the teachers are really trying to work with every child based on their strengths. So for example, in language arts class, you will see students writing essays at slightly above grade level to what you would expect from three levels above. But the teacher isn't grading everyone to the standards of three levels above."

Although students are capable of working at an advanced level, teachers are very well aware that the students are still youngsters. "For example, our fourth graders start dissecting fish and frogs in biology and they are meticulous about keeping lab journals following the scientific method. But then they build a construction paper frog to take home, because they're just nine years old. So they're doing very advanced conceptual work, but we do it in ways that are very child-friendly methods."

Nysmith certainly has a distinguished reputation among DC-area independent schools, and those students who don't go on to TJ often attend some of the most prestigious independent high schools in the area. However, Nora sees a growing trend of increased stress over applying to independent schools, especially when Type A parents are raising Type B students. "Part of the stress comes from the parent's commitment to trying to find the very best fit. No one place is going to answer all concerns. It is important for parents to rank their priorities, but also to consider what they really think is best for their child." While Nysmith begins enrollment in pre-kindergarten, Nora stressed that, even from an early age, it's important to balance the family values and priorities along with the best environment for the student. "The most important question a parent can ask is, 'Where will my child learn best and how does it align with our family priorities?'"

Consider the International Perspective

Anna Ellenbogen is the director of admissions at the British School of Washington (BSW), located in picturesque Georgetown. The school offers families in the DC area an entirely international experience, culminating with the International Baccalaureate (IB) program in high school.

Since students from all over the world attend the British School, no specific standardized testing is required. Anna says, "Almost two-thirds of students applying are from international families and we've found that standardized tests have a cultural bias." Instead of relying on standardized admission testing, entrance assessments are based on strong teacher recommendations, a pattern of progressively more challenging coursework, and solid grades.

Anna and her staff want to be sure students can handle a heavy workload and have the capacity to develop strong writing skills. Along with these abilities, BSW is looking for an open mind and a willingness to accept an international perspective. "It is no longer a cliché to say the world is getting smaller, that's the reality. Therefore, our students here are very aware of becoming global thinkers. Because we are an international school, cultural and racial diversity happens almost by default.

"A concern families may have when considering an international school is the preconceived notion that because the school is international, there will be a high turnover rate among students." Interestingly enough, Anna states, "Our attrition is about the same as other schools. Once an international family is here, they are likely going to stay as long as possible. Our American families tend to stay because they are looking for an international education, specifically the IB program. It really helps to set us apart."

Understand That the Admission Process is Just That—A Process

Vince Rowe has worked in independent school admissions for more than 18 years and is currently the director of admission and financial aid at Georgetown Day School (GDS) in Washington, DC. Coming from a public school background himself, Vince says that it doesn't so much matter which school a student is coming from when they apply, but rather whether or not the student is "taking full advantage of the resources available to them at their current school." Vince acknowledges that students coming from an independent school often have access to many more resources than those attending some public schools, but notes that GDS loves to see students going out to "advocate and create opportunities" for themselves.

In regards to standardized test scores, Vince says that the weight they carry varies depending on who you're talking to. He notes that the school goes through the selection process as a committee, "so you have me as the admission chair, along with principals, learning specialists, teachers, as well as the head of the school. So I think if you ask that question, you're going to get a different answer from different people—as it should be."

In Vince's view, the admission process is a juggling act of making sure that the student is both academically and socially a good fit for the school culture. When asked how the school can ensure that a student is socially a good fit, Vince replied, "You would be surprised what you can learn when you ask the right questions in the right context to a young person or a family." In terms of how a student approaches the school admission process, he says it varies depending on the entry year, since

GDS is a K-12 school. "When students are young, the parents are doing the decision making, but in middle school, it's more of a partnership between the parents and the student. Certainly by high school, I would say that most of our highly motivated and fully engaged students drive the entire process—everything from finding what schools they want to apply to, to coming in, and doing their own interviews."

Due to the school's 97-98% retention rate, it has a waitlist in place. However, Vince is quick to highlight that "it's not really a waitlist, it's a wait pool. We just call it a waitlist to be consistent," but in reality, there is no ranking for students as to who is offered admission from this wait pool. Interestingly, the decision changes year by year and day by day. Vince added, "The decision is usually driven by criteria as specific as race/ethnicity, just to balance socioeconomic diversity and ability." Vince elaborated, "If there's a class, for example, where there were more boys than girls, then clearly the girls are going to come out with a leg up in terms of chances of getting in. We try to factor that in while also keeping in mind that we want to find the best match."

Vince provided a metaphor that admission is a lot like a merry-go-round, "where you bring people in and then they leave. We want people to come in and stay until they graduate, but sometimes an acceptance or rejection results simply due to the time you got on the ride."

Delivering a Traditional Curriculum in Non-Traditional Ways

The McLean School of Maryland is well known for its ability to offer a traditional curriculum in a non-traditional way to bright students with a learning disability or ADHD. According to Judy Jankowski, the former director of admission, McLean looks for students with "solid cognitive scores who are in the average-to-above-average range on a WISC, but we realize that despite high scores in some areas, a student may have a weakness in processing speed or working memory and that's okay. We're also looking for motivation, perseverance, and a willingness to try new strategies. Aside from test scores and report card grades, the students who stand out are the ones who are enthusiastic and active participants."

Judy encourages parents to spend as much time as possible at the school and to talk to members of the school community outside of the admission office. McLean frequently puts prospective families with current families, but Judy also recommends talking to outside professionals as well. "Look at all your options, and keep an open mind.

There are times when people say, 'I went to X type of school and I turned out well, so that's where my child is going to go, too.' Parochial schools, for example, are great for kids that are right in the middle of things, but exceptional kids on either side are not always going to be best placed there. Going in with preconceived notions about how your child will learn doesn't necessarily serve him or her well."

The admission staff and teachers keep detailed notes on each candidate's shadow visit. "During the shadow visit, we want to see how comfortable they are in the environment. Every teacher receives a form that evaluates the students academically and socially so that we get feedback from multiple teachers in multiple environments."

The instructional approach is unique. "McLean seeks to create a balance between oral presentation, visual learning, and hands-on instruction. In math, for example, students utilize manipulatives and games frequently. The other day I observed a science class in which the teacher was explaining the structure of a cell. She had all the students standing up and a group of them were in a circle on the outside and they were the cell wall. There were individual students inside the cell wall who were acting as the various organs within the cell." She also gave an example of fifth-grade students studying World War I. "A teacher had the students turn their desks sideways to simulate bunkers and used Nerf balls to simulate and better understand trench warfare. This type of teaching causes students to really internalize the material actively, as opposed to simply being passive observers in a classroom." Whether your child needs an alternative approach to learning or not, the key is to look for student engagement as you observe classes.

When parents initially tour McLean, some ask about how colleges view the school's non-traditional approach to education. The staff believes that success in college actually starts in the elementary grades. "The lower school is about competence and confidence. It is very hands-on and the teachers use manipulatives and games to a large extent. In the middle school, the focus is on understanding who you are as a learner and what you need to become successful. Here, students get a lot of tools and strategies to keep themselves organized. Does the student need to use graph paper in math? Should they color-code their notes using highlighters? In the upper school, there are college guidance counselors who start working with students in the ninth grade. These students begin preparing for the SAT and ACT in the ninth grade. McLean also has a very traditional AP and honors track."

Judy encourages parents who are interested in a school that addresses learning differences to think outside the box. "Just because you learned one way, doesn't mean your child will do it the same way. Parents need to get information from a lot of sources, including a psycho-educational or neuro-psych evaluation to determine learning differences. Testing can indicate what a child's stronger learning suit is going to be. Having hard data is really helpful."

Consider the Catholic Option

Since its doors opened in 1957, Bishop O'Connell High School has grown into one of the largest Catholic high schools in the metropolitan area. As director of admission (and also an alumnus), Michael Cresson has the responsibility of reviewing hundreds of applications throughout the year. "We receive well over 500 applications and enroll about 300 students. One of the first things I look for is the teacher recommendation letter. Foremost, we want children with good character who are also good students.

"After reviewing the recommendation, I look at the student's grades and test scores. Our students take the High School Placement Test (HSPT). The HSPT has five sections split between English and math. It's a very hard test because each section is timed and students aren't allowed to use a calculator. They just aren't used to that type of test." Because so much anxiety can go along with standardized testing, O'Connell has begun offering students a practice test that is taken at the end of the seventh-grade year. "It gives them a feeling for what the real test will be like in the fall. It's the same amount of sections, just fewer questions. It's designed for any seventh grader who is applying to Catholic school. Parents will get a report of their scores so they will know what their student needs to work on over the summer."

Michael determines how a student's test scores compare to his or her grades. "We do understand that kids may not have the best test day." Some students have good grades, but weak test scores, "so we do have a couple of alternatives where students do a summer bridge program, if their scores aren't quite what we're looking for, to help them get adjusted to high school."

Students do not have to be Catholic to attend O'Connell, and Michael encourages students of all religious backgrounds to consider the school. "During the admission process we look at all students equally. That includes religion as well." Nonetheless, O'Connell's population is heavily Catholic at 82%, yet it's also quite diverse. "We have 90 international students enrolled on average every year, so we truly have this unique group coming into the school. We have local students who travel great distances, from as far north as Bowie to as far south as Fredericksburg."

Although O'Connell's athletic program is at the top of any list, academics take center stage. "We offer 26 AP classes and more than 50 honors and elective courses. So the strength of our academic program is something that's of interest to parents, but this is also a welcoming and enjoyable school. There's a community atmosphere." Michael believes that a sense of community is just as important as the number of honors and AP classes. He encourages parents to evaluate these two factors equally.

O'Connell encourages families to begin looking at high schools in the spring of the child's seventh grade. "I would definitely suggest a head start. I think most parents will go to the open houses, but on a tour, they get to see what it's like on a normal school day. At an open house, you aren't going to get to see the kids in the rooms and get their true feeling of what the school is like. So I always recommend doing the tour in the spring or the fall the year before—the earlier, the better. If the school allows a shadow visit, consider it. Here, they shadow as seventh graders so they get to see what it's like to be an O'Connell student for a day."

Coming to Terms with LD or ADHD and Finding a School to Match

Commonwealth Academy is a college preparatory school in Alexandria for students who benefit from small classes and instruction designed to address various learning styles. Most students who attend Commonwealth have a diagnosed learning disability or ADHD.

As the director of admission, Josh Gwilliam is on the lookout for the "average-to-superior student with a mild-to-moderate learning disability or ADHD. Being a smaller school—about 150 students total in grades three through twelve—I need to make sure that the student is going to be able to fit into the culture and the community of the school."

Learning how to learn is a focus at Commonwealth, but in the end, they want students to be fully prepared for college. "Because we are a college prep school, everything leads up to that place. That actually starts in our lower school—grades three, four, and five. Our students become very aware of who they are as learners, and then they get to this acceptance place where they say, 'I learn a little bit differently, I require a different environment, and I need to be okay with that.'"

At Commonwealth, students learn how to develop their executive functioning skills in order to get better organized, plan ahead, and focus. "Learning executive functioning skills is a key benefit for our students, even our twice exceptional students or our students coming out of GT (Gifted and Talented) programs. For example, we have a matching notebook system. From grades three to twelve, each student has an assigned color-coded binder to stay organized. In addition, every student has an advisor. The advisor meets with the student in the middle school twice a day, and in the high school once a day; they look at the notebooks one day, the lockers the next day, and the backpacks the next day." When visiting schools, Josh encourages parents to ask how teachers help students stay organized, plan ahead, and develop good study habits.

For some parents, realizing that their child may need a different kind of academic setting isn't always easy. "What we're really looking for are parents who are coming to grips with an understanding of who their child is. I can tell you that I've had parents in my office who have found it extremely difficult to accept that their child needs a different learning environment. But once they take that leap of faith and trust the school, and their child is happy, successful, and thriving, they come to understand exactly who their child is and what they need to learn. It really gets back to the question of does your child feel safe and secure. Is she happy, thriving, and finding academic success? These are all key components. Especially within DC we have a lot of Type A personalities, parents who are very successful, very well educated, who all of a sudden have a student who has a learning disability or ADHD. So, it's not an easy process, but it definitely is a good process and a healthy process for the child."

Opportunities for Leadership Are the Name of the Game

Just off of River Road in Bethesda you will find Norwood School, a popular choice among parents seeking a K-8 education for their child. Maralyn Marsteller's own children attended Norwood and now she serves as the school's assistant director of admission. She and the other administrators believe that there are many important benefits to a school whose primary focus is educating students from kindergarten to eighth grade. "When you have a young child, it's hard to know if the school you're considering now is also going to be the best one years from now when your child is, say, 14 years old, because children change and grow. I firmly believe—having done it twice with my own children—that it's best to choose for the now rather than the maybe based on what you *think* they might become.

"Like other K-8 schools, our seventh and eighth graders are really like juniors and seniors. They become the leaders at the school and are the buddies to the younger children. The third and fourth graders are the leaders at the lower school. We want children to try everything and this is a safe place to do it. Our middle schoolers aren't constantly looking over their shoulder saying, 'Gee, I wish I was a high schooler.' When you don't have the influence of the older children, I think it's a little bit easier. Kids are more willing to try new things and take on leadership roles."

Getting into Norwood is competitive. "The first step is for the family to visit, either on a tour or at an open house. We like to take our tours into the classroom so families can see the kids in action and see how the classroom works. It's usually just a gut feeling if they can envision their child here. That's what happened to me. I'm a fourth-generation Washingtonian and I went to very different schools from Norwood as a child, but when I came to Norwood as a prospective parent, I just felt at home. You want a place that feels warm and inviting and a place where your child will be happy."

Whether parents are considering a K-8 school or one which progresses through high school, Maralyn believes that "the great thing about independent schools is that there isn't a 'you have to do it this way' belief system." At Norwood, "every year is different. For example, this year we had one math group that was going to be almost all boys with two girls, so we made it all boys. We would describe ourselves as traditional and innovative combined. I think we have a lot of the structure of a traditional school, but we do try to think outside the box."

Besides flexibility being a key component in any good school, Maralyn believes that finding a place where students have close ties with teachers is vital. On a personal level, she has experienced how small class sizes and student/teacher relationships can make all the difference. "My son was a quiet guy. In seventh and eighth grade we had advisory groups instead of homerooms. He had a great advisor who is a science teacher here.

"The students were doing *A Midsummer Night's Dream* for the seventh and eighth-grade play. My son would never have tried out for a play, but his advisor told the play director, 'You should really try to get Wylie to audition for the part of Bottom, because he's so funny.' Once he heard that from the director, Wylie thought, 'Oh, well, maybe I can.' So he went home and worked on it, got the part, and he had leads in every play all the way through high school. Now he's in an all-male a cappella group at college. What I love about that is, if someone notices you, even if you're a quiet little guy, you are more willing to take the risk. If you do, then you can find something that you end up loving. That's a neat thing about independent schools. In a large place he would have just gone on in his own quiet world."

CHAPTER 11

Tips from Veteran Parents

SOMETIMES, THE BEST WAY TO learn about something new is through others' experiences. This chapter is a look into the independent school world by parents in the area who have gone through a similar admission process and can offer unique insight. Some of their tips may surprise you as well.

Engage Your Child

This area mom has had experiences at Field School, Green Hedges, and Georgetown Visitation. Her daughter is a senior at Visitation, commonly referred to as Visi, which is known for its challenging academics and college matriculations to show for it. "Many graduates have said that college is easier than Visi and that the workload is actually lighter in college." The Visi program is incredibly rigorous, sometimes with four hours of homework a night. The family's daughter is very driven, so it's a great fit. The campus is gorgeous (as is Field School's, the mom points out) and Visi even has a system for girls to take college courses at Georgetown University. Catholic mass is once a week and students take a religion class every year. There is a heavy Catholic population, but if you're not Catholic, there are many other families at Visi and they are all accepted into the community.

Her son, however, took a different academic path through Green Hedges and Field School. Green Hedges offers a Montessori program for young children and a more traditional curriculum beginning in first grade. By the third grade, her son was beginning to struggle, but she waited to get him tested until the following year, believing that he'd grow out of it. He was eventually diagnosed with a learning disability. "I should have had him tested going into third grade because it would have been better to know earlier on."

Although Green Hedges was a wonderful, nurturing experience, this mom knew that her son needed more differentiated instruction. As for her experience at Field School, she says it is "very diverse and applauds individuality." Students call teachers by their first name, and students are very comfortable asking for help. The relationship between students and teachers is unique. The school has a Latin-based trip to Rome, special Winter Internships to get students real-world job experience, and a wealth of learning support. Expect two hours of homework a night, and sports are required after school. Many of the sports are non-competitive, though, and as far as academics, there are extra study halls built into lunch. The school even opens from 9 a.m. – 12 p.m. on Saturdays for extra help for every student.

As for tips in your school search: "Applying to three schools is ideal, but really make visits and see as many as possible." Most importantly, "Engage your child." Their son didn't want to make the switch from Green Hedges to Field at first, but it ended up being fantastic. "Always talk to families currently at the school, and get psycho-educational testing done early to find out how he learns." Once you're in, "If the school has an ambassador family program, definitely take advantage of it." The family accompanies you to parent picnics and school functions before the school year starts. For a student, getting to know someone in her class beforehand makes a huge difference in confidence on the first day of school.

As for getting your child into a school like Visi, "Get a tutor for the SSAT or HSPT. Ideally, you should start a year before, or at least the summer before. If the results aren't the greatest, you still have time to make it up."

Trust Your Instincts

Connie has a son at Maret School, considered by many to be one of the top K-12 schools in the area. "Maret is great so far, it's very welcoming," Connie says. "It's not a cookie-cutter school. It accepts all different kinds of personalities while still being rigorous and exclusive." Although her son is not yet in high school, Maret has a double language requirement, which can be intimidating for many families. "The school has actually been very accommodating. I'd say about one-third of the new students are in a language class that is remediating, or rather helping them catch up to students who have been under Maret's language requirements since kindergarten. If you're trying to get into Maret, I'd definitely recommend starting on a foreign language earlier than normal."

Prior to Maret, Connie's son was at Nysmith. "The math and science program is very strong, mainly because every family is trying to get into TJ. I loved the teachers, too. They were the kind of people you'd cast as teachers in a movie—highly qualified and very caring." Despite the strong academic program, Connie and her husband, Greg, decided to consider a switch to another school in eighth grade after they started previewing schools while Mitch was in seventh grade. They had planned to transition Mitch in ninth grade, but when they started looking at potential options, they "absolutely fell in love" with Maret and decided to apply for eighth grade. It's the only school to which Mitch applied because they were not overly impressed with the other independent schools they looked at and would have been very happy with him continuing at Nysmith.

According to Connie, the students at Maret are "confident, outgoing, well rounded, and shake your hand when you meet them." Students are required to take choir, band, or guitar, and the list of high school electives is so impressive that it played a big factor in the family's decision. "[Our son] was actually excited when he read the course offerings. He's a self-starter, and he was so energized by Maret's options that he already has his high school classes mapped out. The school really can accommodate a wide variety of students. Maret is a good fit for a student who is very focused and well rounded, but doesn't want a pressure-cooker school."

Connie's best advice is to trust your instincts when looking at schools. When she first visited Maret, she felt that it would be a good fit for her son, but he wasn't completely on board with a move. "Kids naturally resist change. This isn't to say you should discount your child's opinion. If a school is too rigorous, too cliquey, or your child is completely opposed to it, you should absolutely listen! Rather, if it seems like your child just has a fear of the unknown, and you feel the school is a good fit academically and socially, it can't hurt to nudge them in that direction. If you supplement everything with encouragement and show that you care, your child will be thanking you sooner than you think."

The Balance of a Single-Sex School

Christine has twin daughters at Connelly School of the Holy Child in Potomac, Maryland. Holy Child is an all-girls school, which offers a unique dynamic for its students. Christine's daughters had a co-ed experience before getting into Holy Child, and so far she believes it was a good switch. "I love the all-girls environment because it feels much more relaxed. Holy Child teachers are very nurturing—they're willing to stay after class and my daughters feel cared for."

Many students are worried that they will not get a "normal" educational experience at a single-sex school, but in reality, there are plenty of opportunities to interact with members of the opposite gender without it becoming overwhelming. Many all-girls schools partner with nearby all-boys schools for co-ed drama programs, dances, and other normal high school experiences like football games and prom. Holy Child girls have dances and mixers with Landon and Bullis, for example. Christine says that the notion that girls at a single-sex school are sheltered is a myth. Rather, they are receiving all the elements of a normal high school experience in a more comfortable environment. "All-girls schools connect you with like-minded people all across the area," Christine says. "Schools like Gonzaga, Georgetown Prep, Stone Ridge, and Holy Child make you feel like you are part of one big family."

Christine has several tips for your school search. "What to look for is different for every family. Know your children and know what you're looking for. Go to open houses and look at what the students are like. Don't forget to consider the commute. If you've lived here for a while, I don't have to tell you about that." When she found Holy Child, she wished she had started earlier. "Do yourself a favor and start looking at schools more than a year before. Eighth grade can take a great emotional toll on a student if she has to leave friends behind. I would've considered making the switch earlier so that my daughters could see that it was where they wanted to go with even more of a head start." As for her daughters' all-girls experience at Holy Child, "I can't speak highly enough about the school and its families. There's just a lot less drama. For me, that's priceless."

If Your Child Has an LD, Traveling Can Be Worth It

Mary Kate's son was diagnosed with dyslexia and dysgraphia (reading and writing disorders). In public school, the family had struggled to get an IEP (Individualized Education Plan) and extra time to complete standardized tests. Mary Kate spoke to one public school teacher, and "he thought that [my son] would be better served in private school, and that if it were his child, it's what he would do." A local independent school was there to provide excellent specialized instruction through great teachers in sixth through eighth grade, but as high school approached, the family looked for an option with even more learning support. This led them to Bullis, which has been a fantastic fit thus far.

"Bullis has been everything we dreamed of," says Mary Kate. Although Bullis is not specifically for LD children, it is able to offer targeted, differentiated instruction. "What I like best is that the students are cared for, but without a lot of hand-holding. They teach students to be independent and productive despite any learning challenges." Students who need learning assistance are not ostracized, and using the learning center is seen as very normal. This can be a big deal for a child with LD. "There is a lot of class unity at Bullis," Mary Kate adds. "I especially like that the homecoming dance is not competitive or exclusive." Bullis has created a friendly, accepting environment for every kind of learner, and it turned out to be the perfect fit for Mary Kate's family, even though it was across the bridge.

"For a student with LD, the closest thing is not always the right thing." For parents considering options in Maryland, Mary Kate wants you to know that "the bridge is not that bad." When it comes to your child's education, it's worth it. When looking at schools, pay special attention to how the school reacts when you talk about LD. "If they cared about your child, they'd want you to tell them. Don't be afraid to talk about it—if you're afraid to talk about it, you shouldn't be there in the first place. The LD isn't going to change in your kid." The best fit is a school that is well equipped and trains its faculty.

Different Schools for Siblings

Abbey is in the unique position of having her two children at different K-12 independent schools. "There are different fits for different kids," she says. "As a parent, trust your gut. You really need to listen to your instincts." Abbey notes that it's also important to take into account your child's opinion as they get older. "It really helps with a school change if your child has a friend in the school ahead of time. This is not always possible, but what you can do is get your child's input and try to match a school that fits his interests and personality."

Transportation is an especially important factor to consider if you have kids in two different schools. "Many of the independent schools offer transportation for an extra fee. Others offer door-to-door busing, or pick-ups at central bus stops. You'll want to make sure the transportation options work for you and your family," she says.

Another thing to think about is where most of the families live that attend the school(s) you are considering. "Remember that that's where your child's friends will be living. So, for example, if you live in Falls Church and are considering a school in Maryland, you may be looking at lots of driving on the Beltway to support your child's social life."

During the application process, Abbey has some tips for the interview. "Be honest. Be prepared to highlight strengths and address weaknesses. If you say your kid is perfect, they'll know you're not being truthful." To a certain extent, you can trust that the school knows what different kinds of students will fit in, so why not be honest? When going on your school tour, Abbey says, "You can tell a lot from the kids—how they dress, how they engage each other, how they act in the classroom." This can tell you a lot about the school and whether or not your child will fit in.

Abbey's last piece of advice is for everyone who's looked for school secrets on the internet: "You can't believe everything you hear, especially on the internet. Every family's experience is different. Drugs and cliques are something everybody deals with. Remember, for every negative story there is a positive one, and vice versa."

A Good Learning Center Can Be Life Changing

Becky, a Flint Hill veteran mom of three, says that having strong learning support in place can make all the difference. "I've referred five families to explore the school's learning center services and several of those families applied, were accepted, and utilized the learning center," says Becky. The family's prior school experience was disappointing. Becky says the workload was not rigorous enough, and although the teachers were dedicated, they were spread thin by high student-to-teacher ratios. Flint Hill has been a positive change for the family, but Becky says to be aware that getting accepted doesn't mean your work is done as a parent.

"I think you get out of a school what you put into it," Becky says. "Fair doesn't always mean equal when it comes to the education you're getting. You have to go the extra mile to get the most out of your school. The families that are taking full advantage of the school's resources are the ones getting the best educational value. Even at a public school, pursuing as many honors and AP classes as possible proves advantageous when the time comes for your college search, applications, and eventual acceptance and attendance."

When looking for a high school, Becky recommends that parents take a close look at the college counseling program. As for Flint Hill's, Becky says, "The college counseling office offers a breadth of information and supports you and your child every step of the way. It is worth its weight in gold." The Flint Hill college counselors are interested in getting to know each student in order to find a college that is the right fit for your child, whether that's an Ivy League or a small, tight-knit local college with a great film department.

Becky has a lot of tips for parents going through the school selection process. If the school has a shadow visit option, where your child can follow a current student for a day, definitely take advantage of the program. It can completely change your child's opinion about a school. "Go to as many open houses as possible, and don't go in blind." Do your research beforehand, and don't be afraid to have specific questions. Do teachers use a multisensory approach? Does the school have an integrated curriculum? Flint Hill, for example, like many other schools, teaches the same time period in its English and history classes simultaneously, which can greatly reinforce learning across the curriculum. Lastly, Becky adds, "Don't go to private if there isn't a need." Situations are different for every family, and the good news is that in this area you have options.

Choose a School with a Positive Emotional Environment

Living in the District, Judy and her husband thought that an independent school might be in their daughters' future, but they decided to try their local public school first for their oldest. They enrolled Julia for kindergarten, but it wasn't a positive experience. Judy switched gears and began looking for a different environment when she stumbled upon Sheridan School. When asked why she chose a K-8 school, she stated, "You don't know what kind of student your child is at that age, so you have to go with the emotional atmosphere and what you sense about the other parents, teachers, and administrators. You want to be sure the emotional environment will be positive for your family. When kids are young, you have to go with your gut instinct. You have testing (most schools require the WPPSI IQ test), but it's a blunt instrument and you don't get a sense of the type of student your child is."

Now that Julia is a freshman in high school, Judy realizes even more that moving schools after eighth grade is a good thing. "Kids have the ability to reinvent themselves in high school. An ongoing school is a lot more convenient and it puts the parents' minds at ease to know that you don't have to go through the application process again, but for the kids themselves, it's kind of nice to have that break, i.e., going to a new school. It may not be true for every kid but it is true for most kids.

"When thinking about a high school, our top priority was that Julia be happy and have a lot of girls like her that she could be friends with. That was the criteria because all the schools she was looking at were all good schools academically, so we couldn't go wrong. It came down to her gut instinct. We looked at Madeira, Georgetown Day (GDS), Maret, Sidwell Friends, and Washington International. She applied to Madeira and GDS. She got into both and went to Madeira because she had just fallen in love with it. It was a fresh start for her and there was nobody else from Sheridan there. Even beyond that, it was just so clearly the right place for her. GDS was a fabulous school and the classes were amazing; a wide variety of very interesting kids there, but the decision felt right. Madeira felt homey to her."

Madeira's academic bar is high. "There are a lot of quizzes and an emphasis on topics that she didn't encounter much before, such as English grammar. It's a hard school." The transition from a progressive curriculum to a more traditional one was particularly challenging for Julia, who has ADHD. "Once we asked for accommodations, which she did not ask for right away, they've been amazingly supportive. They don't make anything easier. The girl has to ask, take initiative, and go through the process. Once she does ask, they (the teachers and administrators) are generous with their time, helpful and smart about strategies, and warm, and supportive. The girls learn to advocate for themselves and to take responsibility for seeking out the help they need. You have to advocate for yourself. I've been really impressed." Judy suggests that when parents work with the school to secure the support their children may need, they also should make sure their children learn to take responsibility for advocating for themselves and finding solutions.

Judy's younger daughter, Emilie, is "very different. She's incredibly creative. She'll do really well at a school where the arts are given as much respect as academics. She is also someone who loves to be able to move around independently in the city, so a suburban school wouldn't be ideal for her. She's only in seventh grade now, so we'll have to see what happens."

You and Your Child are Two Different People

For Ray, his wife Brianna, and his stepson Brian, the school application process had a number of ups and downs. This turbulent journey was primarily caused by Ray's and Brian's differences. Ray says that he was always "academically, extremely competitive. I didn't just assume I would get an A, I assumed I would get a 99 or 100." Ray represents a number of parents who are extremely Type A, but have the responsibility of raising a Type B child. Ray's innate ambition and competitive nature caused him to become discouraged with Brian. Ray discussed how he would spend hours helping Brian with his homework, only to feel that Brian wasn't motivated. It left both of them feeling frustrated.

When it came time for the family to begin looking at independent schools for Brian, Ray and Brian once again failed to see eye to eye. Ray pushed for Brian to go to a school known for a high degree of academic rigor in the high school years. "I love academics and like being in the elite group, but Brian isn't impressed by that." The one thing they could wholeheartedly agree upon was a co-ed environment. Both Ray and Brian believed that boys and girls working together, side by side in the same classroom, better prepares them for the reality of college and work life.

Even though they were in agreement on this factor, Brian felt pressured about the process in general. He became reluctant to go to any independent school due to the fear of his friends' reactions. "He didn't want to be harassed by his friends about going to a place other than McLean High School."

While tensions rose between Ray and Brian, Brian's mother Brianna suggested another approach. Ray initially believed the school selection was something for parents to decide. "I didn't think Brian should have much of a choice—you're going here, you're going to work it out, that's the decision, let's move on. That would be more my style." Brianna thought it would be helpful to expose her son to the positive aspects of private education by introducing him to two students who had left the public school system to transfer to an independent school.

The family ultimately decided on Flint Hill because it seemed like the right fit for Brian. "Flint Hill had the most nurturing environment and also an excellent academic program. The selling point to me, what I finally realized, was that the environment of learning and matching the learning style is just as important as the quality of academics, which is not something I would have naturally thought of. I was able to walk away understanding that you can be in an excellent environment, but if you're not inspired to learn, it's a waste. It needs to be the product of those two factors."

Brian himself is "really looking forward" to his move to Flint Hill. Two aspects that Brian is particularly excited about are the role of technology and getting to know his teachers. Brian said, "Each student is given an Apple laptop. The environment seems so open, too. There are tables in the middle of the atrium area that kids use to gather and do work. I also like that there are periods after school when you can meet with teachers. They seem really approachable."

Ray encourages others to go into the process with an open mind and consider hiring a professional if you're struggling to do so. "You think you know your child, but you really don't because you're not objective. You don't know how people learn and you need professional advice." Ray reiterated the importance of valuing the environment of the school as much as the academic reputation. "I would say parents, especially Type A, tend to judge schools based mostly on the academic component. So they look at where the kids go to college, test scores, etc. While academic excellence is important, it's just one factor in your child's educational experience." In the end, he realized that you can get academic excellence at many schools in the area.

A Learning Disability Can be a Gift in Disguise

Teresa learned pretty early on that her son, Christopher, learned a little differently than the other students in his class. "We had a wonderful preschool teacher who red-flagged his ability to learn letters and process reading." Despite these concerns, "the elementary school was not willing to do any type of testing on him since he was so young (first grade), so we went to a private testing group and he was diagnosed with dyslexia. We provided the private test information to the public school and that's when they were willing to work with us and provide Chris with an IEP."

Despite having an IEP in place, Christopher continued to struggle during second grade. "We had a child who did not want to go to school and seemed very depressed." Both Teresa and her husband are proponents of the public school system and were hesitant about pursuing an independent school education. "We realized that we were losing our child and that we needed to help him. We found a very small, nurturing school that had a great teacher/student ratio—fourteen students to two teachers. We moved Christopher over to McLean School in Potomac to be in an environment where he would begin to believe in himself and his ability to learn."

After several years in an independent school, "Christopher made the decision to switch back to public school, Cooper Middle School, at the beginning of seventh grade. He felt that the independent school was beginning to feel too small. He wanted a larger environment." Both Teresa and her husband were worried about the switch back to public school, primarily due to the class size. "We spoke to both the McLean School and the Cooper administrators and it was McLean that told us that we as parents need to show Christopher that we have the confidence in him to make this move—that's very impressive, because we were money walking out the door. We followed Christopher's lead and have never looked back."

Both Teresa and Christopher are happy with his decision to switch back to a public school. "Because of this move, we believe that college will be easier for him because he has had to learn to be his own self-advocate in a larger environment. McLean School was a great tool for him to build his confidence to go out and take on a bigger challenge."

By high school, Christopher made the decision to drop his IEP and applied to many colleges and universities. "As a parent with a child that struggles with learning, I have had to hold my breath and take that leap with him every step of the way. I worried about the move from the small private school to a big public school—then the move to our larger public high school, Langley. Chris has taught me how to believe in him. In a unique way, Christopher's disability has become somewhat of a gift. It has taught him how to work and to never give up."

Christopher will attend Indiana University in the fall and Teresa believes his confidence and motivation to enter a competitive college is because of the school options he had available to him at a young age. "His work ethic is as high as it gets—he can outwork any 4.3 GPA student. He puts his head down and just makes it happen."

CHAPTER 12

Pointers from Kids: The Real Pros

As I researched information for this book, one of my favorite parts was talking to students who had recently gone through the process. What I found was in line with what I've always seen as a consultant, that parents view independent school education through the lens of an adult. They care mostly about academics. On the other hand, children care more about friendships and the social implications of changing schools. Common concerns included: Would they make new friends at their new school? Would they be accepted by existing cliques? Who would they sit with at lunch? Would they lose their current friends as they went off to a new school?

Before embarking on this book project, I knew that social relationships meant a lot to kids, but I didn't realize exactly *how* much and to what a large extent they would influence a child's school selection. Read on to see how these kids handled the application process and eventually moved from one school to another.

Wanted: A Middle School with Small Classes and Hands-On Instruction

Sean is an eleven-year-old fifth grader at Nottingham Elementary in Arlington, Virginia, where he earns average grades. His experience in elementary school has been a positive one, but in his public school district, middle school begins in sixth grade. Ordinarily, he would move onto Williamsburg Middle School, but due to the school's size, the family decided to look at independent school options.

Sean's mom recognized that Sean tended to perform better in smaller classes in which there was more discussion and hands-on learning. His parents considered McLean School, Field School, and The New School because they knew each of these schools understood how to deal with students who work best when instruction is kinesthetic. Although McLean and Field were good options, Sean's mom and dad worried that the commute to Potomac or south Alexandria would be a strain;

therefore, they only had Sean shadow at The New School. In addition, the tuition was lower, which was a nice added benefit. As luck would have it, Sean loved his day there and the Head of School, John Potter, thought he'd be a great fit.

Sean said, "When I went into each classroom on my shadow visit, there were fewer kids than in my crowded school. I noticed that it was a lot quieter. Everyone was really nice—the teachers and the kids.

"Now I'm excited when I think of going to my new school in the fall. I love trying new stuff. Sometimes, I'm nervous when I meet people for the first time, but I usually make friends easily after that. I think learning will be fun at my new school, especially in science!"

Adjusting to a Longer Day and Challenging Academics

Joe was a student at a public middle school in Northern Virginia when his mom approached him about moving to an independent school. Joe's mother had attended Georgetown Visitation as a girl and knew that her children could get a challenging and individualized education at an independent school. In the fall of his eighth-grade year, they visited and applied to a number of schools, both co-ed and all-boys. Although his parents were gung-ho, Joe wasn't so convinced that a move would be such a good thing. "I was worried that by not going to Madison (the public high school he was slated to attend), I would lose all my friends." Despite his worries, he went to a number of shadow days.

"Before I shadowed at St. Albans, I was thinking that I really didn't want to go because it's all boys, but after the visit, I found the environment surprisingly different than I thought it would be. I really liked it. Now I'm a freshman and I've been there for almost a full year. Being at an all-boys school is a big help. I can concentrate a lot more. The environment is better and they expect a lot more from you. Plus, it's right next to an all-girls school, so that makes it easier. We can take classes with girls at NCS, too."

Joe's concern about losing his friends ended up to be a non-issue. "I made it out to be much bigger of a deal than it really was. That was the main reason I had hesitation. But that hasn't happened. I still hang out with my old friends and we still have a lot of fun. Once I got to St. Albans, I made friends easily. We only have about 80 kids in our grade, where at Madison, there are about 500. I adjusted pretty easily to the social aspect of a new school."

When asked about other adjustments in the beginning, Joe said, "The academics are so much tougher. The first month was a slap in the face to wake me up. We get a lot of homework each day, but grading-wise, the work that I'd do to get an A at my old school would get a much worse grade at St. Albans."

The other adjustment Joe encountered wasn't academic; it was the length of the day. "I was used to going home at 2:00, but now I get home at around 7:30 because of sports. Although school technically ends at 2:00, it's connected to the after-school activities. After school, you have about an hour to do whatever you want, but then sports start every day at 3:30. Every season you have to do a sport at St. Albans. I'm playing lacrosse now."

When asked if he felt St. Albans is too competitive or difficult, Joe replied, "In some ways it does feel very competitive, but it also brings the boys closer. I'm really happy there and I'm so glad I made the move."

Going with Your First Instinct

Joe's sister, Katie, was excited about switching schools from the beginning. She attended her local public elementary school from kindergarten to sixth grade. From grades three to six, she was part of Fairfax County's Advanced Academic Program (AAP), which accelerates instruction for bright children.

Katie knew National Cathedral School (NCS) was a fit for her when they arrived at the campus, which sits next to St. Albans on the grounds of the National Cathedral in downtown DC. "I was in awe when I went there for the first time. I loved the buildings. Everything was really bright and the energy was good."

When asked about the biggest challenge in going to a new school, Katie replied, "In the AAP, we did a lot of math, so I'm a year ahead of my classmates, but we didn't do as much English. Now I'm writing a lot more papers than I did last year. English is harder than last year."

She went on to say, "My new environment was different at first, but I got into the groove quickly. It wasn't an issue meeting new people." I asked her if NCS had established cliques, which are common with middle school girls, and she gave a surprising answer: "It's actually the opposite of what people think. The good thing about NCS is that everyone can talk to anyone about anything. It's very open. Everyone has their own friends, but it's not exclusive."

What has taken some adjustment is the commute into DC. Katie said, "The drawback is that it's far away, but we have a carpool, so in the morning I'm just with one other person who's not in my grade. In the afternoon, I carpool with a girl my age that I've gotten to know better. My mom is great about driving us a lot of places."

Katie was quick to share advice with other girls who are looking for a new school. She suggests, "Whatever your first instinct is, that's probably your best one. If you had a good first instinct, that's where you should go."

Transitioning from Catholic to Public School

Alex was a student at Our Lady of Good Counsel (OLGC) Catholic School in Vienna, VA for nine years, from kindergarten through eighth grade. But when his final year ended, he was excited to move on to high school from his small K-8 school for a couple of reasons. "I didn't like how strict OLGC was. There were a lot of rules and we got in trouble for small things. That was the biggest drawback."

Like most of his classmates, Alex applied to Paul VI (PVI) in Fairfax and Bishop O'Connell in Arlington for high school. Alex felt a nudge in that direction by his father. "My dad went to Catholic schools his whole life, so that's what he wanted for me. But my mom is Muslim, so she didn't really care if the school was religious or not. She just wanted me to go to the school I'd excel most at. I also thought of applying to Gonzaga as well, but I was too late with the application. My parents ultimately said the decision was up to me and one day I heard that my public school was having an open house, so my dad took me. I saw all my friends from the neighborhood, which was great, and then I reviewed the course offerings. The public school offered a lot of classes and more electives. At PVI or O'Connell, I would have to take a religion class each day, which would take away one of my electives. With public school, I had more choices. I loved it and my parents were supportive of my decision to go."

Alex was quick to say that when he entered ninth grade and compared notes about his transition with many of his friends entering from public schools, he was actually grateful for the education he had had. He realized that although his teachers in elementary and middle school were strict, he benefited from a tough academic program. "The curriculum (at OLGC) was different than what my friends were exposed to. It prepared me well. The work I had was a lot more challenging. I had more homework and more independent work, such as a big science fair project. That helped me to learn organizational skills. We also had to do certain things like note-taking. We learned Cornell Notes, which is what we use now in high school."

Looking back, Alex is thankful for a Catholic education and feels that it made him the good student he is today. His advice to other kids who are thinking about high school: "Most of my friends went on to Catholic high schools or other private schools like Potomac, but I think it's important to consider public schools, too. I've just finished my freshman year now and I've already learned a lot, not just in class, but how to adapt to kids from different cultures. In my case, I love a big school and all the class choices, social events, and diversity that it brings."

Sometimes the Choice is Made for You

Catherine is a sophomore at the British School in Georgetown, but her journey to get there has been an arduous one in many ways. Catherine is the youngest of five children and she and her family have lived in five countries around the world because of her father's job. They moved to Virginia from Belgium seven years ago. "When we first got here, my mom put me and my siblings in The British School of Washington (BSW) because we've always gone to a British school while abroad, so it seemed to be the obvious choice. Things were going well until I got really sick. After lots of tests and doctor visits, I found out I had diabetes, which was devastating. The only way to control it was with insulin shots, which I still give myself three times a day. When all of this happened, I was so scared and my parents were, too. I had a hard time regulating it and sometimes, I'd fall ill at school and my mom would have to come and get me because there wasn't a nurse on campus to help. We live in Oakton, so the drive to Georgetown can be well over an hour one way. It was becoming too hard to manage."

Luckily, Flint Hill School was just around the corner and most importantly, it had a full-time nurse. "Right away, I loved Flint Hill, not because of the nurse, but because everyone was so nice and the teaching was so different. And it was only seven minutes from my house! The academics were challenging for me at Flint Hill, but there were lots of teachers there to help out. The main difference at BSW is that we spend three, four, even five days on a topic until everyone gets it. For example, in math, we learn one concept, but really in depth, before moving on, but at Flint Hill, you go quicker. Each day we'd learn a new topic and the next day it would be something else. The American way of learning is much faster paced."

Catherine's bliss lasted two years at Flint Hill. Her diabetes stabilized and she and her family knew that she would need to return to the British School. "We all realized that my dad would get transferred again and that I'd go to university in the UK. They would not accept my American credits and I'd need to repeat two years. There's no way I was doing that. So for ninth and tenth grade, I went back to BSW. I don't like the commute because I have to get up at 5:30 in the morning and I don't get back until 5 p.m., but I love the teachers there and my friends. It's also different because in American schools, kids think of each other on grade levels, like 'I'm an eighth grader, so I won't talk to sixth graders because they're beneath me,' but at BSW, everyone is friends with everybody. And it's a good school for Americans, too. A lot of people think that BSW is just for Brits, but about half the school is American kids and the other half is international, from countries all over the world."

When asked if she had advice for other families considering a new school, she said, "You should look at all different kinds. BSW and Washington International, our rival in sports, are awesome. Americans don't consider them as much, but they are great schools and the IB [International Baccalaureate] program is well respected here and around the world."

Catherine and her family are on the move again. Her father was just transferred back to Belgium.

Consider All Options, Including Boarding School

Eric and his family live in Frederick, Maryland, quite a distance from many of the independent schools that surround the DC area. With the traffic in the metro area, commuting wasn't a good option, so they began to broaden their options to look at boarding schools. "I wanted to get the best education possible, and there wasn't necessarily a school like that in my hometown. So we started to look at boarding schools. I was nervous about the possibility, but I knew there were some amazing boarding schools that had a compilation of things to offer, from a great education to sports. I went to Phillips Academy in Massachusetts for an overnight visit, knowing nobody. I made a really good group of friends that I hung out with. It was virtually impossible *not* to make friends. I've visited a lot of schools since then and I've realized that you're going to find people like you and people not like you, but you're going to learn a lot from the people not like you. Diversity is one of the good things about going to a boarding school. You can learn from other people who are different from you."

Eric is confident in his academic abilities, but he's also relieved that there are safety nets even at the most rigorous of schools. "All the schools are going to provide you (the student) with all the tools you need to be successful. There are support networks established with tutors and academic advisors. That's another good thing about a boarding school. Your teachers are living on campus. Everyone wants to help you. These are a group of adults who have dedicated their lives to helping young people."

One of the best things Eric says he and his family did was to start looking at schools early. "If I could give advice to kids, it would be to not wait until the last minute. A lot of my friends did that and it didn't work out too well for them. Get on the process in the spring of seventh grade. Start investigating and continue through the summer. Talk to your family about it so that it's not as stressful when you do your visits and interviews in the fall."

His next tip is about interviews. "Kids can really get stressed out. I was talking to my friends about it. My number one tip is to be yourself. I noticed that the schools want to know who you really are. They want to know your character, your personality. They're not interested in seeing someone blow themselves up to be someone they're not."

When asked about missing his family, Eric paused. "That's one of the most prominent and very real disadvantages of a boarding school. You're going through all these years of living with your family and suddenly you're plopped into this intense academic environment without your family. But you're able to call them as often as you want and you can Skype with them. I think the student will get enough contact not to be really homesick. But a parent would have to judge the maturity level of their kid. It's up to the family to make a decision together, as a unit," he said.

"One last thing—don't hesitate to look at a wide range of schools. That's what we did. Push your comfort zone a little bit so that you can learn about all the different opportunities that are out there. You will find a school that fits you." This fall, Eric will be off to the prestigious Lawrenceville School in New Jersey.

Good Advice from Mom

Alek is an eighth grader in his last year at Norwood School in Bethesda, Maryland. "My parents always wanted me to go to Georgetown Prep, but we looked at a number of other schools. For me, a good education is the first priority. I applied to Prep, Potomac, St. Andrew's, and Landon. I was accepted at all the schools except for Potomac, where I was waitlisted. Although I liked St. Andrew's, I thought it was too much like Norwood—too small. I wanted a bigger school. My top choices were Landon and Prep. I knew I'd get a great education at both schools and I really liked both campuses and their sports programs, but I decided to go with Prep. I had a great shadow visit and everyone was really nice and I also preferred a Catholic school, but religion didn't play a huge part in my decision."

Alek said that there were a number of things during the admission process that were especially stressful. "I was really nervous before the interview at Prep because my friend told me that the questions they asked were really hard, but once we got engaged in conversation, I realized there was nothing to be nervous about. I just needed to act normally." The other tough part of the process was the application essay that Prep required. "The question I had to respond to was deep, much different than the other schools. It was along the lines of, 'How would you pursue excellence at Georgetown Prep?' I rewrote and edited it many times until it was just right."

When asked about the SSAT, Alek replied, "I took it three times. I kept trying to improve my score, especially in the vocabulary section. That was the hardest for me. In the beginning, I would study and memorize the words and then I wouldn't see them on the test. It was really frustrating! But the more words I studied, the more I saw them on the test later on. I ended up scoring around the 70th or 80th percentile, so it worked out in the end."

Reflecting back, Alek said the best advice he could give another student was actually from his mother. "My mom told me, 'You will hear lots of things from your friends and other people about which schools are good or the best, but you have to visit them all and then choose the one that *you* like the most. That's the one you'll end up doing best at. If you're happy, you're going to do well academically.' And I think my mom was right."

Considerations of a Sophomore Year Transfer

Naina is a high school freshman in Rockville with an active social and extracurricular life. She was a straight-A student in middle school, despite little effort. Academics came easily to Naina. She was eager for her adventures in high school, especially since she had just earned a coveted spot on the junior varsity soccer team.

When school began in the fall, Naina was busy with after-school games, practices, and her social life. She says, "I got home from soccer at around seven o'clock every day, ate dinner, did homework, and on the weekends, I hung out with my friends. My first quarter grades weren't good, mostly Cs and Bs, but I wasn't worried because everyone told me there'd be an adjustment period."

Although Naina realized that strong grades are the result of studying, not merely completing homework, she continued to believe she could improve with minimal effort, just like at middle school. "It wasn't until the end of the second quarter when I knew I was in trouble academically. I had a 2.9 GPA and my parents were mad. What I got away with before wasn't working. I was taking three honors classes, which were much harder. I was totally unprepared for high school. At the start of the third quarter, I tried to focus more. Every day I'd go to class and listen and take notes. I'd review the study guides for tests, but that was only helping a little bit. I honestly wasn't sure how to study effectively. Also, my classes were really big, like 30 kids, and I was distracted in class. When I stayed after school for extra help, there were lots of other kids with problems, too. I needed more help. I felt overwhelmed."

Naina's parents realized that their daughter would probably benefit from a smaller school and smaller classes. On a whim, they went to visit a couple of local independent schools and realized that if their daughter were to be accepted, another school might better equip Naina for success. Naina says, "I was actually excited about the thought of moving schools. I loved my friends and my team, but I knew I wouldn't get into a good college at the rate I was going. When I found out that my GPA would be reported to colleges from the new school, I was relieved. Basically, colleges would see my freshman grades, but my GPA would be based on tenth through twelfth grade."

Naina ended up applying late to two schools. So far, she's been accepted to one and is waiting to hear from the other, which is her first choice. "I really like both schools, but one is definitely more convenient and their soccer team is more competitive. Honestly, I could be happy at both. I'm looking forward to getting to know new friends, my teachers, and having a fresh start."

Present the Best Version of Yourself

Ben and Max were stunned when they found out that, due to their dad's job, they were going to have to relocate to Northern Virginia from New York. The boys felt the timing couldn't be worse. Ben was going to be a high school junior and Max was just about to start middle school. After quickly recovering from the shock, they visited Northern Virginia and met with a consultant. After considering public and independent options, they decided that, to make the transition easier, an independent school would be best.

Though the family looked at a number of excellent schools, they ultimately decided on Potomac for both boys. Ben said that he immediately felt at home with the students there. "The community was incredible. They are very focused on math and science, which is what I excel at." Math and science are both important to Ben, who is passionate about computer programming. "I could just see myself there more. It just kind of looked more like my style than the other schools."

Ben is a big advocate for being the best version of yourself during the school admission process. He says, "Be yourself, don't try being something you're not. Schools do not want to see that. As long as you're trying to be yourself and show them what you're made of, I think that's good advice." Ben also stressed the importance of making a good first impression: "Try to introduce yourself to everyone, and to all the teachers. Be as nice as you can." Ben argues that to present the best version of yourself, preparation is necessary. "You need to prepare for everything, like the interview and the SSAT."

Prepare, Ben did. He reports that he studied for the SSAT for about six months. Having struggled a bit in ninth grade (which was reflected to some degree on his report card), Ben knew that to be a serious contender for some of DC's most prestigious schools, he would have to knock the SSAT out of the ballpark—and he did. Ben received a perfect score on the math portion of the test and extremely high marks in both the verbal and the reading sections.

Max follows his brother's lead with his own advice. He believes that approaching the entire admission process with a positive outlook is crucial to finding the right school. "Don't try to think about all the bad things, like being lonely in a new school. Try to think about all the new friends you'll make and that it's going to be a completely new experience." Max agrees with his brother that preparation is necessary, but he believes that it's important to check your nerves at the door: "Try your best and don't be nervous. Nervousness is going to make you choose poorly."

Ultimately, both boys add that you have to be accepting of the school's decision and know that whatever happens is for the best. Max adds, "Just remember that there are so many other kids trying to get in too and that at least you tried. There are a lot of great schools in DC!"

Part IV

Schools at a Glance

The DC area is home to a wide range of educational options. With almost 100 independent schools profiled in this section, you will see examples of rigorous academic programs targeted towards self-motivated students. You will also find schools targeted towards those who may need support in the classroom, whether it be through full remediation or an academic safety net. This section includes traditional schools, progressive schools, single-sex schools, co-ed schools, religiously affiliated schools, secular schools, primary schools, secondary schools, and everything in between. I firmly believe that the right match for your child is just beyond the next few pages.

This section contains the following chapters and school profiles:

Chapter 13

Making Sense of School Profiles

The first step in creating this book was to draft a list of schools to be included. One of the benefits of living in the DC area is the number of education options available for families, each with their own specialized approach to learning. However, due to the overwhelming quantity of school options, it was impossible to include every school. Schools that solely educate preschoolers, that are so small they serve a very limited population, and others that are just too far out of our geographic area were not included. In addition, there are a tremendous number of Catholic schools that do a fantastic job of educating children from all backgrounds, but I found it difficult to include each and every school due to the sheer volume.

In fact, there are approximately 1,000 non-public schools, counting preschools, in the metro area. In the end, my staff and I included schools that are well known and capable of serving diverse needs, or that serve a significant number of students. We also added schools that we felt have a loyal following of families and are highly regarded in the community. A vast array of schools is included to meet the needs of every type of learner and most every family's personal values.

While we've included a fairly comprehensive list of schools, I also believe that there is a local school option available for every type of family and student, and I urge families not to discount a school solely based on its omission from the school profiles section.

Understanding the School Profiles

This section is designed to be informative, not promotional in any way, in order to provide parents with an objective overview of each school. The profiles contained in the next few chapters are intended to help you create an initial list of schools; however, they should not be used as your sole source of information. There are aspects of each school that aren't best reflected in a brief summary. In fact, you may not even get a true realization of a school by reading its entire website word-for-word. You need to step foot on the campus. I encourage you to visit each school of interest to gain a true understanding of the school's culture, academic programs, and student life.

The information you will read on the following pages was obtained by speaking to directors of admission, reviewing the schools' websites, and when possible, visiting campuses. As a caveat, parents will need to verify the facts as information can change. It's not unusual for schools to modify curriculum or programs offered as their needs change throughout the year.

As you peruse each school's description, you'll find its general contact information including the address, phone number, and website so you can follow up directly with the school if you would like more information. Also included in each profile is the school's core information: grades covered, religious affiliation, enrollment, average class size, admission deadline, required testing, tuition, and financial aid. All information applies to the 2013-2014 school year.

Mission Statement

The mission statements are quoted from the schools (though some have been shortened) and should give you an idea of their educational philosophy and approach to learning. Take these mission statements seriously. A school should live and breathe its values, vision, and educational philosophy. If you find that a school's mission statement does not resonate with you, I would think twice about that school. A clearly defined mission statement is essential to a properly run school.

Curriculum

The curriculum section is essential to your understanding of the school. This will tell you what to expect as far as rigor, academic emphasis, and course offerings. The idea is to give you a picture of what's actually going on inside the classroom.

In the curriculum section, you may come across important, yet unfamiliar terms. Some of this educational jargon will help you to better understand the unique aspects of each school's programs. Here are some common terms you will see:

Montessori: Montessori schools offer a different approach to early education (typically ages preschool through third grade, although it varies by program). The main elements of a Montessori program are multi-age classrooms, choicc of learning activity, and long blocks of uninterrupted work time. In a multi-age classroom, students learn to develop socially with students who are both older and younger than they are. Within the classroom, the teacher presents students with a range of educational activities, and students are then free to choose which activity best suits their interest. The aim is to allow students to discover concepts through hands-on experience and working directly with multi-sensory materials.

Advanced Placement (AP): AP classes offer high school students a college-level curriculum with the possibility of earning university credit. Students take a challenging class which culminates with a national AP test in May. Depending on a student's score (on a scale of one to five), colleges may grant credit upon enrollment and exempt students from introductory level courses in that field. AP classes cover a wide variety of subjects, from mainstays like European History and Calculus to more creative pursuits like Music Theory and Studio Art. AP classes look great on a college resume, but take care that your student is not overloaded.

International Baccalaureate (IB): You'll find the exacting IB program at international schools like British School of Washington and Washington International School, but also at American schools, such as Holy Cross. The IB program is based on challenging international education guidelines that are popular in European educational systems. The high school program includes some unique practices. For instance, students take classes in ethics, write an extended essay, and enroll in a Theory of Knowledge (TOK) seminar. IB programs place a high emphasis on writing, critical thinking, and the humanities. Colleges and universities around the world respect the IB program for its rigor and high standards.

AP vs. IB

Both the AP and IB programs are considered equally attractive to a college admission board. They are rigorous and intensive, but there are some differences. Many AP courses cover a vast amount of material in a short period of time, and focus on memorization and critical analysis. IB, on the other hand, tends to be a deeper curriculum because less information is generally covered. There is a greater focus on writing. That doesn't mean that one is better or worse than the other—rather they take slightly different approaches.

STEM: The goal of STEM (science, technology, engineering, and math) education is to integrate technology into daily classroom teaching so that American students can be more competitive in a global workforce. Recent studies have found that U.S. students rank far lower in math and science than others in much smaller and less wealthy nations such as Estonia, Slovenia, and Finland. The STEM initiative includes a greater emphasis on technology, beginning in elementary school all the way through unique STEM classes in high school. Examples of high school coursework include: Digital Electronics, Aerospace Engineering, Computer Integrated Manufacturing, and Engineering Design/Drafting.

Differentiated Learning: Differentiation is a form of instruction that assumes that no child has the same road map to learning. In a differentiated classroom, teachers can modify content (what's being taught), process (how they teach it), products (ways they assess learning), or the classroom environment itself (quiet areas or places for small group learning). For example, if you walk into a differentiated classroom, you may see some students peer editing an essay, others working with a teacher to develop simple paragraph writing skills, while others are on the computer editing their final copy. At most schools, every classroom includes some degree of differentiation. Further examples at the elementary level include: different spelling lists based on ability, leveled books for various reading levels, learning centers based on student interest, and different types of assessments (projects, oral reports, etc.) to demonstrate the student has learned the topic.

Responsive Classroom: Responsive Classroom is a research-based approach that reinforces an elementary classroom environment that is safe, respectful, and predictable. Strategies include a daily morning meeting and the creation of classroom rules by students. Teachers use a specific, positive dialogue instead of punitive words to guide students to appropriate behaviors. Logical consequences are in place for misbehavior, but they are used in a way that allows children to learn from their mistakes. Students are allowed input into their education, especially when it comes to demonstrating their knowledge. For example, at the end of a unit students can show their mastery of the topic by choosing to create a poster board, write a short story, or create a PowerPoint. The idea is that when students develop social skills, such as cooperation and empathy, they are more likely to be successful academically.

Primary Source: A primary source is a document, speech, or other work that was produced during the time period being studied. Instead of or in addition to using textbooks, some schools rely on primary sources so that students obtain knowledge directly from the original source. Examples of primary sources are Plato's Republic, The Declaration of Independence, The Diary of Anne Frank, and film footage from the assassination of President John F. Kennedy.

Classical Education: This curriculum style emphasizes reading classical books, especially of Greek origin, and studying Latin, logic, math, science, rhetoric, and the fine arts. There is also an emphasis on grammar, astronomy, music, and geometry. Some schools use this approach throughout every grade level and in almost every subject, while others will simply utilize classical readings in their humanities classes.

Phonics-Based Reading: Students using a phonics-based approach to reading learn how to effectively "sound out" words by breaking them down into individual sounds or syllables. For example, when a young child sees an unfamiliar word such as 'flash,' using a phonics-based approach he decodes the word into the units 'fuh-luh-ah-sh,' thereby reading the word accurately. Phonics is a valid method of teaching children in primary grades reading and spelling.

The Whole Language Approach: The whole-language approach strives to teach children to read words as units instead of individual sounds. The idea is that when children are consistently exposed to literature, they will begin to memorize what words look like and mean. For example, if a child comes to the unfamiliar word 'flash,' he may recall it from previous exposure or sound out the first letter and determine what word might make sense given the context. This form of instruction is taught using a holistic approach, meaning that children do not learn to break down sounds individually but to take words at face value and associate them with prior knowledge.

Everyday Math: Everyday Math is a pre-k and elementary school math curriculum developed by the University of Chicago's School Mathematics Project in the early '80s. The idea of Everyday Math is to make studying math as relevant to the real world as possible, as hinted by the name. The curriculum emphasizes concepts using practical problems such as sharing a bag of M&M's to demonstrate division. The program seeks to avoid rote memorization, and instead help students understand the way math is used each and every day in life. When students are introduced to new problems, they are encouraged to try to use what they know to find solutions instead of simply being told the correct method.

Singapore Math: Singapore Math takes an in-depth, methodical, and thorough approach to instruction beginning in first grade. Traditionally, most math education in the United States begins each grade with an extensive review of topics covered during the previous year. In contrast, Singapore Math eliminates the need for review by taking extra time to cover each concept in significant depth. Additionally, Singapore Math focuses on mathematical concepts that build on each other and are therefore essential to progressing to higher levels. It also places an emphasis on understanding word problems at an earlier age, in order to prepare students for more complex problem solving they will encounter at higher levels.

Arts

Almost every independent school has some type of artistic requirement for students and this section will elaborate on those offerings. You will find that some schools have very comprehensive art programs including options in areas such as woodworking, pottery, photography, advanced dance and choreography, graphic design, and so on.

Athletics

For many families, athletics is an influential factor when selecting a school. This section includes the athletic options a school offers and also sheds light on any athletic requirements, tryout policies, and standout programs.

Student Life

The type of information contained in the student life section varies from school to school, mainly because activities outside of the classroom are so vast. This segment includes offerings in character development, community service, clubs and organizations, study abroad opportunities, school traditions, and weekend activities.

Campus

The campus section gives you an overview of the major facilities including technology labs, libraries, and sports fields. You'll want to visit the school yourself to gain your own impression, but for instance, if your student is a field hockey player and the school is limited to an urban campus with no off-campus fields, this makes it that much easier to cross it off your list.

Learning Support

For some families, a deciding factor in selecting the right school is the amount of support the school can provide. This section gives a basic overview of the school's learning support services from fully staffed learning centers to schools that offer virtually no accommodations at all.

Schools Attended by Most Graduates in the Past Five Years

This list includes the schools that have been most attended by graduates over the past five years. For example, if the school ends in eighth grade, this section will provide a list of schools most attended by rising freshman. If the school continues through high school, the colleges that most students have attended are provided. **Take note that the data is self-reported by the schools and is not a comprehensive list**. For a number of reasons, some schools did not wish to publish this data. To obtain this information or a full matriculation list, please contact the school directly.

Takeaways

The last section contains general summary information and highlights of the school. In addition, I tried to provide you with a general idea of the type of student or family that may be a good fit for that school community. You'll find all of this information in one place, conveniently laid out for you, as you embark on your school search.

Chapter 14

Finding Your Fit: Schools by Category

On the following pages, you will find schools grouped by category. Some schools fit into multiple categories such as Independent Catholic and All-Girls; therefore there will be overlap within the groups. This information will make it easier for you to find the schools that might best fit your child as you peruse the school profiles found in the next few chapters.

All-Boys Schools: The schools in this category educate males only.

The Avalon School, page 151
DeMatha Catholic High School, page 173
Georgetown Preparatory School, page 180
Gonzaga College High School, page 344
The Heights School, page 189
Landon School, page 196
St. Albans School, page 373
St. Anselm's Abbey School, page 376

All-Girls Schools: Likewise, these schools include only females.

Academy of the Holy Cross, page 148
Brookewood, page 158
Connelly School of the Holy Child, page 170
Foxcroft School, page 262
Georgetown Visitation Preparatory School, page 342
Holton-Arms School, page 191
The Madeira School, page 286
National Cathedral School, page 360

Secular Schools: These schools are not religiously affiliated. It's not to say that spirituality doesn't play a role, it's just that these schools do not identify themselves with any one particular religion.

Loudoun School for the Gifted, page 284
Lowell School, page 355
The Madeira School, page 286
Maret School, page 357
McLean School of Maryland, page 199
Middleburg Academy, page 291
The New School of Northern Virginia, page 293
The Newton School, page 296
The Nora School, page 204
Norwood School, page 206
Nysmith School for the Gifted, page 299
Oakwood School, page 304
Parkmont School, page 365
The Potomac School, page 309
Primary Day School, page 209
Sheridan School, page 368
The Siena School, page 214
Wakefield School, page 319
Washington Waldorf School, page 229
Westminster School, page 322

Catholic Diocesan Schools: These are schools directly tied to a Catholic diocese (Archdiocese of Arlington, Washington, or Baltimore). These schools will often offer tuition assistance for church members, and there is a sense that all of the schools see each other as part of a family—once you're in a Catholic primary school, it often leads to acceptance at a Catholic middle and upper school. For the right student, schools on this list can be a great fit.

Academy of the Holy Cross, page 148
The Avalon School, page 151
Bishop Denis J. O'Connell High School, page 244
Bishop Ireton High School, page 246
DeMatha Catholic High School, page 173
Gonzaga College High School, page 344
Paul VI Catholic High School, page 306

Catholic Independent Schools: These schools are run by an order of the Catholic Church, such as Jesuits. They do not have to follow strict curriculum guidelines set forth by the Catholic Church. They have the highest level of autonomy. Because they do not receive funding from the local diocese, their tuition is higher than Catholic diocesan schools. Class sizes are smaller, too.

Brookewood, page 158
Connelly School of the Holy Child, page 170
Georgetown Preparatory School, page 180
Georgetown Visitation Preparatory School, page 342
The Heights School, page 189
Oakcrest School, page 302
St. Anselm's Abbey School, page 376
St. John's College High School, page 379
Stone Ridge School of the Sacred Heart, page 223
The Woods Academy, page 232

Other Christian Non-Denominational Schools: There are other Christian religious schools, ranging from Lutheran to Protestant to Episcopalian, which are tied to their local church. These schools follow their own guidelines and some receive funding from their affiliated religious institution.

Ad Fontes Academy, page 238
Beauvoir, The National Cathedral Elementary School, page 325
Episcopal High School, page 256
Grace Episcopal Day School, page 184
Merritt Academy, page 289
National Cathedral School, page 360
National Presbyterian School, page 363
Sandy Spring Friends School, page 211
Sidwell Friends School, page 370
St. Albans School, page 373
St. Andrew's Episcopal School, page 217
St. John's Episcopal School, page 220
St. Patrick's Episcopal Day School, page 381
St. Stephen's & St. Agnes School, page 312
Trinity Christian School, page 315
Virginia Academy, page 317
Washington Episcopal School, page 226

Jewish Schools: As the title suggests, these are schools that focus on providing an education in Jewish heritage including Hebrew, Jewish history, and religious instruction.

Learning Differences Schools: Every parent deals with learning issues at some point during their child's school career; however, when these obstacles are more than just a bump in the road, other schooling options can be considered. In a more supportive, specialized school, children with learning disabilities or ADHD are taught vital strategies by specially trained teachers. Gaps in learning are remediated, strengths are honed, and "learning to learn" takes place. All of these schools are also secular.

International Schools: These schools are designed for international families or families with students who hope to study abroad after high school. International schools provide an international diploma, typically an International Baccalaureate, and place a heavy emphasis on foreign language study. These schools are all secular.

Boarding Schools: Students live on campus in dormitories, similar to college. Most faculty members also live on campus and there is a significant amount of structure in terms of oversight and planned activities. Some of the schools below have a robust boarding population while others have just a few dorms available.

CHAPTER 15

Maryland Schools

Academy of the Holy Cross

4920 Strathmore Avenue, Kensington, MD 20895
301.942.2100 | www.academyoftheholycross.org

"The Academy of the Holy Cross, a Catholic college preparatory school sponsored by the Sisters of the Holy Cross since 1868, is dedicated to educating young women in a Christ-centered community that values diversity. The Academy is committed to developing women of courage, compassion, and scholarship who responsibly embrace the social, spiritual, and intellectual challenges of the world."

Grades 9 – 12 | All Girls
Catholic | Archdiocese of Washington, DC

Enrollment: 530 | **Average Class Size:** 19
Admissions and Testing: Deadline December 6; HSPT (9-12)
Tuition and Financial Aid: $19,550; financial aid budget of $1.6 million; uses SSS form.

Curriculum: The Academy of the Holy Cross (AHC) offers honors and AP classes and the IB diploma program. Along with study in six subject groups, IB core requirements include the Theory of Knowledge course—which explores the nature of knowledge as human construction; the Extended Essay—which is a fully researched and documented essay of global significance; and Creativity, Action, Service (CAS)—which emphasizes experiential learning outside traditional classroom methods. All students are required to take English, math, and theology courses all four years. Before graduation, all seniors complete a 60-hour internship program, the Senior Project, in which they work at an area business or organization in a field of their interest. AHC offers a variety of elective courses including Computer Programming, Web Design, Peer Ministry, Personal Finance, and Public Speaking.

Arts: AHC's performing arts program hosts several main stage performances a year, including dance concerts, music concerts, and improvisational shows. The Adrenaline dance team allows more experienced dancers the opportunity to perform and compete throughout the year while gaining additional dance experience. The Madrigal Singers a cappella group provides students who have a passion for vocal performance an outlet to improve their skills. AHC is a member of the Tri-M Music Honor Society, the International Thespian Society, and the Nu Delta Alpha National Dance Honor Society.

Athletics: AHC is a charter member of the Washington Catholic Athletic Conference. Athletic offerings include basketball, crew, cross-country, equestrian, field hockey, golf, ice hockey, lacrosse, soccer, softball, swimming and diving, tennis, track, and volleyball. Most sports offer both junior varsity and varsity level competition with tryout seasons taking place in fall, winter, and spring.

Student Life: The school provides many opportunities for students to cultivate their interests in more than 20 co-curricular clubs. As a Catholic school, AHC hosts on- and off- campus initiatives such as the Christian Service Commitment program and an active Campus Ministry. The Moreau Advisory Program extends learning beyond the classroom with a guidance counseling curriculum that prepares students to be self-advocates and leaders.

Campus: Located in Kensington, Maryland, AHC's 28-acre campus includes art studios, a dark room, a kiln room, and rehearsal rooms. The school has a 400-seat theater that includes a rigging system, acoustical treatment, fly space, scenery storage, and large dressing rooms. The campus is a five-minute walk from Grosvenor Metro station and a Ride-On stop is located at the school entrance.

Learning Support: AHC provides access to the Student Resource Center for academically capable students with diagnosed learning disabilities on a semester-by-semester basis.

Schools Attended by Most Graduates in the Past Five Years: University of Maryland—College Park, University of South Carolina, University of Maryland—Baltimore, Towson University, Saint Joseph's University

Takeaways: AHC's college prep program aims to provide opportunities and challenges necessary for girls to achieve their full potential in today's society. Students have a variety of learning experiences in liberal and creative arts, mathematics, science, and career education, and are encouraged to consider the rigorous IB program. The IB program is available either through individual certificate courses or the full diploma offering. Unique programs such as the Senior Project and Madeleva Scholars demonstrate the school's dedication to fostering learning experiences beyond the classroom. AHC is worth considering for students who are looking for an all-girls environment, strong academics, a Christian community, and a commitment to service.

The Avalon School

200 West Diamond Avenue, Gaithersburg, MD 20877
301.963.8022 | www.avalonschools.org

"Established in 2003, The Avalon School brings the spirit of adventure and friendship to boys grades two through twelve in an independent day school featuring a challenging liberal arts curriculum. The school seeks to cultivate in its students a sense of intellectual freedom and personal responsibility; to foster the gifts of faith and culture that are within each boy's reach; and to help them fulfill the deep desire to live a noble life that resides in all men."

Grades K – 12 | All Boys (Co-Ed Kindergarten)
Catholic | Archdiocese of Washington, DC

Enrollment: 200 | **Average Class Size**: 15
Admissions and Testing: Rolling admission; no testing required
Tuition and Financial Aid: $5,975 (Half-Day K), $12,450 (Full-Day K), $12,450 (Lower School), $13,950 (Middle School), $14,500 (Upper School); 33% of students receive aid.

Curriculum: The liberal arts-centered, college prep curriculum focuses on cultural literacy and academic mastery. This means that boys are trained in the arts, literature, poetry, languages, the sciences, and religion. Boys in the lower school are introduced to nature, literature, drawing, and sports by male teachers who serve as enthusiastic role models.

Middle school boys go on frequent field trips that allow them to explore their surroundings and feed their adventurous spirits. The upper school curriculum covers Shakespeare, as well as literature from western civilization. Students also participate in language studies, and Calculus is required of all seniors. Students must graduate with three credits in Latin, Greek, Spanish, or Italian. Nine AP classes are offered to juniors and seniors.

Arts: Aside from the poetry program, the arts program at The Avalon School includes an acting guild in partnership with the Brookewood School. The two schools hold a Spring Gala each year at which the students perform musical numbers.

Athletics: Avalon competes in the Capital Area Football Conference, the Old Line Baseball Conference, and the Mid-Atlantic Christian Conference. Baseball, soccer, basketball, football, and cross-country are offered. Avalon holds tryouts and makes cuts, although this is rare at the middle school level. Avalon's baseball team has won four state championships. These programs are not mandatory.

Student Life: Avalon follows a house system in which groups of boys compete against each other in intramurals and take part in school traditions. Moreover, Avalon has a particularly strong poetry program. Beginning in the lower school, students create, recite, and sing poetry. In every grade, students participate in regular poetry competitions. Additionally, all lower school and middle school students compete in a poet laureate competition each winter. Students are encouraged to see poetry as an emotional outlet and learn to express themselves.

Campus: Avalon shares a building with the First Baptist Church of Gaithersburg. Avalon has plenty of access to sports fields as well as facilities for its arts programs.

Learning Support: Learning differences are handled on a case-by-case basis. Parents and consultants meet and decide on a course of action for the student. Other support offered is after-school time with the teachers and extra time allotment on tests. In some cases, a course may be substituted with a study hall or extra work with a tutor.

Schools Attended by Most Graduates in the Past Five Years: University of Maryland, Catholic University of America, United States Military Academy, Benedictine College, St. Mary's College of Maryland

Takeaways: Avalon features small class sizes, and the poetry program is emphasized heavily. Additionally, the liberal arts focus provides boys with a challenging academic experience. The school's baseball and football teams have had a significant amount of success, and students are encouraged to engage in competition through the school's house system.
Avalon is a good fit for traditional families looking for instruction focused on literature, poetry, languages, and arts, all within a Catholic setting.

The Barnesville School

21830 Peach Tree Road, P. O. Box 404, Barnesville, MD 20838
301.972.0341 | www.barnesvilleschool.org

"We are dedicated to providing a joyful and supportive learning environment for the development of excellence in each of us."

Preschool – Grade 8 | Co-Ed
No Religious Affiliation

Enrollment: 196 | **Average Class Size:** 11
Admissions and Testing: Priority Deadline January 15; SSAT or ISEE (5-8)
Tuition and Financial Aid: $15,200 (K), $18,130 (1-4), $19,440 (5-8); financial aid available; uses the SSS form; merit scholarships available.

Curriculum: Barnesville's lower school is divided into two pods. Pod A consists of preschool through first grade and Pod B comprises students in second through fourth grade. The pods meet individually to celebrate birthdays, play games, and listen to stories. The core curriculum includes language arts, math, science, social studies, writing, Spanish, art, music, library, technology, and physical education. Additionally, Barnesville utilizes iPads in preschool, kindergarten, first, fifth, sixth, and seventh grade.

The middle school offers an integrated program with core subjects (language arts, math, science, etc.) as well as music, art, Spanish, and physical education. A special emphasis is placed on critical thinking, organization, speaking, and writing. The school is focused on building its science and environmental curriculum and is certified as a Maryland green school. While Spanish instruction begins in preschool, the language program culminates in middle school when fifth and sixth graders have the opportunity to participate in a foreign language program with St. Andrew's School in Bolivia. Additionally, seventh and eighth graders have the opportunity to participate in the school's exchange program with the Leonardo Da Vinci School in Lima, Peru.

Arts: Students partake in regular music classes at Barnesville and have the chance to work in the art studio beginning in kindergarten. Students in the lower school are encouraged to participate in the Winter Holiday Musical Production as well as the May Day Musical Production. The middle school students can participate in chorus, band, the fall theatrical production, and the spring musical.

Athletics: Barnesville competes with schools in the Maryland Junior Athletic Conference. Basketball, soccer, cross-country, and lacrosse are offered for both boys and girls. Team rosters are limited, and the program is not mandatory.

Student Life: With fewer than 200 students in preschool through eighth grade, the students and teachers alike are able to build close relationships. The school has a "buddy program" that partners younger students with older students to reinforce the sense of community. Barnesville hosts a variety of after-school activities for students ranging from Club Yoga to Math Counts, but there is an additional fee associated with these clubs.

Campus: Barnesville is located on 50 acres within Montgomery County's Agricultural Reserve. The campus includes a museum building, a science lab with a weather station, two technology labs, a gym, a library, athletic fields, a drama stage, a ropes course, and an outdoor classroom.

Learning Support: Barnesville staffs one learning specialist, a tutor, and a speech therapist.

Schools Attended by Most Graduates in the Past Five Years: Poolesville HS Magnet Program, Our Lady of Good Counsel School, St. John's Catholic Preparatory School, St. Andrew's Episcopal School, Georgetown Preparatory School

Takeaways: Barnesville is a traditional school in nature but differentiates itself by its small student population and its focus on community. The small student population enables students to have more access to the school's resources, including individualized time with teachers. The school places a big emphasis on studies outside of the classroom and offers several field trips throughout the year for all grade levels. Barnesville may be a match for families that want their students in a supportive setting with an integrated academic program with special attention to the environment.

Barrie School

13500 Layhill Road, Silver Spring, MD 20906
301.576.2800 | www.barrie.org

"Empower individuals to expand their intellectual abilities, develop their creative talents, and discover their passions to make a positive impact in a rapidly changing world."

---

18 months – Grade 12 | Co-Ed
No Religious Affiliation

Enrollment: 350 | **Average Class Size:** 12
Admissions and Testing: Deadline January 17; testing is optional
Tuition and Financial Aid: $14,500-19,650 (Primary), $22,350 (1-5), $25,350 (6-8), $27,000 (9-12); 12-15% of student body receives aid with an average grant of $7,600; uses SSS form.

Curriculum: Barrie seeks to offer students a progressive educational experience beginning in nursery school through its Montessori program. Lower school Montessori students are divided into four groups: toddler, primary, lower elementary, and upper elementary. Within these levels students are grouped into multi-age classrooms that reflect their stages of development. Primary classes include students of ages three through six, lower elementary includes students in first through third grade, and upper elementary consists of students in fourth and fifth grade. This approach allows younger students to learn from older students, gives older students leadership opportunities, and provides teachers a deep understanding of the children in their classrooms.

The middle school integrates a thematic curriculum that encourages interdisciplinary collaboration and connection. For example, students may be learning about environmental studies while also learning about a respect for the environment. Barrie's philosophy is to "respect the environment, yourself, and others."

Students who attend Barrie's upper school are given the opportunity to challenge themselves with college prep classes. Barrie offers various pathways for students to fulfill their graduation requirements, seeking to place importance on students' intrinsic motivation. The humanities, in particular, offer students a number of unique elective choices ranging from American Popular Music to A History of the World through Food. Barrie's dedication to experiential learning continues to be a focus throughout its upper school curriculum. Through the Experiential Education program, students partake in internships and complete a total of 75 hours by their senior year.

Arts: The arts are actively integrated into daily life at Barrie. Students have the option to take classes in art history, chorus, dance, drama, music, studio art, watercolor, painting, ceramics, woodworking, sculpture, digital photography, and technical theater. The school's black box theater partners with the Olney Theater Company throughout the year for several workshops and seminars.

Athletics: The upper school competes in several athletic conferences and offers interscholastic teams in soccer, volleyball, cross-country, basketball, lacrosse, tennis, equestrian, golf, and track and field. The school specifically boasts an equestrian program with stables and equestrian grounds on campus. There is an athletic credit requirement for students, but competitive sports are not mandatory.

Student Life: Barrie offers students various ways to explore their interests outside of the classroom. The school has a weekly clubs and activities period built into the schedule for upper school students. Students can take part in leadership positions within various school organizations or start a new club. Students are also encouraged to participate in community service and creative opportunities such as the Barrie Slamstation, a poetry slam tradition.

Campus: Barrie is located in Silver Spring, Maryland. The 45-acre wooded campus is well suited for outdoor education. It includes a black box theater, athletic fields, an art house, an outdoor pool, and stables. Barrie has recently added a learning studio and a research learning lab.

Learning Support: Barrie's learning support staff includes a college counselor, a school counselor, and a learning specialist.

Schools Attended by Most Graduates in the Past Five Years:
No matriculation information is available.

Takeaways: Barrie focuses on student-centered learning and experiential education. It features a Montessori education through fifth grade while also providing a smooth transition into a progressive, college prep curriculum in the middle and upper schools. With multi-aged classrooms beginning in preschool and continuing until students reach middle school, students are given opportunities to be leaders from a very early age. Students in the middle and upper schools at Barrie will find that the curriculum is driven by the school's philosophy and that moral development is interwoven with the content in every class.

The faculty at Barrie strives to provide a modern, relevant educational experience for all students who attend. If you are looking for a progressive preschool through twelfth grade school for your child with a Montessori foundation, then Barrie may be a good fit.

Brookewood

10401 Armory Avenue, Kensington, MD 20895
301.949.7997 | www.brookewood.org

"The Brookewood motto is Nolite Timere ("Be not afraid"), a frequent injunction of John Paul II to the world's youth. It captures both the spirit and goal of the school . . . that a Brookewood student, armed with the knowledge and faith, imparted at school and home, and with the grace of God, should not be afraid to go out into the world."

Grades 1 – 12 | All Girls
Catholic | Independent

Enrollment: 150 | **Average Class Size:** 15
Admissions and Testing: Rolling admission; no testing required
Tuition and Financial Aid: $11,000 (1-5), $12,250 (6-12); $250 activities/materials fee; financial aid available; uses FACTS form.

Curriculum: The lower school is based on the guidelines of the Core Knowledge Series, which emphasizes an integrated liberal arts curriculum to develop literacy and math fundamentals. Here students begin to memorize poetry. Literacy skills are built, in part, by reading classic children's stories. All students are required to study Italian.

In the middle school, the English curriculum is centered on critical reading, writing, and rhetoric. Algebra is introduced. Middle school biblical studies focus on both the Old and New Testament. Latin courses begin in eighth grade and students continue to study Italian.

The upper school curriculum includes college prep classes with an emphasis on critical-thinking skills. Upper school students also take courses in ancient, medieval, and modern history. The religion classes include courses such as Christology, Church History, and Ecclesiology. In the upper school, students can choose to either continue on with Latin or switch to Spanish.

Arts: Musical training is a priority at Brookewood. There are several performances each year, and there is a strong emphasis on musical education for all girls. Instruction begins in the lower school with weekly classes. Students learn songs from all over the world, musical history, and music literacy skills. Students can also study piano and violin.

Athletics: Brookewood competes in the Independent School League. It offers lacrosse, field hockey, cross-country, basketball, and volleyball. The program is not mandatory. Brookewood is known more for its outdoor hiking trips (to Sugarloaf Mountain, Old Rag Mountain, Harper's Ferry, etc.).

Student Life: Brookewood implements a house system, which assigns every student to one of four houses. The house system is designed to encourage cooperation and collaboration. Middle and upper school students are responsible for helping younger students, taking on the role of "older sisters."

Campus: Brookewood is located in the educational wing of St. Paul's United Methodist Church and uses nearby parks and fields for athletics. The church offers space for mass and worship meetings as well as chorus practice.

Learning Support: Brookewood is not specifically equipped to handle students with learning disabilities.

Schools Attended by Most Graduates in the Past Five Years:
No matriculation information is available.

Takeaways: The standout program at Brookewood is its musical training program. All girls at the school receive musical training starting in the lower school. Brookewood provides a liberal arts-based education with a focus on critical thinking and a heavy emphasis on Catholic teachings. Founded in 2006, Brookewood is a relatively new school in the area. The school is a good fit for a girl who is musically-oriented and looking for a single-sex, Catholic education.

Bullis School

10601 Falls Road, Potomac, MD 20854
301.299.8500 | www.bullis.org

"Bullis School provides a student-centered balanced experience in academics, arts, athletics, and community service. Bullis uniquely prepares all students to become caring citizens and creative, critical thinkers who will thrive in tomorrow's world."

Grades 3 – 12 | Co-Ed
No Religious Affiliation

Enrollment: 725 | **Average Class Size:** 15
Admissions and Testing: Deadline January 10, then rolling admission; WISC-IV (3-5), SSAT or ISEE (6-12)
Tuition and Financial Aid: $31,580 (3-5), $33,680 (6-8), $35,050 (9-12); uses the SSS form.

Curriculum: The Bullis lower school curriculum is very individualized. Small class sizes allow teachers to use a wide variety of formal and informal assessments to develop appropriate academic challenge and support. The curriculum strives to develop critical readers, strong writers, and confident problem solvers with solid numeracy and computational skills. The Responsive Classroom methodology used by each homeroom teacher places a strong emphasis on the social curriculum. In addition to the homeroom teacher, students also work with dedicated specialists in reading, science, Spanish, art, general music, and instrumental music.

In the middle school, teachers seek to create a strong foundation of reading, writing, research, and critical-thinking skills. Meeting the individual learning style of each student is a key component of classroom success. Students are exposed to a curriculum that encourages collaboration and leadership. STEM, entrepreneurship, and global studies are areas of emphasis that are integrated into the curriculum. Students emerge from the middle school with strong technology and presentation skills. An effective advisory program strengthens students' sense of diversity, social awareness, and community service.

In the upper school, students begin to focus on more complex skills like analysis, synthesis, evaluation, and application. Students in the upper school can continue with Latin or Spanish, or they can begin studying French or Chinese. There are 17 AP courses offered including computer science, psychology, and studio arts. Bullis offers signature programs in entrepreneurship for students interested in business. Bullis's teachers employ a wide variety of teaching styles, including the flipped classroom, meaning that students have the main lecture at home (using technology) and "homework," which is hands-on time, in the classroom.

Arts: Students have the opportunity to take art classes on a variety of topics ranging from ceramics to digital video to stagecraft. Furthermore, Bullis has staggered its classes in dance, music, theater, and visual arts so that students can take different levels as their skills develop, just as they would a foreign language.

Athletics: Bullis competes in the Interstate Athletic Conference and the Independent School League. Fall sports include football, cheerleading, boys' and girls' soccer, girls' tennis, field hockey, and cross-country. Winter sports include boys' and girls' basketball, wrestling, ice hockey, and swimming. Spring sports include softball, baseball, boys' and girls' lacrosse, boys' tennis, golf, and track and field. Participation is mandatory; upper school students must participate in a sport or an approved after-school activity two out of every three seasons.

Student Life: Bullis offers opportunities for student leadership through their two student body governments—one in the middle school and one in the upper school. The school also offers a variety of in-school, co-curricular, and extracurricular options from the Global Studies and Service program, which gives students opportunities from traveling to different countries during school holidays to holding Skype conferences with NASA.

Campus: Bullis is located in Potomac, Maryland, and spreads out across a spacious campus that includes athletic fields and facilities, a terrace area, academic buildings, The Blair Family Center for the Arts, and the Marriott Family Library.

Learning Support: The school employs learning, writing, and math specialists, as well as academic advisors. Bullis works to accommodate students with all types of learning needs. The Academic Center is located in a brand new facility equipped with technological resources for state-of-the-art learning. Bullis's learning center is not solely reserved for those students with learning disabilities. The school encourages the entire student body to use the center's services. Students are allowed to have a private tutor come work with them during the school day.

Schools Attended by Most Graduates in the Past Five Years: Syracuse University, Miami University, University of Maryland—College Park, Georgetown University, Pennsylvania State University

Takeaways: Bullis seeks to maintain a diverse student body by offering a wide range of courses and paths a student can take at his or her time at the school. Bullis is a good option for families looking for a broad curriculum that offers both academic rigor and balance. Students are able to pick options that work best for them, from taking a full course load of AP classes to receiving learning support. Bullis fits the needs of diverse learners. Because the school is so accommodating in its approach to education, many different types of students can succeed at Bullis.

Butler School

15951 Germantown Road, Darnestown, MD 20874
301.977.6600 | www.butlerschool.org

"Butler's mission is to provide a learning environment where children think, choose, and act to realize their full potential."

Preschool – Grade 8 | Co-Ed
No Religious Affiliation

Enrollment: 138 | **Average Class Size:** 18
Admissions and Testing: Rolling admission; no testing required
Tuition and Financial Aid: $13,100 (Primary), $13,900 (Elementary), $14,390 (Intermediate)

Curriculum: Every student at Butler, from preschool through eighth grade, is learning in a Montessori classroom. Students do not receive grades for their class work and are divided into developmental levels: primary (preschool and kindergarten), elementary (first through sixth grade), and intermediate (seventh and eighth grade). Each level is designed to match the students' developmental needs and characteristics. Elementary classrooms are centered on social development, curiosity, and imagination. Students in the intermediate level focus on social and emotional development.

Arts: Students are encouraged to express themselves through art in every subject area at Butler. This can mean drawing and decorating math sheets or decorating the backdrop for the upcoming school play. Music is integrated into the curriculum as an additional way to foster creativity, and students begin having at least weekly classes in music beginning in preschool.

Athletics: Butler's main sport is equestrian, which includes vaulting. Vaulters compete on the American Vaulting Association circuit. Other after-school programs include soccer, mountain biking, and creative movement.

Student Life: The equestrian program is a big part of the student experience at Butler. Students have the opportunity to take yearlong lessons.

Campus: The campus sits on 22 acres adjacent to Great Seneca State Park. Students at Butler have access to climbing walls, rope courses, equestrian riding and vaulting facilities, a tennis court, an organic egg-laying chicken hutch, a garden harvested by students, ponds, creeks, and miles of wooded trails.

Learning Support: Within every classroom, instruction is individualized and every student is working at his or her own pace. Students do not receive time limits on work and they are encouraged to get up and move as needed. Butler has a full-time educational specialist on staff who consults with teachers and parents. The school employs a private speech therapist and arranges for private tutoring. Both services cost an additional fee, but can take place during the school day.

Schools Attended by Most Graduates in the Past Five Years: Quince Orchard High School, Northwest High School, Wootton High School, Damascus High School, Magruder High School

Takeaways: Butler has one of the longest running Montessori programs in the nation (33 years). The school differentiates itself from other Montessori schools in the area because it offers Montessori classes for students from preschool through eighth grade. One question many parents ask is how students make the transition to a traditional high school. The school states that students transition well and leave as strong critical thinkers. Butler is a good option for a family looking for a Montessori school and a student who will succeed in a non-traditional environment.

Charles E. Smith Jewish Day School

1901 E. Jefferson Street, Rockville, MD 20852 (K-6)
11710 Hunters Lane, Rockville, MD 20852 (7-12)
301.881.1400 | www.cesjds.org

"The Charles E. Smith Jewish Day School is dedicated to creating an environment in which students can grow to their fullest potential as responsible and dedicated members of the Jewish community and of American society."

Grades K – 12 | Co-Ed
Jewish | Pluralistic

Enrollment: 1,200 | **Average Class Size:** 18
Admissions and Testing: Deadline January 15, then rolling admission; no testing required
Tuition and Financial Aid: $21,310 (K-6), $27,340 (7-11), $13,970 (Grade 12 first semester); 35% of the students receive aid; uses the PSAS (Private School Aid Service) for initial evaluations and analysis.

Curriculum: Charles E. Smith Jewish Day School (CESJDS) offers a balanced curriculum with strong general coursework and a comprehensive Judaic studies program. Lower school students start on the journey to become skilled readers, writers, mathematicians, scientists, and artists, anchored in Jewish values and knowledge. The upper school offers students college prep and advanced classes on both secular and Judaic topics. There are a wide range of electives and a variety of class choices to satisfy credit requirements in English, science, Jewish history, and Jewish text, thought, and practice.

Hebrew instruction gives students the opportunity to learn a second language while connecting to Jewish history and culture. Further, there is a strong reliance on technology to support learning in all content areas. The everyday incorporation of technology strives to develop problem-solving skills that will be applicable to future academic and professional settings.

Arts: Lower school students are exposed to music, dance, and a variety of media including drawing, painting, collage, printing, sculpture, and weaving. Art from a different era and culture is incorporated into the curriculum at each grade level. The arts are an integral part of the upper school experience. Students have numerous opportunities for self-expression in the form of ceramics, drama, music, photography, sculpture, painting, printmaking, and creative writing.

Athletics: CESJDS is a member of the Potomac Valley Athletic Conference. The middle and upper schools offer a range of teams including soccer, volleyball, cross-country, tennis, basketball, track, dance, softball, golf, wrestling, and indoor track. Basketball, baseball, tennis, and volleyball have all won championships in the past three years. The program is not mandatory.

Student Life: The school offers a wide variety of opportunities for learning outside of the classroom. In the lower school, students enjoy enrichment programs including robotics, Israeli dance, Odyssey of the Mind, and Shakespeare club. After-school clubs and activities in the upper school include business club, yoga club, math team, debate, student council, and mock trial. There are multiple student publications such as a school newspaper, a literary magazine, the yearbook, a Hebrew literary/art magazine, and a publication featuring student work in Romance languages. Students across all grade levels participate in community service with their classes or families; however, upper school students are required to complete 80 hours of community service upon graduation. Many students fulfill this requirement through partnering with nonprofits that work to advocate for social justice both at home and abroad.

Campus: CESJDS is located on two campuses (K-6 and 7-12) in Rockville, Maryland. Both campuses feature wireless access, athletic fields, art studios, and music rooms. The upper school building has a 700-seat-capacity gymnasium, theater, and fully equipped pottery, photography, and recording studios.

Learning Support: The Educational Support Services Department (ESS) is equipped to help students who need basic accommodations and additional learning support. The ESS team develops Educational Plans that include yearly individualized goals. The majority of learning support focuses on honing writing and reading comprehension skills and developing effective study habits and organizational skills. CESJDS is not a school for students with emotional needs or behavioral challenges.

Schools Attended by Most Graduates in the Past Five Years: University of Maryland—College Park, University of Michigan, Indiana University Bloomington, Washington University in St. Louis, Northwestern University

Takeaways: As one of the largest K-12 Jewish day schools in the country, CESJDS is well regarded and hosts a strong academic program. The study of Hebrew as both a living and ancient language is integral to the experience of all students. For students who enter laterally, the school offers a Hebrew ramp-up program; the upper school also features a ramp-up Judaic class for students new to a Jewish day school. Skill building is woven into every aspect of the dual curriculum, with 40% of all instruction dedicated to some aspect of Judaic and Hebrew studies, and the other 60% to general academic subjects. One standout program at the school is the senior semester abroad. Seniors end their formal studies in the winter and visit Eastern Europe for one week. Then they embark on a three-month program in Israel that comprises their spring semester. The school is geared towards families who are looking for rigorous academics interwoven with Jewish culture, heritage, values, and community.

Chelsea School

2970 Belcrest Center Drive, Hyattsville, MD 20782
301.585.1430 | www.chelseaschool.edu

"Chelsea School educates promising students with specific language-based learning differences in a rigorous, individualized college preparatory environment to become lifelong, independent learners."

Grades 5 – 12 | Co-Ed
No Religious Affiliation

Enrollment: 70 | **Maximum Class Size:** 8
Admissions and Testing: Rolling admission; requires full battery of psychological testing (WISC-IV or Stanford-Binet IV) and normed standardized educational testing
Tuition and Financial Aid: $36,964.85; able to offer limited financial assistance from a financial aid budget of about $210,000.

Curriculum: The college prep curriculum, which incorporates reading remediation into most subjects, is traditional but relies on the use of assistive technology such as Kurzweil 3000, WordQ/SpeakQ, Inspiration, etc. Every teacher at Chelsea is a reading and writing specialist and there is an academic advisor for every student who also serves as the student's advocate and case manager. Each student is placed into one level of the three-tiered reading tutorial program and has an individual plan crafted. The literacy and writing remediation program is inherent to every subject. There's an optional five-week summer program that also focuses on remediation in reading, writing, and math.

Arts: Classes are available in music and media production, computer graphics, fine arts, painting, drawing, and ceramics.

Athletics: Chelsea competes in the Independent Small Schools Athletics Conference. Chelsea offers basketball, softball, soccer, and track. All sports are co-ed. The program is not mandatory.

Student Life: Clubs and other after-school activities are important components of the student experience at Chelsea. Technology club, artisans club, and crafts club are some examples of the opportunities available. Service learning is taken seriously at Chelsea. Students are required to meet hourly community service requirements as part of the school's commitment to developing the "whole" student.

Campus: Chelsea relocated to Hyattsville, Maryland, in August of 2013. The new facility is located at the Prince George's Plaza, across the street from the Prince George's Plaza Metro station. It has 23,000 square feet of space that includes computer graphics and media production labs, a fine arts studio, a fitness center, a student lounge, and middle and upper division classroom space.

Learning Support: Every teacher is either certified in special education or is a content area specialist. There are counselors, occupational therapists, speech and language pathologists, and reading specialists available at all times for help with a student's personalized program.

Schools Attended by Most Graduates in the Past Five Years: University of Maryland—Eastern Shore, Davis & Elkins College, West Virginia Wesleyan College, Muskingum University

Takeaways: For students who have been diagnosed with a language-based learning disability, Chelsea is tailored to their needs. Many Chelsea students have difficulty with reading, spelling, writing with grammatical accuracy, and translating their ideas to paper. The DC public school system (DCPS) is unable to accommodate many of its students with special needs and it pays for these students to attend schools that are able to meet their needs. Roughly half of Chelsea students come from DCPS. Reading remediation is interwoven into everything the school does, which helps students build confidence to move on to higher education.

The individualized attention given to each student in the academic, social, and emotional arenas is well suited to students with language-based learning disabilities. Students who find that more traditional school environments do not offer adequate support often find Chelsea to have the programs they need.

Connelly School of the Holy Child

9029 Bradley Boulevard, Potomac, MD 20854
301.365.0955 | www.holychild.org

"Connelly School of the Holy Child is a Catholic, college preparatory school, committed to the intellectual, spiritual, artistic, physical and social development of young women in grades 6-12. The school emphasizes academic challenge, joy of learning, and the education of well-rounded women of faith and action. The Holy Child community welcomes students and families of different faiths and diverse backgrounds. In keeping with the philosophy of our founder, Cornelia Connelly, Holy Child values the uniqueness of each individual and fosters a life of service to others."

Grades 6 – 12 | All Girls
Catholic | Independent

Enrollment: 300 | **Average Class Size**: 15
Admissions and Testing: December 6 (9-12), January 31 (6-8); SSAT
Tuition and Financial Aid: $24,950 (6-8), $27,220 (9-12); financial aid budget over $1 million serves about 30% of the student body; uses SSS form.

Curriculum: The middle school program is focused on laying a solid academic, social, and emotional foundation. Students have one homeroom teacher whom they meet with daily. Religion and Latin courses begin in sixth grade and students can choose French or Spanish for a foreign language in seventh grade. The curriculum emphasizes a differentiated approach to instruction with a robust experiential component.

Upper school students have a single advisor throughout their tenure and are counseled through their college planning as they choose from more than a dozen honors courses and eight AP classes. This coursework is supplemented by numerous electives, including Forensics, Oceanography, Global Issues, and Personal Finance. Students also have the option of adding courses from the school's local independent school Consortium, which offers a variety of choices including AP Economics, AP Psychology, Mandarin Chinese, and AP Art History. The students are required to take four years of English and religion, and three years of social studies, science, foreign language, and math. Fine arts are required for two years.

Arts: Every ninth grader at Holy Child samples classes in art, music, public speaking, and theater so that she can find her passion and discover her talents. The arts begin in middle school, with regular art class, an elective block, and the annual middle school musical. Each April, the entire school celebrates artistic endeavors with the Evening of the Arts gallery that showcases students' visual art, dance, theater, and music. Concerts and recitals are also held throughout the year, with joint performances with the boys of Gonzaga College High School.

Athletics: Holy Child competes in the Independent School League with 34 teams in 13 sports. Holy Child offers an equestrian program, cross-country, dance, field hockey, soccer, tennis, volleyball, basketball, swimming/diving, lacrosse, softball, and track and field; golf has just been added on the JV level.

Student Life: Holy Child is a school that has many respected traditions. There are tea and ice cream socials welcoming new families during the start-of-school orientation days, Blue/Gold games in October, a Big/Little Sister program, weekly prayer-block assemblies run by students, spirit week, and other events throughout the year. Each school year, students are anonymously assigned a prayer partner. Although a student never finds out who her prayer partner is, she is supported by prayer, small gifts on a holiday, or a card on her birthday. Clubs are a very important part of student life and every student is required to belong to at least one of the 30 clubs offered each year. All clubs meet during the school day to facilitate membership. Retreats are attended by all students, with the Kairos retreat for juniors being a high point.

Campus: The nine-acre campus in Potomac, Maryland, includes a chapel, a library, two art rooms, a fitness center, a dance studio, a theater "green room," and a turf field stadium. The school has two computer labs and wired classrooms throughout.

Learning Support: The Academic Support Center (ASC), which employs five learning specialists as well as tutors, regularly trains both teachers and students in current best practices and methods. In addition to counseling on individual learning plans and course selection for the entire school, the ASC advises parents on testing and other topics regarding learning differences. The ASC offers a special program that allows students with a documented language-based learning disability to forego a foreign language requirement in place of another elective class.

Schools Attended by Most Graduates in the Past Five Years: Georgetown University, Smith College, University of Maryland, University of Virginia, Wake Forest University

Takeaways: One of Holy Child's strengths is that it allows students to take different paths. The school offers rigorous college prep classes as well as a comprehensive learning support structure. This allows the school to work with girls of all different academic abilities. The school strives to provide a strong Catholic education through activities such as prayer partners and required theology courses. Additionally, Holy Child offers a wide array of athletic and fine arts options for girls. Holy Child seeks to provide a warm, personalized environment and is a good option for girls searching for an all-female, faith-based education with a balanced approach to academics.

DeMatha Catholic High School

4313 Madison Street, Hyattsville, MD 20781
240.764.2200 | www.dematha.org

"DeMatha Catholic High School is a college preparatory institution dedicated to educating young men in the Trinitarian tradition. DeMatha's historic and ongoing mission is to serve students of differing abilities, interests, and backgrounds from the culturally rich and diverse greater Washington Metropolitan area. [. . .] DeMatha cultivates a respect for other people that finds its most complete expression in students who become gentlemen and scholars."

Grades 9 – 12 | All Boys
Catholic | Order of the Most Holy Trinity

Enrollment: 880 | **Average Class Size**: 22
Admissions and Testing: Deadline December 15; HSPT
Tuition and Financial Aid: $14,750; DeMatha tuition assistance is offered as work-study grants based on financial need. Families apply using the FACTS Grant and Aid Application and are also required to apply to the Archdiocese of Washington for aid.

Curriculum: DeMatha offers a college prep curriculum dedicated to educating young men in the Trinitarian tradition. The school offers over 175 courses in theology, English, social studies, science, math, world languages, computer science and technology, fine art, business, and health and physical education. In addition to core graduation requirements, DeMatha offers semester-long elective options including Biotechnology, African-American Literature, Mythology, Cross-Cultural Literature, Psychology, Philosophical Issues in Western Thought, and Mandarin.

The school's technology and business departments are unique. Students have the option to take Accounting, Business Law, Finance, Marketing Concepts, HTML, Java, Object-Oriented Programming, CADD, and Advanced Topics in Programming. In total, DeMatha offers 15 AP classes and 45 honors classes. Students are required to complete three years of a world language and may choose from French, Spanish, German, Latin, or classical Greek.

Arts: The DeMatha music program consists of five concert bands, three choruses, three percussion ensembles, two string ensembles, two jazz groups, a pep band, and a Sinfonia. DeMatha's wind ensemble was rated the number one Catholic band in the United States for 18 of 20 years. The fine arts program is divided into two areas: creative arts and photography. Students can pursue art history, post-modern art history, fundamentals of art, drawing, painting, watercolor, mechanical drawing, photography, darkroom basics, photojournalism, and Photoshop. The school also supports the DeMatha Players for those students interested in theatrical arts, but does not have any drama classes in place.

Athletics: DeMatha's athletic program has twice been recognized by *Sports Illustrated* as one of the top two high school programs in the country. DeMatha competes in the Washington Catholic Athletic Conference and offers 15 sports, including crew, football, soccer, cross-country, basketball, wrestling, ice hockey, tennis, rugby, swimming, indoor track, golf, baseball, and lacrosse. DeMatha teams have captured over 200 conference championships, as well as national championships, in basketball, soccer, and wrestling. Almost all sports have multiple levels (varsity, junior varsity, and freshman).

Student Life: Students are required to complete 55 hours of community service upon graduation. The Christian Service Program includes a number of sponsored service sites primarily consisting of hospitals, homeless shelters, soup kitchens, and nursing homes. Overnight service trips to the Trinitarian parishes in Texas and New Jersey and the fall Urban Plunge provide additional opportunities for service. The Campus Ministry program conducts overnight and day retreats, and helps plan liturgies and student convocations. Students are encouraged to explore and participate in the numerous clubs and organizations at DeMatha including Campus Ministry, Big Brothers, ACE Ecology, National Honor Society, Mock Trial, Quiz Bowl, and Science Scholars.

Campus: Located just south of the University of Maryland, DeMatha's campus consists of a main building, St. John DeMatha Hall, the Brendan McCarthy Center (home to the music program), the Fotos Art Center, and the new 72,000-square-foot Convocation Center, which provides additional classrooms, physical education facilities, a weight room, a batting cage, a wrestling room, athletic locker rooms, an alumni lounge, athletic offices, a bookstore, and a snack bar.

Learning Support: DeMatha's Counseling Center provides students services in academic, emotional, and career counseling. Counselors can arrange opportunities for peer tutoring and each serves as an additional point of contact for conversations between, teachers, parents, and students. The counseling staff works in collaboration with the Academic Support Center (ASC) staff to assist students in their journey toward becoming independent learners. The ASC teaches study skill strategies and techniques that allow students to mobilize their full strengths.

Schools Attended by Most Graduates in the Past Five Years: University of Maryland—College Park, University of Maryland—Baltimore County, Catholic University, St. John's College, Pennsylvania State University

Takeaways: DeMatha has a challenging curriculum in place, with 98% of graduates enrolling in college. The school has twice been recognized as an Exemplary Private School by the U.S. Department of Education. DeMatha's philosophy is informed by a dedication to faith, community, and service. Over 60% of the teaching staff has been at the school for over 10 years, with an average of 16 years at DeMatha and 20 years in education.

DeMatha is a good fit for a family looking for an all-boys Catholic education in Maryland. The school has a number of academic, social, athletic, service, and artistic options and seeks to produce well-rounded, Catholic young men.

The Diener School

11510 Falls Road, Potomac, MD 20854
301.299.4602 | www.thedienerschool.org

"To teach through experience, stimulate academically, prepare socially, and create a successful educational journey that motivates minds and inspires capabilities for a lifetime."

Grades K – 6 | Co-Ed
No Religious Affiliation

Enrollment: 25 | **Average Class Size:** 8 or fewer
Admissions and Testing: Deadline January 30; full psycho-educational evaluation and report within the last 18 months required
Tuition and Financial Aid: $34,000 (K-6); some aid is available, but the financial aid budget varies from year to year; partial scholarships are available.

Curriculum: The Diener School's academic curriculum is remedial in nature. The staff has knowledge of several specialized reading programs including Read Naturally, Phono-Graphix, Orton-Gillingham, and Great Leaps. Reading instruction is individualized; therefore, a variety of programs can be used based on a student's needs. Instruction in social skills, speech and language, sensory movement, and the arts are integrated throughout each school day. Therapist recommendations and learning specialist input is worked into the daily schedule of each student.

The Diener School believes strongly in the connection between movement and learning. It provides students with daily movement including two fitness classes for health. During fitness classes, instructors emphasize skills such as visual motor coordination, motor planning, sensory activities, and hand-eye coordination through creative and fun activities. The fitness program includes yoga and dance classes.

Arts: Students participate in weekly art, drama, music, and art clubs that emphasize fine arts and art history.

Athletics: Diener offers a daily fitness program, but no competitive sports programs are in place. Diener believes in a strong mind-body connection and the ability of movement to influence learning in a positive way.

Student Life: Diener students can participate in after-school clubs that emphasize fine arts, art history, hands-on science, cooking, and inventing.

Campus: Diener's facilities are small and located in the basement of a church, but the school is expanding every year to incorporate a new grade of rising students.

Learning Support: Diener aims to integrate therapeutic strategies within its curriculum. Therapists and academic tutors meet with teachers regularly to discuss academic goals, themes, and lessons. Therapists are in classrooms each morning to incorporate sensory, language, and motor exercises. Speech therapy, occupational therapy, and academic tutoring are all available and included in the tuition. Diener is equipped to handle mild learning disabilities, students with Asperger's, students who are high on the autism spectrum, and students who have anxiety issues.

Schools Attended by Most Graduates in the Past Five Years:
No matriculation information is available.

Takeaways: The Diener School started in the basement of a church as a result of Jillian Copeland's belief that the DC area lacked a school that could provide solid academics and the social and developmental support needed by students with language, learning, and social deficiencies. The "Diener Pyramid of Learning for the Whole Child" was born and the school continues to expand as that group of students gets older. A sixth grade class was recently added.

The amount of attention given to each individual student by teachers, counselors, therapists, and learning specialists is high. Diener fully believes that each child deserves a shot at an education that promotes real life skills. Classes are small and the environment is nurturing. Teachers post weekly blogs to keep parents up to date on new developments and what's happening at the school. Diener is an ideal school for students with learning challenges who need support and encouragement to realize their full potential.

French International School (Lycée Rochambeau)

7108 Bradley Boulevard, Bethesda, MD 20817 (Nursery School)
3200 Woodbine Street, Chevy Chase, MD 20815 (Lower School)
9600 Forest Road, Bethesda, MD 20814 (Upper School)
301.530.8260 | www.rochambeau.org

"To offer a curriculum (reflecting standards and guidelines in effect in France, as defined by the French educational authorities) that prepares students for the French baccalaureate examination and for admission to higher education institutions in France and French-speaking countries; to qualify students for admission to colleges and universities in the United States by offering a curriculum including courses focusing on the English language, and American history and civilization; to promote the diffusion of French language and culture in the context of American society in a manner that reflects the cultural diversity of the school."

Nursery – Grade 12 | Co-Ed
No Religious Affiliation

Enrollment: 1,100 | **Average Class Size:** 20
Admissions and Testing: Rolling admission; no testing required
Tuition and Financial Aid: $16,875 (Nursery-K), $15,025 (Lower), $17,030 (Middle), $20,045 (Upper); over $300,000 available for financial aid. The school is also able to offer scholarships for French citizens through the French Consulate in Washington.

Curriculum: The French International School follows the traditional education model imposed by the French National Ministry of Education. With three different levels of schooling—maternelle (nursery), elementary, and secondary (middle and upper)—the coursework gradually gets more challenging with the central theme being French culture and language. Students are expected to be fluent in French by first grade and all courses are taught in French with the exception of English and United States History. The curriculum is traditional and rigorous. Like many international schools, the French International School follows the IB program. In the final three years of secondary education, students are expected to take on between 37 to 40 hours of school work per week. German, Italian, Latin, Spanish, and English are all offered as second languages.

Art: The French International School integrates the arts into its curriculum. Art and music projects are included in elementary classrooms and students partake in art classes with subject matter experts, beginning in middle school with the introduction of Plastic Art. Though there is a cultural lens focused on French artwork, the curriculum includes the study of various types of art and artwork from different nations.

Athletics: The French International School competes in the Independent School League. Basketball, swimming, soccer, track and field, and volleyball are offered. Rugby and gymnastics are also available as after-school clubs. Participation is not mandatory and there is a fee for every sport.

Student Life: Community service is built into the curriculum. Various activities are organized by different student groups, from chess club to the annual talent show. Movies are also screened at multiple times during the school year.

Campus: The French International School has three different campuses—one for kindergarten, one for elementary students, and one for secondary students. The facilities are very traditional and include athletic fields, a gymnasium, classrooms, and administrative offices.

Learning Support: The French International School is designed to be rigorous and the school does not employ a learning specialist. Teachers will work individually with students as much as possible.

Schools Attended by Most Graduates in the Past Five Years: McGill University, University of Maryland, American University, Boston University, George Mason University

Takeaways: The French International School was founded to meet the demand of French-speaking families located in the Washington, DC area. The primary language at the school is French, though English instruction is required in kindergarten. For a family that desires the French education model, the French International School will likely be a good fit.

Georgetown Preparatory School

10900 Rockville Pike, North Bethesda, MD 20852
301.493.5000 | www.gprep.org

"Forming men of competence, conscience, courage, and compassion; men of faith, men for others, since 1789."

Grades 9 – 12 | All Boys
Catholic | Independent

Enrollment: 490 | **Average Class Size:** 16
Admissions and Testing: Deadline January 15; SSAT, TOEFL if applicable
Tuition and Financial Aid: $29,625 (Day), $50,465 (Boarding), English as a Second Language Program: $6,620 (additional); 26% of the student body receives financial aid from an aid budget of over $2 million.

Curriculum: Georgetown Preparatory School (Prep) offers young men a challenging college prep program with an emphasis on the liberal arts. In total, the school offers 24 AP classes. The curriculum at Prep has requirements in English, math, art, music, social studies, lab science, modern language, and physical education. Added to this are requirements in religion and 90 hours of Christian service.

Prep upholds a tradition in the classics. All students are required to take two years of Latin, and Ancient Greek is offered as an elective. Although classical languages are an important part of the Prep experience, the school does offer courses in Spanish, French, and German.

Arts: Art classes include Art History, AP Studio Art, Graphic Design and Media, Glass Art, and Digital Photography. For music, students can audition for the concert band, jazz band, string ensemble, or the Prep Singers. Prep also offers an AP Music Theory course in which students learn the fundamentals of music such as melody, harmony, texture, rhythm, and composition in a more in-depth manner than a traditional music class.

Athletics: As a member of the Interstate Athletic Conference, Prep offers 28 sports teams. Freshmen and sophomores must participate in at least one season of athletics each year. Most athletes participate in two sports. Some sports have no-cut policies, but Prep is considered a competitive sports school with the goal of improving fitness and teaching school spirit.

Student Life: Prep offers traditional clubs like the National Honor Society and student government but also unconventional clubs such as the fencing club and the Best Buddies club. There are charity trips to New Orleans; Ivanhoe, Virginia; Dominican Republic; and an immersion trip to Argentina.

Campus: Prep sits on 90 acres, with a state-of-the-art athletic center (weight room, indoor track, pool, wrestling room, basketball courts), stadium, theater, baseball field, nine-hole golf course, tennis courts, chapel, recording studio, film room, and an art studio.

Learning Support: There is a tutoring center on campus where students can receive one-on-one assistance with a learning specialist. Prep also has a writing lab that is open three days a week.

Schools Attended by Most Graduates in the Past Five Years: Georgetown University, University of Notre Dame, University of Virginia, University of Maryland—College Park, Boston College

Takeaways: The expectations at Prep are high and the curriculum is demanding. Students must be motivated and have a strong work ethic. The curriculum places an emphasis on the classics and both Greek and Latin are offered as a foreign language. One thing that stands out about Prep is its extracurricular program. The school seeks to enroll students who are willing to take on a big role in the community. Most students are involved in leadership opportunities and athletics, and they take advantage of the school's hour between extracurricular activities and classes at the end of the day to work on homework. For a young man who is self-motivated, looking to dive into a community and be challenged, and able to learn in a traditional environment, Prep is worth considering.

German School of Washington, DC (Deutsche Schule Washington, DC)

8617 Chateau Drive, Potomac, MD 20854
301.365.4400 | www.dswashington.org

"First, German language and culture have a high priority at our school. They form the basis for teaching and dealing with each other. Second, the school sees itself as a bridge between different cultures and perspectives of German-American focus. We cooperate with American institutions and international non-school institutions. Third, we educate multilingualism, tolerance, and openness. Fourth, our students are empowered to develop their individuality in responsibility towards society and the environment. Fifth, the education at our school is based on mutual respect, respect for human dignity, and responsible use of the earth's resources. Sixth, the educational work is based on partnership and cooperation and supported by parents and guardians. Seventh, the quality of teaching at our school is ensured by regular evaluation and targeted staff training. Eighth, all committees and groups at our school see themselves as part of a team. Ninth, we teach and learn modern methods and use for the latest technologies."

Preschool – Grade 12 | Co-Ed
No Religious Affiliation

Enrollment: 550 | **Average Class Size:** 20
Admissions and Testing: Rolling admission; no testing required
Tuition and Financial Aid: $14,350 (Preschool), $16,040 (Kindergarten), $16,350 (1-4), $17,850 (5-6), $18,410 (7-9), $18,940 (10-12), new student fee $2,000; about 8% of students receive aid; uses SSS form.

Curriculum: The German School of Washington's (GSW) teaching philosophy incorporates technological, scientific, cultural, and social developments into class work. The goal of the curriculum is to prepare students to obtain the German Abitur (a secondary graduation certificate), which is equivalent to a Maryland high school diploma. GSW is a bilingual school (German and English) but most courses are taught in German and follow the German national curriculum. In kindergarten, children begin to learn German (if they do not know it already). In fifth grade, students choose to learn either French or Spanish.

Arts: GSW offers a variety of art classes, culminating in studio art. Students study and practice music on a regular basis. They learn songs that correlate with their everyday activities, mainly to aid language acquisition.

Athletics: The school competes in the Independent School Athletic Conference. Soccer, gymnastics, basketball, badminton, field hockey, beach volleyball, handball, table tennis, and track and field are offered. Participation is not mandatory, but students must acquire an athletic credit through competitive sports or an after-school activity.

Student Life: GSW annually conducts a social skills training for students in fifth through eighth grade. Boys and girls receive separate training with the same goal in mind: to allow students to practice positive social skills. The program serves to boost self-confidence, improve communication skills, and teach methods for solving conflicts constructively. Students have the opportunity to join the student council beginning in fifth grade. Each grade has two representatives who are elected at the beginning of the school year by the student body.

Campus: Located in Potomac, Maryland, GSW's facilities include three gyms, two libraries, two playgrounds, an indoor swimming pool, a beach volleyball field, two soccer fields, and a computer lab.

Learning Support: GSW is not equipped for students in need of remediation. The school staffs a learning support teacher who works with students outside of the classroom in private lessons. The school also employs tutors to aid students struggling in their foreign language classes.

Schools Attended by Most Graduates in the Past Five Years: University of Virginia, McGill University, Tufts University

Takeaways: GSW's emphasis on a rigorous, German curriculum is an advantage for those families looking for a versatile, European-based education. In line with German standards, the school day is two hours longer than a typical day at an American school. While a large portion of the students have ties to Germany, it is not a requirement. Some families choose GSW in hopes of one day moving to Europe. The school places a heavy emphasis on preparing students to succeed in the European economy or the European university system.

Grace Episcopal Day School

9411 Connecticut Avenue, Kensington, MD 20895
301.949.5860 | www.geds.org

"Grace Episcopal Day School will provide every student the opportunity for academic excellence in a caring, nurturing, moral environment that embraces diversity and promotes creativity, self-confidence, and service to others."

Nursery – Grade 5 | Co-Ed
Episcopalian | National Association of Episcopal Schools | Mid-Atlantic Episcopal School Association

Enrollment: 100 | **Average Class Size:** 12
Admissions and Testing: Deadline January 15, then rolling; testing required for kindergarten through fifth grade, WPPSI-IV/WISC-IV required
Tuition and Financial Aid: $18,500 (K), $19,000 (1), $19,750 (2), $20,350 (3), $20,500 (4-5); financial aid budget of over $400,000 serves about 40% of the students; uses SSS form.

Curriculum: At Grace Episcopal Day School (Grace Episcopal), the curriculum is fairly traditional and individual attention is highly valued. Kindergarten and first grade students receive a balanced literacy approach to language arts, including word study, guided reading, and writing. Math lessons provide the foundation for higher-level thinking skills. Outdoor play, art, music, Spanish, physical education, and chapel foster the social and emotional, cognitive, physical, and spiritual development of the students. Second through fifth grade students are offered a challenging academic program that includes a continuation of a balanced literacy approach, daily math, and an emphasis on developing a spirit of inquiry through science and social studies.

Arts: Students receive weekly instruction in art in order to promote self-expression, creativity, and global awareness. Students work with a wide variety of media including printmaking, watercolors, pastels, and clay. The study of art is closely integrated with the language arts and social studies curriculums. Music is also a large part of the experience at Grace Episcopal. Students learn to read and write music, play instruments, and folk dance.

Athletics: Fourth and fifth-grade students are encouraged to participate in team sports. Kickball, soccer, basketball, and track and field are offered with the goal of teaching students teamwork, confidence, and leadership skills. Students play against other schools in the metropolitan area.

Student Life: Providing students with the opportunity for spiritual growth is important at Grace Episcopal and chapel is held weekly for each division. The school has an After-Class Enrichment (ACE) program, which offers various classes in partnership with programs throughout the metro area. Some options available are cooking, drama, yoga, soccer, piano, martial arts, French, Mandarin, and chess. Students also have the opportunity to serve on the student council.

Campus: The 11-acre campus in Kensington, Maryland, contains a large art studio, science lab, library, multipurpose room with a stage, and a computer lab. Outdoor spaces include two playgrounds, a nature trail, and playing fields.

Learning Support: A full-time reading specialist works in all classrooms with all students. The school also employs a part-time psychologist.

Schools Attended by Most Graduates in the Past Five Years:
St. Andrew's Episcopal School, Bullis School, The Field School, Sidwell Friends School, Holton-Arms School

Takeaways: Grace Episcopal is known for its nurturing school environment. Two standout aspects of the school are the intimate setting and the dedicated staff. The teachers aim to differentiate instruction and make sure that every student's needs are addressed. The school is very proud of its After-Class Enrichment (ACE) program; students are given freedom to pursue drama, music, yoga, soccer, and so on. For families looking for a Christian atmosphere, a tight-knit community, and a traditional curriculum, Grace Episcopal is a school worth considering.

Green Acres School

11701 Danville Drive, North Bethesda, MD 20852
301.881.4100 | www.greenacres.org

"Green Acres is a co-educational, progressive school for grades preschool through eight, dedicated to fostering the natural curiosity of students, engaging them actively in the joy of learning, and facilitating problem solving. Based on an understanding of child development, Green Acres' program is cognitively, physically, and creatively challenging. Valuing acceptance of a variety of viewpoints, this community promotes socio-economic and cultural diversity. An environment of trust, cooperation, and mutual respect encourages students to become increasingly independent thinkers and responsible contributors to an ever-changing, multicultural world."

Preschool – Grade 8 | Co-Ed
No Religious Affiliation

Enrollment: 320 | **Average Class Size:** 12
Admissions and Testing: Deadline January 17; no testing required
Tuition and Financial Aid: $30,215 (Preschool-8); can match up to 80% of the tuition needs with grants.

Curriculum: Green Acres offers a progressive curriculum that is integrated across the core subjects. This means that students are frequently studying the same topic in all of their core classes. For example, if students are learning about ancient Egypt, they may be reading a book about a mummy in English, creating a project on King Tut in social studies, and working on a project on the human body and mummification in science.

Students participate in outdoor learning on the school's 15-acre campus utilizing its gardens, playgrounds, fields, and woods. The use of the outdoors is directly tied into the school's environmental program, which emphasizes composting, recycling, and saving energy. The school has a 1:1 iPad program for all eighth graders. Spanish and musical instruction begins in third grade and drama is introduced in fifth grade.

Arts: The music program includes general music, handbells, and chorus. Recorder is taught in third and fourth grade and guitar is covered in sixth. Performing arts offerings include creative movement classes for the youngest students and drama classes for middle school students. Performances are frequent and all seventh and eighth graders put on a Broadway production as part of the school curriculum.

Athletics: Outside of physical education classes, which are held four times a week, middle school students can take part in the after-school, no-cut athletic program. The program offers students an opportunity to participate fully on a number of teams including soccer, cross-country, basketball, softball, and lacrosse. The program is not mandatory but participation is encouraged.

Student Life: There are multiple traditions throughout the school that foster a community spirit. Examples include assemblies in the outdoor amphitheater, a school-wide Thanksgiving Lunch, the Family Heritage Fair, and the Family Picnic.

Campus: Green Acres is spread over 15 acres of land in North Bethesda. The school has recently renovated its classrooms and installed new science labs and art studios. The school has outdoor facilities, enabling extensive outdoor education.

Learning Support: Three part-time counselors and two learning coordinators regularly enhance, enrich, and update the strategies used by the teaching staff. The four support specialists attend weekly planning meetings at each grade level and join the division heads and the Head of School weekly to discuss how to best serve students.

Schools Attended by Most Graduates in the Past Five Years: Georgetown Day School, St. Andrew's Episcopal School, Sandy Spring Friends School, Walter Johnson High School, Bethesda-Chevy Chase High School

Takeaways: Green Acres is a progressive school that has a commitment to outdoor learning and environmental sustainability. The school was the first racially integrated school in Montgomery County when it was founded in 1934. A cornerstone of the Green Acres curriculum is "authentic learning," meaning that teachers seek to relate the material being taught in class to students' life experiences. With an average of 12 students per class, Green Acres offers a small, diverse, and unique learning environment. It's a good match for hands-on learners seeking a progressive curriculum.

The Heights School

10400 Seven Locks Road, Potomac, MD 20854
301.765.2093 | www.heights.edu

"Our mission is to assist parents in the intellectual, moral, physical, and spiritual education of their sons, with dedicated teachers training boys rigorously in the liberal arts. This formation in virtue fosters respect for every person, a desire to serve God and others, and an optimistic attitude towards life's challenges."

Grades 3 – 12 | All Boys
Catholic | Independent

Enrollment: 465 | **Average Class Size:** 15
Admissions and Testing: Deadline: January 25; SSAT (Upper School)
Tuition and Financial Aid: $17,000 (Lower School), $20,750 (Middle School), $22,850 (Upper School); uses FACTS for tuition management and grant and scholarship assessment.

Curriculum: The Heights' lower school encourages students to be adventurous and to learn through exploration. Classes are taught in log cabins and students in the lower school are placed in a homeroom where they have one male teacher. Students study religion, natural history, history, language arts, literature, music, mathematics, art, and physical education. Students in the middle school study a variety of subjects within the core content as well as Latin, art, and physical education.

In the upper school, students are expected to take four years of history, English, religion, and math and three years of science and foreign language. All students are required to take Latin and may also elect to take Spanish or Greek. To fulfill the elective requirement, students can choose from a variety of classes including Microeconomics or Macroeconomics, the American Revolution, the Cold War, Russian History, Computer Programming, Art History, Carpentry, or World War II.

Arts: The arts are integrated into the curriculum at every division. Beginning in the lower school and continuing through the middle school, students take classes in art and music regularly. In the upper school students are required to take one art class to fulfill their elective requirements. They can choose from art, AP Art History, band, carpentry, men's chorus, or drama.

Athletics: Students at The Heights School can participate in twelve different sports throughout the school year. Options include soccer, golf, basketball, squash, swimming, wrestling, baseball, lacrosse, rugby, tennis, and track and field.

Student Life: Extracurricular clubs include archery, rock climbing, book club, philosophy club, wrestling, yearbook, ping pong club, and math club. Students in third through eighth grade take an annual camping trip. At the end of eighth grade, students have the opportunity to take part in a student exchange trip to Spain. Additionally, the junior trip is viewed as a rite of passage at The Heights. It consists of a 100-mile hiking, running, biking, canoeing, and swimming journey to St. Clement's Island, where Maryland's first Catholics landed.

Campus: The Heights campus, located in Potomac, Maryland, was designed with all-boys learning in mind. All homeroom classes in the lower school are located in log cabins and the boys have access to the surrounding woods, which are used for outdoor learning.

Learning Support: Although The Heights is not a school that specializes in learning support, the school can support some students with mild learning disabilities.

Schools Attended by Most Graduates in the Past Five Years: The University of Virginia, University of Notre Dame, Virginia Tech, University of Maryland, Catholic University of America

Takeaways: The Heights' male-oriented atmosphere enables boys to learn best while the teachers and administrators implement exploration and movement into the classroom. The school provides a challenging academic experience through comprehensive studies and a significant amount of after-school work. The Heights is a good match for families looking for a traditional Catholic environment that encourages high levels of mutual respect among all students and staff.

Holton-Arms School

7303 River Road, Bethesda, MD 20817
301.365.5300 | www.holton-arms.edu

"Holton-Arms School cultivates the unique potential of young women through the 'education not only of the mind, but of the soul and spirit.'"

Grades 3 – 12 | All Girls
No Religious Affiliation

Enrollment: 645 | **Average Class Size:** 15
Admissions and Testing: Deadline January 10; WISC-IV and CTP (ERB) (3-5); SSAT or ISEE (6-12)
Tuition and Financial Aid: $33,560 (3-6), $35,200 (7-12); financial aid budget over $3.5 million serves about 25% of the students.

Curriculum: The Holton-Arms curriculum is centered around the core subjects with an emphasis placed on learning strategies. Teachers work with students to develop their skills in following directions, note-taking, test-taking, studying, organizing, and time management.

The middle school strives to bridge the gap between childhood and adolescence by continuing to offer students structured classrooms but with choices as to their content studies. For example, students can choose between French, Chinese, Spanish, or Latin as a foreign language to pursue.

Holton-Arms boasts a number of electives such as Forensic Science, Intro to Engineering, Earth and Space Science, Molecular Biology, and Computer Programming and Robotics. Additionally, the school offers an independent study program to juniors and seniors. All seniors at Holton-Arms are required to partake in the Senior Project during their senior year. This project requires students to undertake a role in a career or service area that is of particular interest.

Arts: The arts are interwoven into the curriculum beginning in the lower school. Art offerings include vocal and instrumental music, ceramics, photography, studio art, drama, dance, music technology, and production technology.

Athletics: Holton-Arms competes in the Independent School League and offers fifteen different sports. Athletic offerings include basketball, crew, cross-country, field hockey, ice hockey, lacrosse, soccer, softball, swimming, diving, tennis, track and field, and volleyball. The tennis team has won the ISL championship four years in a row, and the volleyball team is also a reigning ISL champion. The athletic program is mandatory for middle school girls only, but is considered an integral part of a balanced education, and practices and games are scheduled not to conflict with academic responsibilities.

Student Life: Girls at Holton-Arms have a number of options to choose from when it comes to their extracurricular activities. For example, the school hosts a student-designed fashion show every year, a Spring Gala, a Winter Play, and a coffeehouse-styled Open Mic Night.

Campus: Holton-Arms is located on 57 acres on River Road in Bethesda. Highlights include two libraries, a performing arts center, a 400-seat theater, a black box theater, natural light art and ceramics studios, and state-of-the-art photography and digital music labs. Athletic facilities include a double gymnasium, an indoor competition-sized pool, seven tennis courts, three athletic fields (including one synthetic turf field), a fitness center, three dance studios, and an all-weather track.

Learning Support: Holton-Arms employs three learning specialists, one for each school division, who aid in the facilitation of accommodations and provide support for students with learning needs.

Schools Attended by Most Graduates in the Past Five Years: University of Maryland—College Park, University of Virginia, Washington University in St. Louis, Dartmouth College, The College of William and Mary

Takeaways: Holton-Arms seeks to provide innovative and challenging academics, dynamic visual and performing arts, and vigorous athletics within an engaging all-girls environment. It has a strong technology program—an iPad initiative introduces students to technology in the lower school and allows them to transition seamlessly into a 1:1 laptop program in middle and upper school. Holton-Arms is a good fit for a girl who is looking to be challenged but does not want a "pressure cooker" atmosphere. A strong set of organizational, time management, and study skills are a necessity for success at Holton-Arms; however, the school begins working on these skills from an early age to ensure that by the time the girls reach the upper school, they are fully capable of managing the workload.

The Katherine Thomas School

9975 Medical Center Drive, Rockville, MD 20850
301.738.9691 | www.ttlc.org/katherine_thomas_school

"To enable students to reach their full educational potential through a multi-sensory, developmental, language-intensive curriculum."

Preschool – Grade 12 | Co-Ed
No Religious Affiliation

Enrollment: 130 | **Average Class Size:** 8-10
Admissions and Testing: Rolling admission; psychological and educational testing as needed, plus speech language and occupational therapy testing as needed
Tuition and Financial Aid: $15,757 (Preschool), $24,951 (Lower and Middle School), $29,568 (Upper School); financial aid budget of $231,000 served 16 students in 2011.

Curriculum: The Katherine Thomas School (KTS) curriculum is developmental and adaptive. It emphasizes the use of multi-sensory methods and specialized language strategies while integrating counseling, speech-language, and occupational therapies. KTS provides instruction and remediation in phonics, as well as reading/listening comprehension remediation. The school aims to not only improve students' academic and cognitive abilities but also their interpersonal and organizational skills. Upper school students receive instruction in the core courses and choose from elective credits in art, music, drama, Spanish, reading, and computer-related and vocational cluster courses.

Arts: Art, music, and drama classes are available to all students. The school houses a black box theater, two music rooms, and two art classrooms with a kiln.

Athletics: Basketball, soccer, and physical education are offered, and students also have the chance to participate in the Special Olympics. The program is noncompetitive and not mandatory. The goal of the program is to support a positive self-image and create a connection between movement and learning.

Student Life: Students are given the opportunity to grow leadership skills through the Student Government Association, Athletic Leadership Program, and Peer Mediation. The environment at KTS strongly encourages students to participate in extracurricular activities and to explore their personal interests.

Campus: The main campus is a two-story building with three gymnasiums and three playground areas.

Learning Support: KTS is a school that concentrates on special education. Twenty-five learning specialists are available plus counselors, occupational therapists, speech therapists, reading specialists, and physical therapists.

Schools Attended by Most Graduates in the Past Five Years:
No matriculation information is available.

Takeaways: KTS is a special needs school that relies on hands-on and multi-sensory instruction. Families from a wide geographic range send their children to KTS for its all-inclusive offerings—the school can address most learning needs, from language and learning disabilities to high-functioning autism. During the school day students have access to speech, occupational, and physical therapists—a one-stop shop of sorts. Most students leave the school prepared for higher education, but others receive technical and life skills training instead.

Landon School

6101 Wilson Lane, Bethesda, MD 20817
301.320.3200 | www.landon.net

"Landon School prepares talented boys for productive lives as accomplished, responsible and caring men whose actions are guided by the principles of perseverance, teamwork, honor and fair play."

Grades 3 – 12 | All Boys
No Religious Affiliation

Enrollment: 685 | **Average Class Size:** 16
Admissions and Testing: Application Deadline January 15, Supporting Documentation Deadline January 31; In-house testing (3-4), SSAT or ISEE (5-12)
Tuition and Financial Aid: $32,516 (3-5), $33,565 (6-12); one in four Landon students receives an average grant of $17,500 from a financial aid budget of $3 million.

Curriculum: Through the academic program at Landon, boys gain foundational knowledge and intellectual maturity. In a small class setting, faculty support and challenge each student, allowing him to ask questions, engage in debate with teachers and peers, and form his own viewpoints. The lower school program (grades 3-5) offers a foundation for each boy's intellectual and moral education, an emphasis on study and organization skills, and a field experience program. Additionally, boys in Landon's lower school are taught by specialists in the core subjects of reading/language arts, math, and social studies.

In Landon's middle school (grade 6, forms I and II), students face a challenging scholastic environment with increased academic, artistic, and athletic demands. Teachers in every discipline reinforce academic and study skills. Students in the middle school are encouraged to develop a personal point of view and learn to advocate for themselves.

In the upper school (forms III-VI), Landon offers a course of study that helps boys build a foundation of knowledge and develop independent critical-thinking skills. Upper school boys take classes in English, history, mathematics, science, and world languages and fulfill requirements in the visual and performing arts, daily athletics, and community service. The upper school offers 19 AP and 17 honors classes.

Arts: Students compete in music and drama festivals, as well as art competitions. In the lower and middle schools, boys enjoy time in the art studio and work with a performance group. In middle school, boys can elect music or drama to fulfill their performing arts requirement. The upper school has a two-year arts requirement. Boys select from choices in music, studio art, and drama.

Athletics: Landon participates in the Interstate Athletic Conference and offers baseball, football, swimming, cross-country, golf, rugby, soccer, riflery, basketball, lacrosse, tennis, fencing, track and field, hockey, ultimate frisbee, squash, water polo, and wrestling. Landon requires daily participation in athletics—either interscholastic or intramural.

Student Life: From third through twelfth grade, students have the opportunity to partake in extracurricular offerings, including: a variety of community service programs; Animal Crew, a club responsible for taking care of all the animals on campus (lower school); the Hiking Club (middle school); Landon Local Heroes; Young Republicans or Democrats; and Investment Club (upper school).

Campus: Landon's campus is located on 75 acres in Bethesda, Maryland, with three school buildings (each with its own library), a Performing Arts Center, a sports complex with separate strength training center and outdoor swimming pool, an outdoor tennis complex, a stadium with turf field, six athletic fields, a world-class azalea garden, a farmhouse, and an outdoor amphitheater.

Learning Support: The Center for Teaching and Learning Resources strives to help students become better learners and faculty become better teachers. Two learning specialists evaluate and assess individual student needs and help boys meet and overcome learning challenges.

Schools Attended by Most Graduates in the Past Five Years: University of Maryland—College Park, Davidson College, University of Virginia, Cornell University, Wake Forest University

Takeaways: Landon provides a comprehensive, well-rounded education for boys and requires participation in sports and the arts. Students leave Landon with a strong foundation in critical thinking, study skills, and self-advocacy that prepares them for college and life. A student who would succeed at Landon would be a self-motivated boy who can juggle multiple activities on his plate.

McLean School of Maryland

8224 Lochinver Lane, Potomac, MD 20854
301.299.8277 | www.mcleanschool.org

"McLean makes education accessible, stimulating, and meaningful for a broad range of learners. Our students flourish because McLean responds to students' learning styles. McLean prepares students intellectually and socially by encouraging self-advocacy and building self-confidence. Our students succeed because they learn how to learn."

Grades K – 12 | Co-Ed
No Religious Affiliation

Enrollment: 360 | **Average Class Size:** 10
Admissions and Testing: Deadline February 1; WISC-IV/Stanford-Binet V, WJ-III
Tuition and Financial Aid: $25,000 (K), $30,440 (1-4), $33,160 (5-8), $35,615 (9-12); financial aid budget of over $1.2 million serves about 22% of students; uses FAST form.

Curriculum: McLean's curriculum is traditional, but teachers have a great deal of flexibility in determining their method of instruction. In addition to standard core classes, arts, physical education, foreign language, and computer technology are part of the curriculum. An individual student learning profile is created for each student and updated consistently to maximize the benefits of the program. In the lower school, instruction is very hands-on, and the use of manipulatives, software, and experiential learning encourages exploration.

The middle school offers a strong curriculum with an emphasis on multi-sensory instruction, and helps students become self-aware of their optimal learning style. The upper school, which offers nine AP classes, prepares students for college and allows them to develop skills to become advocates of their learning styles and needs.

Arts: Students have various options for pursuing artistic endeavors. Some class options include Foundation Art, Principles of Design, Ceramics,

AP Studio Art, Web and Graphic Design, Animation and Video Exploration, Chorus, Music Theory, Classic Guitar, and Drama.

Athletics: McLean is a member of the Potomac Valley Athletic Conference. McLean offers volleyball, lacrosse, soccer, basketball, track and field, cross-country, and wrestling. The program is not mandatory, but all students in grades K-8 take part in daily physical education. McLean's teams frequently make the semifinals of the PVAC tournaments in their respective sports, and the soccer team has the strongest competitive tradition.

Student Life: McLean School has a great number of opportunities available outside of the classroom. The selection of clubs and activities ranges from cooking classes to Tae Kwon Do. Clubs such as Student Government, Discipline Committee, Environmental Club, Prom Committee, and Student Ambassadors keep students involved both in and outside of school.

Campus: The McLean School's nine-acre campus is tucked away in a Potomac neighborhood by the I-270 spur. The campus has three art rooms, three music rooms, three technology labs, seven science labs, a gym, athletic fields, and a weight room.

Learning Support: The entire curriculum is geared towards assisting students who have different learning styles and are not optimally served in a traditional school environment. McLean School staffs two reading specialists, four learning specialists, two speech and language pathologists, a math specialist, an occupational therapist, four counselors, and a college guidance counselor. Outside providers are brought in when necessary.

Schools Attended by Most Graduates in the Past Five Years: High Point University, Susquehanna University, Denison University, American University, Muhlenberg College

Takeaways: The McLean School is very student centered, and students are given ample leadership opportunities at every turn. Seniors, for instance, complete a two-week, self-directed project as part of their graduation requirements. The school is a great option for students with learning disabilities who still need to be challenged academically and who can thrive in a classroom environment when given the right support. There is a great amount of teacher training, and every student is given personal attention. Students are viewed holistically at McLean School—instruction targets the academic, physical, and social/emotional realms. McLean accepts students with all different learning needs and is a good fit for a bright child with ADHD or a learning disability. McLean also serves remedial students and is flexible with outside tutoring options. Relative to its size, the school has a fairly broad list of course offerings, comparable to that of a more mainstream school.

Melvin J. Berman Hebrew Academy

13300 Arctic Avenue, Rockville, MD 20853
301.962.9400 | www.mjbha.org

"Melvin J. Berman Hebrew Academy is an Orthodox Day School that provides a comprehensive Jewish and secular education in an atmosphere of reverence, good citizenship, and love of the Jewish people and Israel. Adhering to standards of academic excellence and exemplary moral conduct, it prepares its graduates to become Halachically observant, well-educated Jews. It provides opportunities for each student to achieve the maximum of his or her potential, engaged with, and contributing to, both the Jewish community and the society at large."

Preschool – Grade 12 | Co-Ed
Jewish | Modern Orthodox

Enrollment: 720 | **Average Class Size:** 17
Admissions and Testing: Rolling admissions; no testing required
Tuition and Financial Aid: \$14,040 (K-5), \$17,350 (6-8), \$20,615 (9-12); financial aid budget over \$2 million serves 25% of the student body.

Curriculum: Melvin J. Berman Hebrew Academy (MJBHA) is the only Modern Orthodox, preschool-12, day school in the Washington area. The dual-curriculum is rigorous and provides students with a very well-rounded academic experience. General studies, Judaic studies, and Hebrew are all interwoven in the curriculum, which encompasses a firm foundation in Torah and Jewish law. Lower school students learn in an environment that promotes self-expression and creativity. The middle school program is geared toward encouraging maturation and begins to more heavily emphasize the dual nature of the curriculum. Students in the upper school take nine courses with one elective. The upper school curriculum is challenging and emphasizes liberal arts and Judaic studies. In the upper school there are seven AP classes, and Arabic and Hebrew are offered as foreign languages.

Arts: Art class offerings include studio art, digital photography, ceramics and sculpture, and drawing and painting. Music classes stress the Jewish tradition.

Athletics: MJBHA competes in the Potomac Valley Athletic Conference. The school offers basketball, softball, soccer, tennis, volleyball, and track and field. The program is not mandatory. The strongest programs are track and field and girls' junior varsity basketball, which has won a conference championship in the past three years.

Student Life: Students can participate in a variety of clubs based in the Jewish tradition such as Chesed club, Hadas, and Shabbat Shiur. There are also specialized clubs to appeal to student interests. Some of these offerings include literary magazine, student government, jazz band, stock market club, and mock trial.

Campus: The 20-acre campus includes a 1,200-seat auditorium, a gym, a music room, an art studio, athletic fields, and tennis courts.

Learning Support: MJBHA prides itself on making accommodations for students with learning difficulties. Under the supervision of the director of special services, eight learning specialists are available, plus counselors and other administrators. For more intensive needs, the school relies on its partnership with the Sulam School.

Schools Attended by Most Graduates in the Past Five Years: University of Maryland, University of Pennsylvania, Cornell University, New York University, Yeshiva University

Takeaways: MJBHA provides students with a college prep curriculum that heavily stresses Hebrew and Judaic studies. The curriculum places a strong emphasis on Israel and tries to instill a love and appreciation of the modern Jewish culture in all of its students. The school has recently expanded its facilities to include a Jewish cultural arts center and a media center. Parents who want their children to receive rigorous instruction in traditional academics as well as Hebrew and Judaic studies should certainly consider MJBHA. The main thrust of the school is an all-encompassing Jewish education with religious instruction woven into every corner of the curriculum.

The Nora School

955 Sligo Avenue, Silver Spring, MD 20910
301.495.6672 | www.noraschool.org

"Our mission is to nurture and empower bright students who learn differently."

Grades 9 – 12 | Co-Ed
No Religious Affiliation

Enrollment: 60 | **Average Class Size:** 8 (12 maximum)
Admissions and Testing: Rolling admission; no testing required
Tuition and Financial Aid: $25,800 (9-12); financial aid budget serves 15% of students with an average grant of $12,600; uses SSS form.

Curriculum: The Nora School offers an intellectually challenging curriculum to students with different learning styles and intends to prepare students for college, community, and professional life. The core curriculum includes English, social studies, mathematics, science, and foreign language (Spanish or German). Core subject classes include general overview-type courses and more specialized offerings. Within the English department, for instance, students can take a generalized class such as Literature and Composition or a more specialized class such as African-American Literature of the 20th Century. Small class sizes and an emphasis on class discussions create a more progressive atmosphere that gives attention to individual needs.

Arts: Nora offers courses in creative writing, poetry, architecture, studio art, computer graphic design, art history, illustration, sculpture, photography, ceramics, and music. One unique course offering examines graphic design and publishing, as well as filmmaking.

Athletics: Nora is a member of the Washington Small Schools Association Athletic League but will also compete out of conference. The school offers basketball, soccer, volleyball, and softball. Teams are co-ed, and the school encourages participation over competition. Students must fulfill an athletic credit requirement, but the competitive program is not mandatory.

Student Life: Nora offers a variety of activities including student government, club sports, and a range of outdoor trips and hikes. Classroom trips with faculty are varied and include visits to Washington, DC area museums, theaters, and the Chesapeake Bay. Juniors and seniors go on autumn retreats in preparation for the upcoming school year, while sophomores go whitewater rafting in the spring. Some students can train to serve as peer mediators and all students are required to complete 32 hours of community service each school year.

Campus: The Nora School is located near the Silver Spring Metro station, which is about a five-minute walk away. Many students take public transportation to school. Sports take place at nearby fields and gyms.

Learning Support: Nora takes pride in helping its students with learning disabilities, and all of its programs are catered to students who need support. A learning disabilities specialist, psychological consultant, and tutors are on staff to support teachers. Instruction is differentiated to address multiple learning styles.

Schools Attended by Most Graduates in the Past Five Years: Bard College, Guilford College, McDaniel College, Dickinson College, Shepherd University

Takeaways: At the Nora School, classes are small, and teachers and students know one another on a first-name basis. Because of its size, Nora's faculty easily creates relationships with each student and thus can cater to individual learning styles. There is an expectation that students will take part in leading class discussions and directing their studies. The atmosphere at Nora is quite informal; however, there is structure as each student's daily schedule is busy with classes, athletics, community service, and extracurricular activities. Nora's programs will resonate with parents whose children have had a difficult time in a more mainstream environment.

Norwood School

8821 River Road, Bethesda, MD 20817
301.365.2595 | www.norwoodschool.org

"Norwood School's mission is to ensure that each of its students grows intellectually, morally, physically, socially, emotionally, and spiritually, while preparing to function productively and generously in our pluralistic society. Norwood's challenging educational program and broad-based activities are designed to help students experience joy in learning, develop self-confidence, and learn respect for the rights and feelings of others. Embracing diversity is integral to the school's tradition that both recognizes the worth of each member of the community and emphasizes the common values of academic achievement, mutual respect, cooperation, and personal responsibility."

Grades K – 8 | Co-Ed
No Religious Affiliation

Enrollment: 491 | **Average Class Size:** 10
Admissions and Testing: Deadline February 1; WISC-IV (K-4), SSAT or ISEE (5-8)
Tuition and Financial Aid: $25,820 (K), $26,210 (1-2), $27,040 (3-4), $29,940 (5-8); financial aid budget over $1.5 million serves about 20% of the students.

Curriculum: Norwood employs a broad-based curriculum, meaning traditional electives (art, music, foreign language, and physical education) are just as important as core subjects (reading, math, language arts, science, and social studies). This approach to education encourages students to explore outside of their comfort zones and try new things. The school strives to create a safe and nurturing learning environment where students are encouraged to take risks, both academically and socially.

One unique aspect of Norwood is that students spend the first fifteen minutes every day in chapel. Though the name "chapel" has religious connotations, the time is secular and used for reflective purposes and moral development. The students and teachers break up into their age-appropriate divisions for chapel meetings Monday through Thursday and then come together for a school-wide assembly on Friday.

Arts: Norwood believes that an education in art and music has a direct correlation to problem-solving abilities and high self-esteem. Students have several options in the arts to explore, from visual art classes to regular dramatic and musical performances. The halls of Norwood are not only full of student art, but the school also posts a majority of students' work online for friends and family to view.

Athletics: The Norwood Blue Hawks compete in the Capital Athletic Conference. Norwood offers basketball, soccer, dance, baseball, field hockey, cross-country, lacrosse, softball, and track. Middle school students are expected to pick a sport in each of the three annual seasons, but may alternatively choose a fitness and conditioning class. There is also an outdoor Summit program that features outdoor education and adventure sports.

Student Life: Norwood presents its students with traditional activities such as yearbook, Model UN, Math Counts, and others, such as GLOW—Growing Leaders of Our World, Girls on the Run, Green Hawks, Kid-to-Kid Giving Circle, Odyssey of the Mind, and the Student-Centered Independent Project. The school intends to develop students' leadership opportunities and encourage them to try new activities.

Campus: Located in Bethesda, Maryland, Norwood's 38-acre campus includes an art and music building, two gyms, including an athletic center with a double gymnasium with two basketball courts, a fitness center, five athletic fields, a 20,000-volume library, and up-to-date technology labs.

Learning Support: While it is not a school that specializes in learning support, Norwood is equipped to work with students with mild learning disabilities. The school employs two learning specialists—one for the lower school and one for the middle school. The lower school specialist works primarily with parents, teachers, and other professionals to identify any possible difficulties and to ensure that the right support is in place. The middle school specialist spends the majority of her time working with students individually on their organizational or academic skills.

Schools Attended by Most Graduates in the Past Five Years: The Potomac School, Walt Whitman High School, Holton-Arms School, Landon School, Georgetown Day School

Takeaways: Norwood strives to develop an open mind, an adventurous spirit, and a high self-esteem in its students. Students have a homeroom class for core courses and are divided into learning groups based on their developmental levels. Outside of the homeroom, students are assigned to different groups for their elective classes. The school believes that this helps students develop relationships and venture outside of their comfort zones. Norwood aims to emphasize the importance of community and family. Daily chapel allows students to create intimate bonds with one another and faculty while discussing important ethical issues. Norwood is a good fit for a family looking for a balance between traditional and progressive learning, a strong sense of community, and a commitment to academic, social, and creative growth.

Primary Day School

7300 River Road, Bethesda, MD 20817
301.365.4355 | www.theprimarydayschool.org

"The Primary Day School, a demonstration school for the Phonovisual Method, is a diverse, co-educational, independent school for children in pre-kindergarten through second grade. The school's warm and supportive atmosphere encourages the development of students intellectually, morally, physically, and emotionally, according to each child's gifts and talents."

Preschool – Grade 2 | Co-Ed
No Religious Affiliation

Enrollment: 145 | **Average Class Size:** 18-20
Admissions and Testing: Deadline January 24; in-house testing (Preschool-K), WISC-IV (1-2)
Tuition and Financial Aid: $17,850 (Preschool), $19,425 (K), $21,000 (1), $22,050 (2); financial aid relies on SSS analysis.

Curriculum: The Primary Day School offers a comprehensive early childhood curriculum for students in preschool through second grade. A cornerstone of the school's program is the use of the Phonovisual Method, which is a phonics-based approach to teaching reading, writing, and spelling and is integrated throughout the entire curriculum. Children learn about the sound/symbol relationship of the consonants and vowels through stories, poems, games, and songs. The school also uses Math in Focus, which emphasizes logical and critical thinking rather than rote memorization and calculation. Students are exposed to Spanish, French, and Mandarin Chinese beginning in preschool with each language having one lesson a week. These lessons are meant to develop students' listening and language abilities.

Arts: Both art and music are integrated into the daily curriculum. In music, students study folk songs from different cultures, traditional children's songs, and classical music to introduce children to basic musical concepts such as rhythm, melody, tempo, and dynamics.

Athletics: The physical education curriculum focuses on the development of motor skills and general movement abilities. Students are encouraged to develop good teamwork and cooperation skills through the STAR (Sportsmanship, Teamwork, Attitude, Respect) values.

Student Life: Primary Day offers students a number of after-school enrichment programs that change based on demand and season. The school also has a number of special events that students partake in such as Second Grade Authors' Tea, Spirit Week, and Colonial Day.

Campus: Primary Day is located at the intersection of River Road and Royal Dominion Drive in Bethesda, Maryland.

Learning Support: Classroom teachers differentiate their teaching based on student strengths and needs. In addition, the learning enhancement specialist works with classroom teachers to develop and implement teaching strategies across the curriculum. Primary Day supports early literacy, provides acceleration for individuals and groups, and offers intervention and remediation strategies as needed.

Schools Attended by Most Graduates in the Past Five Years: Holton-Arms School, Landon School, Georgetown Day School, Sidwell Friends School, Norwood School

Takeaways: Primary Day may be a match for a family looking for a school that specializes in early childhood development and emphasizes early reading skills. The Phonovisual Method is a hallmark of the school and all of the faculty members are extensively trained in the approach. Primary Day focuses on cultivating well-rounded, active learners. The school seeks to create a positive learning environment to allow for students' curiosity and confidence to develop. Students who attend Primary Day will leave with a strong academic foundation across the board.

Sandy Spring Friends School

16923 Norwood Road, Sandy Spring, MD 20860
301.774.7455 | www.ssfs.org

"Sandy Spring Friends School provides a welcoming and nurturing learning community with Friends testimonies and meeting for worship central to its life and vitality. A challenging academic curriculum, enriched arts program, inclusive athletics, and service opportunities promote intellectual excellence and strength of character. Recognizing the unique worth of each person, the school strives to develop individual talents and foster caring and effective citizens of the world."

Preschool – Grade 12 | Co-Ed | Boarding Option for Grades 9 – 12
Quaker | Society of Friends

Enrollment: 550 | **Average Class Size:** 12-15
Admissions and Testing: Deadline January 1, then rolling admission; BRIGANCE Early Childhood Screening (Preschool-1); WPPSI-III/ WISC-IV (2-5), SSAT or ISEE (6-12)
Tuition and Financial Aid: $15,500 (Preschool), $19,900 (K), $23,800 (1-5), $26,350 (6-8), $29,200 (9-12, day), $43,000 (9-12, five day boarding); $53,800 (9-12, seven day boarding); financial aid budget over $3 million serves about 23% of the student body; uses SSS form by NAIS.

Curriculum: Sandy Spring Friends School's (SSFS) programs are grounded in an ethical framework of the six Quaker "SPICES": service, peaceful resolution of conflict, integrity, community, equality, and stewardship. The lower school curriculum includes the traditional core courses but also instruction in Spanish, technology, and wellness and life beginning in preschool.

The middle school curriculum continues to build upon the skills developed in the lower school. The school combines social studies and English classes for middle school students into one joint humanities program. In the middle school, students experience a progressive, academically challenging, college prep program infused with Quaker values.

In the upper school, SSFS offers college prep classes and several semester-long elective classes. In eleventh and twelfth grade English, a student may have the opportunity to take the following classes: Banned Books, Native American Literature, Literature and Film, Satire, Literature of the Wild West, or Visual Texts. In line with its college prep curriculum, SSFS offers sixteen AP classes and Spanish, French, and Chinese for foreign language options.

Arts: Art and music classes are integrated into the curriculum beginning in preschool. As students advance, they have the opportunity to take classes such as Play Production, Modern Dance, Stagecraft, Video Production/One Acts, Handbells, and Ceramics. SSFS's most unique art offerings are in woodworking, weaving, and fiber classes, which are each offered for a full year.

Athletics: Middle school boys and girls and upper school boys compete in the Potomac Valley Athletic Conference (PVAC). Upper school girls compete in the Independent School League (ISL). Baseball, basketball, cross-country, golf, hockey, lacrosse, soccer, softball, tennis, track and field, volleyball, and wrestling are offered in the upper school. Baseball, basketball, cross-country, softball, and lacrosse are offered in the middle school. The school also has several outdoor education and leadership offerings, including rock climbing and outdoor leadership courses in both the middle and upper schools.

Student Life: As a Quaker school, one of the most important activities is student government. Students have the opportunity to become involved with student government beginning in grades four and five when they can join SPARK, the student government for the lower school. Two representatives are elected from fourth and fifth grade for SPARK and from sixth through eighth grade for FLAME, the middle school student government. The student government program culminates with the upper school's TORCH program, which sets the agenda for monthly town meetings and sponsors school events throughout the year.

Campus: SSFS is located on 140 acres in the heart of Montgomery County, Maryland. The campus has 14 academic buildings and six dormitories. A dining hall, athletic facilities, an indoor rock climbing wall, a fine arts center, a performing arts center, a library, science labs, and the meeting house are all included. The school is adjacent to the Sandy Spring Adventure Park, an outdoor aerial park.

Learning Support: There are three full-time learning specialists at SSFS, one in each division. Working together, counselors and learning specialists make up the Student Support Services Group (SSS). The group works with students, parents, faculty, and staff to provide education, information, and resources. This includes testing information and providing referrals to outside resources when situations arise beyond the capabilities of the student support team members.

Schools Attended by Most Graduates in the Past Five Years: Dartmouth College, Guilford College, Haverford College, Occidental College, Washington University

Takeaways: SSFS is a progressive, co-ed, college prep Quaker school serving students from preschool through twelfth grade, with an optional boarding program in the upper school. Founded in 1961, SSFS offers a deep and rigorous academic curriculum that focuses on a global education, 21st century skills, character education rooted in universal Quaker principles, and a diverse and international student body. SSFS's K-12 structure may be a good fit for a family who is looking for continuity in their child's education and an emphasis placed on fairness and equality.

The Siena School

9727 Georgia Avenue, Silver Spring, MD 20910
301.592.0567 | www.thesienaschool.org

"The Siena School offers a rich educational program for bright, college-bound students who are challenged by language-based learning differences, such as dyslexia. Our program is designed for students with mild-to-moderate needs who experience a discrepancy between their intellectual abilities and academic achievement in one or more areas such as reading, writing, oral expression, or math."

Grades 4 – 12 | Co-Ed
No Religious Affiliation

Enrollment: 80 | **Average Class Size:** 10
Admissions and Testing: Deadline February 10; needs full psycho-educational testing, WISC-IV and an achievement/academic test such as WJ-III
Tuition and Financial Aid: $31,718 (4-8), $33,225 (9-12); 15% of the budget is used for financial aid, and 33% of the students use it.

Curriculum: The curriculum at Siena is geared toward preparing students with language-based learning disabilities, especially dyslexia, for college. The school generally follows the Common Core Standards. In reading, language arts, and math, students are grouped by ability level rather than age or grade level. Instruction revolves around several principles: high academic standards, best practice teaching, individual attention for each student, research-based curriculum, multi-sensory instruction, character development, and community service. Study skills and organization techniques are embedded in the curriculum. Curriculum integration is a key component at Siena. For example, courses in history and literature are thematically and topically connected. AP classes are not currently offered at Siena.

Arts: In the arts, students learn to draw, paint, sculpt, and use mixed media. All students take drama, as it is built into their coursework. The integration of art in the curriculum is important at Siena. For instance, geometry, art, and photography students all collaborate together in creating a "human spirograph" art piece, based on the work of da Vinci's Vitruvian Man.

Athletics: Siena competes in the Maryland Independent School Athletic League. The school offers soccer, softball, basketball, volleyball, tennis, and track, with jujitsu as an after-school activity. The program is not mandatory. The jujitsu team competes in local tournaments. The girls' varsity basketball team has won a league title in the past three years.

Student Life: Siena stresses service learning and requires student participation. There is a strong emphasis on experiential learning and curriculum-related field trips are common. Upper school students visit the various sites in Washington, DC, such as the Supreme Court, war memorials, and art galleries. Further, upper school students participate in yearly two-week volunteer internships to explore career interests. Recent internships have been conducted at art studios, veterinary clinics, and law firms.

Campus: Siena has very recently undergone an extensive renovation to relocate its campus. The new school building opened at the end of January 2013 and includes a number of new features including a photography room and a piazza for lunch.

Learning Support: The entire school is geared towards assistance with language-based learning disabilities, such as dyslexia. All staff members are trained in specific instructional strategies for students with language-based learning needs.

Schools Attended by Most Graduates in the Past Five Years: High Point University, Goucher College, McDaniel College, University of Maryland—Eastern Shore, Lynn University

Takeaways: Although Siena believes in improving a student's reading skills, it believes children will get further in life by focusing on growing their strengths. It offers a special class called STRENGTHS in which students select topics of interests on which they do yearlong projects. Siena offers a tight-knit community with an emphasis on personal attention. Parents receive a phone call or email at least once every three weeks from their student's academic advisor. To further develop and strengthen the school's ties with the contemporary art community, Siena maintains an Artist-in-Residence who organizes annual student art exhibitions and creates a commissioned piece for the school. Siena is known in the area as being a flagship school for the remediation of dyslexia. The type of student best served by Siena is bright and college bound, has mild-to-moderate language-based learning needs, and is emotionally and behaviorally stable.

St. Andrew's Episcopal School

10033 River Road, Potomac, MD 20854 (Preschool-2)
8804 Postoak Road, Potomac, MD 20854 (3-12)
301.983.5200 | www.saes.org

"The mission of St. Andrew's Episcopal School is to know and inspire each child in an inclusive community dedicated to exceptional teaching, learning, and service."

Preschool – Grade 12 | Co-Ed
Episcopalian

Enrollment: 489 | **Average Class Size:** 11
Admissions and Testing: Deadline January 15; WPPSI-III/WISC-IV (Preschool-3), SSAT or WISC (4-5), SSAT or ISEE (6-12)
Tuition and Financial Aid: $13,990 (Preschool), $20,990 (Pre-K), $24,750 (K-3), $29,990 (4-5), $33,990 (6), $33,990 (7-8), $35,990 (9-12); financial aid available.

Curriculum: St. Andrew's provides a comprehensive college prep program that exemplifies the views of the Episcopal Church. The academic calendar consists of three 12-week trimesters. St. Andrew's believes a liberal arts approach to education—based on four pillars: academics, art, athletics, and spiritual life—encourages students to become independent thinkers and lifelong learners. Because of the flexible framework, teachers and administrators can adjust as necessary to maximize the effectiveness of the program.

The middle school and upper school programs include a core curriculum of English, history, language, math, and science. The upper school offers 14 AP classes and four consortium classes. The instruction of library, research, and technology skills is integrated within all courses. The end of each day includes an hour of interscholastic sports as part of the required program. Further, all students must fulfill art, religion, physical education, health, and service learning requirements.

Arts: Students choose from a wide variety of classes within visual and performing arts and they explore traditional and unconventional methods for making art. Upper school students can take AP Studio Art as well as interesting electives such as Protest Art and Critical, Media, and Digital Literacy. Further, there are many avenues for middle and upper school students to explore within performing arts, including the school musicals, plays, dance company, chorus, band, and technical theater.

Athletics: St. Andrew's competes in both the Independent School League and the Mid-Atlantic Athletic Conference. St. Andrew's offers equestrian, golf, baseball, basketball, soccer, softball, tennis, track, volleyball, cross-country, lacrosse, and wrestling. Students must participate in one team sport or athletic activity each year, and ninth and tenth graders must participate in two. Over the past decade, St. Andrew's has won championships in golf, cross-country, soccer, basketball, and lacrosse.

Student Life: Service learning and religion are fundamental pieces of the St. Andrew's experience. Students participate in service initiatives from holiday toy drives to international relief trips. Extracurricular activities include student governments, model UN, yearbook, debate, cooking club, comedy club, and more. Also, twice per year upper school students go on leadership retreats.

Campus: St. Andrew's is situated on two campuses in Potomac, Maryland. The main campus, located on 19 acres, houses third through twelfth grade and includes visual arts studios, a darkroom, a gym, a basketball court, a weight room, a dance studio, a wrestling room, tennis courts, theater space, and a 75,000-square-foot academic building. There are also two new, state-of-the-art evergreen turf fields for soccer, lacrosse, softball, and baseball. The Potomac Village campus, located at the intersection of River Road and Falls Road, is home to preschool through second grade and provides dedicated space for academics, the arts, athletics, and spiritual life.

Learning Support: The academic support team for each student includes teachers, an advisor, the grade-level academic dean, the division head, the school psychologist, and the director of the education center. Learning specialists and tutoring services are available to support students.

Schools Attended by Most Graduates in the Past Five Years: Carnegie Mellon University, University of Maryland—College Park, Oberlin College, Syracuse University, Wake Forest University

Takeaways: St. Andrew's provides a friendly teacher-student environment with a lot of personal attention. The school's Center for Transformative Teaching and Learning (CTTL) brings together all the latest research on how the brain learns and works to get that knowledge to its teachers. The staff is trained in a unique program called "All Kinds of Minds," which helps to determine a student's unique learning profile and how it can affect school performance. Instruction is tailored to individual student needs and students meet regularly with their faculty advisors to discuss areas of growth and concern. The academic program can be challenging, and students should expect a sizeable workload. Students need well-developed organization and time-management skills in order to handle large amounts of homework. The school is a good fit for families who want a great balance between solid academics, arts, sports, and social life, in an intimate setting.

St. John's Episcopal School

3427 Olney Laytonsville Road, Olney, MD 20832
301.774.6804 | www.stjes.com

"It is the mission of St. John's Episcopal School (STJES) to graduate students of character and faith. The Traits for Success are the foundation for students to fulfill their unique potential through intellectual, moral, and spiritual challenge. We balance the need for individual growth with the responsibility of citizenship and community service."

Preschool – Grade 8 | Co-Ed
Episcopalian

Enrollment: 200 | **Average Class Size:** 15
Admissions and Testing: Deadline February 1; testing done only upon request
Tuition and Financial Aid: $12,225 (Preschool), $16,950 (K-1), $17,850 (2-4), $18,350 (5), $18,990 (6-8); 22% of the student body receives financial aid; uses SSS form.

Curriculum: The lower school (kindergarten through fourth grade) curriculum focuses on the cognitive, social, emotional, spiritual, and moral development of students. The school offers traditional instruction in the major academic core areas, plus religion, Spanish, music, physical education, art, library and technology, and weekly chapel services. The upper school (fifth through eighth grade) entails an intense four-year program intended to prepare students for a challenging high school curriculum. In addition to the traditional core subjects, the curriculum emphasizes technology, study skills, group work, and presentations.

Religion is a large component of the student experience. Lower school students attend weekly religion classes and middle school students, through their four years, gain a deep understanding of Christianity, its history, and its place among world religions. St. John's is well suited to differentiate learning to meet a range of needs. Instruction can be enhanced through the accelerated curriculum program or slowed down for students who may need extra time. St. John's uses the Montgomery County school system's standards for its gifted and talented program.

Arts: Art offerings include art, drama, and music, with the drama program incorporating video production and musical theater. Music is an important component of the lower school curriculum, and students are taught literacy, performance, and appreciation. Those students with an increased interest in drama, singing, or instrumental music have the option to audition for the Olney Arts School in a School (OASIS), which provides intensive, individualized training.

Athletics: St. John's competes in the Independent School League. St. John's offers cross-country, soccer, basketball, and lacrosse. There is also a co-ed running team that participates in 5K races. The athletic program is not mandatory, but all students are encouraged to participate in some physical activity every year, whether competitive or noncompetitive. The program is built to encourage enthusiasm for fitness and teamwork.

Student Life: St. John's requires sixth, seventh, and eighth graders to fulfill yearly service requirements. The school sponsors service learning trips for students to locations such as New Mexico. Study abroad opportunities allow sixth graders to travel to Costa Rica and seventh graders to travel to Belize. These trips intend to build on previous ecological knowledge and Spanish language skills. Every other year the school offers a summer family travel opportunity to Italy. The school has a number of age-appropriate after-school activities ranging from Mathematics Jumpstart Camp to Model UN. Parents are often invited to participate in community activities such as parent coffee and family dances.

Campus: St. John's academic facilities include an arts center, a science lab, a computer lab, a gymnasium, and access to athletic practice fields.

Learning Support: A reading specialist is available to assist with reading remediation. St. John's is able to provide basic accommodations to students through the school staff or through external partnerships. The school has implemented several programs such as Traits for Success and the 6 Trait Writing Program.

Schools Attended by Most Graduates in the Past Five Years: Our Lady of Good Counsel High School, The Academy of the Holy Cross, Georgetown Preparatory School, Gonzaga College High School, Landon School

Takeaways: St. John's strives to provide its students with a well-rounded education. The school-wide Traits for Success program incorporates one trait per month into the classroom. September's lesson, for example, focuses on the importance of organization. Other programs of interest include H.E.R.O.E.S., which develops skills of respect, kindness, and courage; World Village Experiences, which aims to introduce students to global issues; and international travel offerings, which take students to Central America and Europe in their studies. The staff at St. John's is well equipped to differentiate instruction, especially to advanced students, many of whom are instructed in material accelerated by one or more grade levels. The school is a good fit for students looking to be challenged academically in a school environment that aims to foster spiritual growth.

Stone Ridge School of the Sacred Heart

9101 Rockville Pike, Bethesda, MD 20814
301.657.4322 ext. 321 | www.stoneridgeschool.org

"Stone Ridge School of the Sacred Heart inspires young women to lead and serve, through lives of purpose that integrate faith, intellect, community, social action, and personal growth in an atmosphere of wise freedom."

Grades 1 – 12 | All Girls
Catholic | Independent

Enrollment: 660 | **Average Class Size:** 14
Admissions and Testing: Deadline December 11, then rolling; WPPSI-III/WISC-IV (K-6), SSAT, ISEE or ERB, HSPT (6-12)
Tuition and Financial Aid: $22,500 (Preschool-4), $24,000 (5-6), $24,900 (7-8), $27,900 (9-12); financial aid budget over $2 million serves about 25% of the student body; uses the FACTS form; merit scholarships are also available for freshmen students.

Curriculum: The lower school curriculum is an integrated curriculum allowing students to explore concepts from all three learning modalities: auditory, visual, and kinesthetic. A phonics-based approach in reading is used in the primary grades. French is the world language of choice for preschool through fourth grade as it is directly tied to the heritage of Sacred Heart.

In the middle school, the engaging curriculum is focused on collaborative learning. There is a strong emphasis on learning how to learn by honing study, research, writing, and problem-solving skills in all disciplines. Grades six through eight have a 1:1 iPad program. Academic extracurriculars are offered such as mathletes and robotics to extend the math and science curricula.

The upper school, now in a four 80-minute extended period schedule, is an academic environment, offering 20 AP classes in total. Stone Ridge incorporates a 1:1 MacBook program, now in its fifth year, and SMART board equipped classrooms, which allow for full technological integration and collaboration in and outside the classrooms. The upper school also incorporates a full service leadership program—Social Action—every other Wednesday of the school year.

Arts: Stone Ridge provides a variety of offerings in the visual and performing arts beginning with its youngest students. An all-school art show opens every April and showcases a rich fine arts program comprised of ceramics, photography, and studio art. Middle and upper school students perform in two plays and two musicals each year. The music offerings include band, string ensemble, handbells, and choir; students perform at the Music Center at Strathmore in December.

Athletics: Stone Ridge competes in the Independent School League. Its athletic program is an integral component of student life. The school offers 19 competitive teams including cross-country, tennis, basketball, field hockey, swimming, diving, soccer, lacrosse, softball, track and field, and volleyball, as well as four club teams (golf, squash, ice hockey, and equestrian). Stone Ridge's swim team holds the ISL title.

Student Life: The leadership program in the upper school is a clear example of Stone Ridge's commitment to community service. The program allows students to bring important issues to the consciousness of the school at large. There is also a large Campus Ministry program in which the students assist in planning, writing, and sharing in faith-filled activities. Each student is a member of either the blue or gold team, which constitutes a significant part of the school's spirit.

Campus: Stone Ridge is located on 35 wooded acres in the heart of Bethesda, MD, neighboring Walter Reed National Military Medical Center and the National Institutes of Health. The campus includes three libraries, three gymnasiums, outdoor tennis courts, playing fields, and a chapel. Stone Ridge has a competition-sized, covered, heated swimming pool. Indoor facilities include three media labs, three science labs, three dining halls, expansive art studios, and a performance theater.

Learning Support: Each division has its own team of learning specialists.

Schools Attended by Most Graduates in the Past Five Years: University of Maryland—College Park, Georgetown University, University of Virginia, Elon University, Syracuse University

Takeaways: Stone Ridge strives to implement technology and best practices in order to inspire students to think critically. The upper school's unique Social Action Program is fully integrated into the curriculum, affording each student the opportunity to engage regularly in service learning. Additionally, students at Stone Ridge can participate in an exchange program at one of over 200 Sacred Heart schools around the world. Stone Ridge is a good option for a girl who is interested in serving her community and can keep up with a rigorous academic program.

Washington Episcopal School

5600 Little Falls Parkway, Bethesda, MD 20816
301.652.7878 | www.w-e-s.org

"Washington Episcopal School believes that learning should be joyful, because academic excellence and happy children belong together. An independent, co-educational school for students from Nursery through Grade 8, WES is committed to helping every child develop his or her fullest potential."

Nursery – Grade 8 | Co-Ed
Episcopal | Episcopal Diocese of Washington

Enrollment: 271 | **Average Class Size:** 14-16
Admissions and Testing: Deadline February 1; WPPSI-IV/WISC-IV (K-6), SSAT or ISEE (7-8)
Tuition and Financial Aid: $24,985 (Nursery, full-time), $30,135 (K-8); financial aid budget serves about 20% of the students; uses SSS form.

Curriculum: Washington Episcopal School (WES) provides students with an academically challenging and broad curriculum. There is an emphasis on global exposure and real-world application. For example, Spanish and French are introduced in preschool, culminating in a trip to either France or Spain by the time students reach eighth grade. Also, fifth graders visit Antietam and Harper's Ferry and eighth graders take a three-day trip to the Chesapeake Bay to further their ecology studies.

Students participate in weekly chapel services and learn about the major themes of the Bible. Core academics, arts, and foreign language instruction all start early at WES as part of a traditional curriculum. Elementary students engage in projects that grow their critical-thinking skills, while the middle school program is academically rigorous and adds programs in secondary school placement, social activities, and community service.

Arts: Chorus, band, digital arts, or a combination of these courses is offered. Speech and drama classes meet once a week and offer students various performance opportunities. Art offerings include painting, clay sculpture, and ceramics, and lessons are interwoven with the history curriculum.

Athletics: WES schedules independently with members of the Capital Athletic Conference, Independent School League, and Potomac Valley Athletic Conference, among others. Interscholastic sports include soccer, cross-country, basketball, lacrosse, and track. P.E. options include tennis, aerobics, rock climbing, martial arts, and biking. The interscholastic sports program is not mandatory and there are no team tryouts.

Student Life: WES offers students various outlets for enrichment beyond the normal school day. Until sixth grade, students can participate in a variety of clubs including art, chess, robotics, karate, and drama. Middle school students can participate in ceramics, film, French and Spanish clubs, the school newspaper, and sewing. Other opportunities include a daily study hall, math labs, community service, and a literary magazine.

Campus: Washington Episcopal's campus sits on ten acres in suburban Bethesda. Facilities include two art studios, a ceramics studio, three gyms, a fitness room and climbing wall, a library, two music rooms, two technology labs, an indoor "Discovery" play space for the youngest students, two playgrounds, one grass athletic field, a soon-to-be-completed turf athletic field, and a sports court.

Learning Support: The school has a full-time learning specialist and a full-time counselor. The school can work with students who require basic accommodations; however, the school is not equipped for students with significant special needs.

Schools Attended by Most Graduates in the Past Five Years: Bullis School, St. Andrew's Episcopal School, The Potomac School, St. John's College High School, Georgetown Day School

Takeaways: WES has a strong commitment to keeping school and learning a joyful experience. Students are exposed to an education that aims to teach ethics and create a strong global awareness through study of religion and foreign languages. Further, competitive athletics are added to the school experience in fifth grade. Athletics make up a large part of the student experience at WES for the purpose of promoting sportsmanship, leadership, and integrity. A noteworthy part of WES's program is its Study Trips initiative. Fifth graders go to Civil War battlefields, sixth graders visit Bryce and Zion National Parks and the Colorado River, seventh graders take a ten-day trip to Italy, eighth graders spend two weeks in France or Spain, etc. These trips are included in the tuition.

WES is a good fit for students looking for an education that broadens their world view, challenges them academically, physically, and spiritually, and encourages exploration of extracurricular interests.

Washington Waldorf School

4800 Sangamore Road, Bethesda, MD 20816
301.299.6107 | www.washingtonwaldorf.org

"At Washington Waldorf, we encourage the connections that broaden students' experience and help them grow in new directions. Our teachers incorporate academic, artistic, and practical elements into every subject, creating memorable lessons—strong individuals and highly successful scholars—along the way. The Washington Waldorf School cultivates each student's capacity to think clearly, feel compassionately, and act purposefully in the world. We are committed to the educational movement inspired by the pioneering work of Rudolf Steiner and advanced by Waldorf teachers worldwide."

Preschool – Grade 12 | Co-Ed
No Religious Affiliation

Enrollment: 240 | **Average Class Size:** 15
Admissions and Testing: Deadline January 31, then rolling; in-house testing
Tuition and Financial Aid: $6,950-$18,900 (Pre-K-Kindergarten), $20,750 (1-5), $22,000 (6-8), $23,200 (9-12); 12% of the budget is reserved for financial aid and serves about 25% of the students.

Curriculum: The Washington Waldorf School (WWS) curriculum is based upon the Waldorf approach to education, in which a long main lesson is taught at the beginning of the day allowing for in-depth exploration of a particular topic. Every three to four weeks the main lesson changes. The school is unique in that it uses only primary sources as texts for classes and instruction often incorporates discussion and storytelling. In the lower school, each class has one primary teacher who continues with the class until eighth grade. Spanish instruction begins in first grade and continues through sixth grade when students can choose to continue or switch to German. Some lower school main lessons include arithmetic, grammar, and plant life.

Students in the upper school begin the day with a double main lesson. These main lessons can include topics such as United States colonial history, art history, organic chemistry, the American Civil War, evolution, the senior play, calculus, poetry, and Dante's work. All students take full-year courses in math, English, and Spanish or German. While students also take a yearlong course in technology, technology is not integrated into the curriculum. The upper school program concludes with a senior project, which students must present to their peers and advisors.

Arts: Beginning in third grade, all students choose a string instrument to study. Private lessons are required for students in fourth through eighth grade. In the upper school, students must participate in either chorus or orchestra. In order to fulfill their graduation requirements, all students must participate in the senior play. Some unique courses offered at WWS include blacksmithing, woodworking, fiber arts, metal work, basketry, and book binding.

Athletics: WWS is a member of the Potomac Valley Athletic Conference and offers baseball, basketball, cross-country, soccer, and softball. It will also compete in the Independent Small Schools Athletic Conference. No cuts are made from any team and every student is given a chance to play. Upper school students are required to participate on one team each year.

Student Life: There are a number of student trips incorporated into the WWS student experience. Beginning in third grade, students take field trips to various local attractions ranging from Washington, DC monuments to Civil War battle grounds. In eleventh grade, all students spend one week at an international community helping handicapped adults.

Campus: The school is located in Bethesda, Maryland, approximately three miles away from the Washington, DC border. It sits on six acres bordering a park and is within walking distance of the Potomac River.

Learning Support: Two learning specialists are available for students with learning needs.

Schools Attended by Most Graduates in the Past Five Years:
No matriculation information is available.

Takeaways: The Waldorf School is one of the most unique schools in the area, both in its curriculum and its course offerings. The main lesson structure and distinctive course offerings such as eurythmy and woodworking are appealing to many students. Teachers develop strong relationships with their students, which enables them to target each student's learning style. Students are required to be artistically involved, beginning with music classes in kindergarten and culminating in the senior play in twelfth grade. The school recognizes the importance of preparing its students for college and offers its own SAT and ACT test prep classes as well as thorough college counseling. WWS is a good fit for students who are individualistic, creative, and open to new ways of learning.

The Woods Academy

6801 Greentree Road, Bethesda, MD 20817
301.365.3080 | www.woodsacademy.org

"The Woods Academy is an inclusive Catholic community preparing boys and girls to lead lives of significance."

Preschool – Grade 8 | Co-Ed
Catholic | Independent

Enrollment: 313 | **Average Class Size:** 15
Admissions and Testing: Deadline March 1; in-house testing (1), WISC-IV (2-5), ISEE or SSAT (6-8)
Tuition and Financial Aid: \$12,225 (Montessori Half Day), \$18,870 (Montessori Full Day), \$18,870 (Lower School), \$19,975 (Upper School); uses the NAIS form.

Curriculum: The Montessori preschool places students of ages three through six in multi-age exploratory classrooms. Students pursue areas of interests at their own pace under the guidance of well-trained professional teachers who implement instructional strategies such as singing, storytelling, poetry, sharing, outdoor play, music, and puppets. In the lower school, teachers capture student interest through journal writing, selecting relevant books, and solving real-life math problems. The Woods employs a number of respected programs in the lower school curriculum, including Everyday Math and the National Science Resource Center's Science and Technology Concepts for Children program.

In the upper school, classes are hands-on and students are encouraged to be actively engaged in their learning. The school employs programs such as the Lego Mindstorm Robotics program in science, the interactive social studies program History Alive!, and the language arts program Words Their Way. Along with core classes, students in grades one through eight take religion courses that teach the foundations of Catholic theology, a variety of art and music classes, and courses on technology and library studies.

Arts: Music and art are integrated into daily academic life at The Woods Academy beginning at a young age. Students are encouraged to use art to express their feelings and experiences, to communicate, and to learn about the world around them. Teachers incorporate seasonal songs, movement, and dance to relate to classroom themes. Students work with a variety of media including drawing, printmaking, architecture, sculpting, painting, and ceramics. In music, students study rhythm, melody, and songwriting.

Athletics: The Woods Academy places a strong value on athletics and movement and encourages all students to be involved in athletics, though it is not required. The school is a member of the Capital Athletic Conference (CAC). Students can participate in soccer, cross-country, basketball, track, and softball (girls).

Student Life: Aside from the artistic opportunities interwoven into the curriculum, students also have the opportunity to take part in a number of extracurricular options including Music in Motion, Chess Club, After-School Sports Club, Flute Ensemble, Math Club, Robotics Team, and Chorus.

Campus: The Woods Academy is located on a six-acre campus in Bethesda, Maryland. The campus includes a number of playing fields for soccer, lacrosse, and baseball, as well as several outdoor playgrounds and a garden surrounding the school building. The campus hosts a Student Activities Center that includes a regulation-size gymnasium, a stage outfitted for theatrical and musical performances, and a music studio. The school is also home to a 15,000-volume library, a chapel, and a computer lab.

Learning Support: All teachers work with students individually and differentiated instruction is used at all grade levels. The school employs two full-time resource teachers who work closely with the classroom teachers in the areas of math and language arts. The math specialist and reading specialist facilitate differentiated instruction at all grade levels.

Schools Attended by Most Graduates in the Past Five Years: Georgetown Preparatory School, Academy of the Holy Cross, Gonzaga College High School, Georgetown Visitation School, St. John's Episcopal School

Takeaways: The Woods Academy stands out among other K-8 schools in the area due to its progressive education model. While the majority of Catholic schools are rooted in traditional education, The Woods offers students a Montessori-based preschool and a lower and upper school that aim to increase intrinsic motivation. The Woods is unique with its overnight trips for students in the upper school. The Woods is a good option for Catholic families looking for a progressive or Montessori education. The school offers a strong core curriculum through a hands-on and exploratory framework. Students are given a number of opportunities in the arts, and the introduction of foreign language in kindergarten enables students to leave The Woods as well-rounded individuals.

CHAPTER 16

Northern Virginia Schools

Accotink Academy Learning Center

8519 Tuttle Road, Springfield, VA 22152
703.644.9072 | www.accotinkcenter.com

"The mission of Accotink Learning Center is to provide each student an individualized education in a safe, supportive environment that promotes self-discipline, motivation, and excellence in learning. The Accotink Learning Center's team joins the parents and community to assist students in developing the necessary scholastic and professional skills for the highest level of success possible."

Grades 6 – 12 | Co-Ed
No Religious Affiliation

Enrollment: 52 | **Average Class Size:** 10
Admissions and Testing: Rolling admission; psycho-educational and standardized testing required
Tuition and Financial Aid: $22,500 (6-12); limited aid is available.

Curriculum: Accotink offers a simplified core subjects program (math, English, science, history, and elective) that is catered to students with learning disabilities. The curriculum is literacy-rich and relies on in-house therapists to work with students with emotional, developmental, and specific learning disabilities. The electives program offers classes in active physics, health, journalism, music, photography, theater, and webpage design, to name a few. Essentially, all students take the four core classes and then select an elective that suits their needs or interests. For students who need extra remediation in reading or math, the elective period offers opportunity for support and specialized tutoring. Students who excel can take college prep courses and foreign language.

Arts: Accotink offers students electives in art, music, theater arts, and webpage design. Art classes focus on basic drawing, painting, and sculpting techniques while tying into art history to provide context for cultural and visual literacy. Music classes provide an overview of music history and theory and give students the opportunity to experiment with drums, piano, and guitar. Theater arts class surveys dramatic literature and allows students to participate in performance and production.

Athletics: Students engage in daily physical activity, but there are no competitive sports programs. Physical activities include softball, rock wall climbing, bowling, basketball, volleyball, and baseball. There is also a swimming club and an all-around sports club during which students play basketball, football, and a variety of other sports. The goal of the physical fitness program is to instill wellness and total fitness.

Student Life: Accotink offers students several after-school clubs for them to explore their interests. Current offerings include music, swimming, sports, cooking, drama, art, and video games. There is also an active Student Council Association (SCA).

Campus: Accotink features a 55,000-square-foot facility that was completed in 2006. It is located in Springfield near many major thoroughfares and was built specifically to allow space for therapy, tutoring, and academic facilities such as science and computer labs.

Learning Support: Accotink Learning Center (ALC) offers a variety of clinical services, including individual and group psychotherapy, speech and language therapy, and occupational therapy. ALC staffs ten licensed clinical psychologists, ten speech and language pathologists, eight crisis staff, two art therapists, and two occupational therapists. Each student is evaluated to determine what services are needed to help that student reach his or her academic and social emotional goals.

Schools Attended by Most Graduates in the Past Five Years: Student destinations are split between local two and four-year colleges and work placement.

Takeaways: Accotink Learning Center caters to middle and high school students with significant learning disabilities and autism. The Learning Center is often confused with Accotink Academy, which is in a different building on the same campus. Accotink Academy is a therapeutic school that serves elementary, middle, and high school students with behavioral issues. Both schools have contracts with several local public school systems that fund students' tuition. For students with a low cognitive profile who feel overwhelmed in more traditional environments, Accotink Learning Center may be worth considering.

Ad Fontes Academy

5649 Mount Gilead Road, Centreville, VA 20120 (K-4)
15450 Lee Highway, Centreville, VA 20120 (5-12)
703.673.1145 | www.adfontes.com

"The Ad Fontes mission is to glorify God by assisting Christian parents in equipping their children to be servant leaders through a superior classical education based on eternal biblical truth."

Grades K – 12 | Co-Ed
Christian | Non-Denominational

Enrollment: 174 | **Average Class Size:** 13
Admissions and Testing: Deadline February 3; in-house testing
Tuition and Financial Aid: $7,800 (K), $8,200 (1-6), $8,750 (7-8), $9,450 (9-12); financial aid available; uses FACTS form.

Curriculum: In the grammar school, students work to develop strong foundations in the core areas of mathematics, phonics, spelling, grammar, literature, science, Bible, history, and Latin. Students also take classes in music, art, and physical education, which are taught as separate courses beginning in second grade. There is a heavy emphasis on memorization and presentation skills, which are taught by using chants, songs, visual displays, and in-class drama.

The curriculum for Ad Fontes's upper school is classical and college prep with a heavy weight placed on developing students' analytical and synthesizing skills. Students in the upper school fulfill their core requirements through honors-level courses in English, math, history, and science as well as Bible, Latin, classical composition, literature, logic, and rhetoric. Students take a full year of logic and civics in eighth grade. In total, students receive five years of rhetoric training. Ad Fontes's program culminates with the Senior Thesis—a 20-page research project defended before a panel of experts and faculty members.

Arts: Beginning in kindergarten, students attend weekly art class. In the upper school, students can take classes in art, choral music, drama, music, and journalism. If a student is particularly interested in music, he or she may join the Praise Band, which the school's music director oversees. The Praise Band runs weekly chapel and performs a variety of spiritual music.

Athletics: Ad Fontes is a member of the National Christian School Athletic Association and the Northern Virginia Independent Athletic Conference. Ad Fontes offers basketball, baseball, cross-country, and soccer.

Student Life: Ad Fontes has a house system in the upper school led by a Junior or Senior House Head. All upper school students are in one of four houses, which have regular social events, competitions, service projects, and small group chapel and prayer time. All students are expected to attend chapel weekly. The school holds different extracurricular events including thematic class parties for the lower school and an overnight retreat for the upper school each year.

Campus: Ad Fontes's upper and lower schools are located on separate campuses. The lower school is housed in Saint John's Episcopal Church in Centerville and the upper school is hosted by Centerville Presbyterian Church. The school uses the church buildings for classroom space and has access to nearby fields for athletics and physical education.

Learning Support: Ad Fontes is not a school specialized in learning support.

Schools Attended by Most Graduates in the Past Five Years: Covenant College, James Madison University, Baylor University, George Mason University, Virginia Tech

Takeaways: Ad Fontes is a small, K-12 Christian school that places a large emphasis on classical education with required Latin courses, cultural studies, and projects. The school strives to actively involve students in classroom discussions and training in Latin, logic, rhetoric and great books. Additionally, Ad Fontes provides a Christian education with required Bible classes and weekly chapel services. The facilities at Ad Fontes are relatively limited and students are fairly confined to a set curriculum. However, the school is a good option for families looking for a relatively low-cost, classical Christian curriculum for a child who learns best in a structured yet engaging environment.

Alexandria Country Day School

2400 Russell Road, Alexandria, VA 22301
703.548.4804 | www.acdsnet.org

"Alexandria Country Day School (ACDS) is a dynamic, K-8 independent school community that values academic excellence, character, independent thinking, citizenship, and respect for others. We inspire in our students creativity, enthusiasm for learning, and confidence through a stimulating academic program, athletics, the arts, and community service."

Grades K – 8 | Co-Ed
No Religious Affiliation

Enrollment: 222 | **Average Class Size:** 13
Admissions and Testing: Deadline January 15; WPPSI-IV/WISC-IV (K-5), ISEE or SSAT (6-8). File Completion Deadline: January 31; (application, testing, transcripts, recommendations)
Tuition and Financial Aid: $24,466 (K-3), $26,569 (4-8); relies on FAST (Financial Aid for School Tuition) analysis.

Curriculum: In the lower school, teachers use guided and independent reading, small groups, read-alouds, journal and book writing, and systematic phonics to teach the basics of reading. In third through fifth grade, students are introduced to literature and comprehension strategies. Students follow the Math in Focus program, which is the American version of Singapore Math, an internationally recognized program that strikes a balance between traditional algorithms and visual representation models that help build critical-thinking skills. The science program at ACDS incorporates studies of earth, physical, and life sciences as well as health, biology, and beginning chemistry. The school also begins Spanish instruction in kindergarten.

In the middle school, a heavy emphasis is placed on language arts including a focus on writing, grammar, vocabulary, and public speaking. In mathematics, students are grouped according to their ability. Social studies focus on understanding ancient civilizations and different world cultures, until the eighth grade, which is centered on American history.

Spanish instruction continues throughout the middle school, and the program culminates in a class trip to Puerto Rico.

Arts: Elementary students attend both art and music classes twice a week. Each trimester, middle school students take art, music, or drama five days out of a seven-day rotation.

Athletics: The ACDS Bobcats are a member of the ABC Athletic League of Greater Washington. Students who choose to participate in the athletic program have the opportunity to partake in cross-country, soccer, basketball, softball, swimming, and tennis. The program has a no-cut policy and any student interested in playing a sport is allowed to do so.

Student Life: ACDS offers extracurricular activities as well as a summer camp. One unique program is the Festival of Learning, a school-wide, yearlong survey of a particular topic that celebrates world cultures, diversity, and historical legacies. The festival allows for students to work together in cooperative projects across grade levels and disciplines.

Campus: The school is located just outside of Old Town Alexandria. All students in kindergarten through eighth grade attend classes in the main building, which includes an art studio, gym, performing arts center, cafeteria, and library.

Learning Support: Though ACDS is not a school specifically designed for children with learning disabilities, the school's Teaching and Learning Center (TLC) is equipped to meet all admitted students' educational needs by working with students individually and in small groups. It also provides teachers with instructional methods to use when working with diverse learning styles.

Schools Attended by Most Graduates in the Past Five Years: St. Stephen's & St. Agnes School, TC Williams High School, Bishop Ireton High School, The Field School, Gonzaga College High School

Takeaways: ACDS strives to develop a deep and rich love of learning from an early age that students will take with them when they depart for high school. The school features small class sizes and a hands-on, integrated curriculum as well as a 1:1 iPad program. ACDS is a good option for families looking for an individualized, traditional education with an emphasis on technology.

The Auburn School

13525 Dulles Technology Drive, Herndon, VA 20171
9545 Georgia Avenue, Silver Spring, MD 20910
703.793.9353 | 301.588.8048 | www.theauburnschool.org

"The mission of The Auburn School is to grow the social and academic potential of bright students with social and communication challenges."

Grades K – 11 (Herndon) and K – 8 (Silver Spring) | Co-Ed
No Religious Affiliation

Enrollment: 45 | **Average Class Size:** No more than 8
Admissions and Testing: February 1; all students are required to have a full psycho-educational evaluation and report completed within the last two years.
Tuition and Financial Aid: $37,570; need based and non-need based; approximately 20-25% of students will receive tuition assistance, with average grant awards of about $7,500-$10,000.

Curriculum: The Auburn School curriculum is based on the Common Core State Standards with a special focus on developing students' social and communication skills along with their academic abilities. Many of the students who attend Auburn are on the autism spectrum. The integrated curriculum emphasizes inquiry-based learning, meaning that students are encouraged to ask questions, make connections, and develop their imagination and intrinsic motivation across all subjects. Along with traditional classes such as language arts, social studies, math, science, physical education, art, and technology, students also take classes such as Social Learning and Thinking and Organizational Strategies.

Arts: The arts are integrated into the curriculum so that students explore different areas. Often students have art projects within the content areas. Some examples of student art projects include creating mosaic pots for a "green curriculum," constructing a model of the auditory pathway for hearing using natural objects, and acting in a reader's theater to depict stories in the literature curriculum.

Athletics: The Auburn School does not have a traditional athletics program, but it does implement physical education into the regular routine of classes. The physical education program focuses on the importance of fitness and an active lifestyle and what it means to be a good team player.

Student Life: The school organizes a number of events for parents and students. Examples of these events include Coffee with the Directors for parents and Read across America Day for students.

Campus: The Auburn School has three campuses in Virginia and Maryland. The school's original campus, located in Herndon, Virginia, opened in 2009. Following the inaugural year, the school opened a campus in Silver Spring, Maryland, in 2010 and a campus in Baltimore, Maryland, in 2011.

Learning Support: The entire school is geared towards helping students with social and communication challenges. The school has an occupational therapist, behaviorists, a school counselor, and a social learning director on staff.

Schools Attended by Most Graduates in the Past Five Years: The school just added a high school and has not yet had a graduating class; therefore, no accurate matriculation information is available.

Takeaways: Auburn's curriculum is integrated across the disciplines, meaning that what students are learning in social studies also applies to what they are learning in mathematics. Social skills are a part of every class and students take electives on topics such as organization and behavioral strategies. Auburn can meet the needs of a student with high functioning autism or other social difficulties who would benefit from small classes and the development of social skills.

Bishop Denis J. O'Connell High School

6600 Little Falls Road, Arlington, VA 22213
703.237.1400 | www.bishopoconnell.org

"Our mission is to provide students an education rooted in the life of Christ and to foster the pursuit of excellence in the whole person."

Grades 9 – 12 | Co-Ed
Catholic | Diocese of Arlington

Enrollment: 1,221 | **Average Class Size:** 19
Admissions and Testing: Deadline January 27 (9), May 1 (10-12); HSPT (9)
Tuition and Financial Aid: $12,585 (Catholic), $15,350 (Non-Catholic); financial aid available; uses FACTS form.

Curriculum: Bishop O'Connell places significant emphasis on college prep by offering 26 AP classes and a dual enrollment program with Marymount University. The school has recently implemented a "Project Lead the Way" engineering curriculum and provides a comprehensive STEM program. Students enrolled in these courses experience hands-on lessons, using real-world problems, supported by state-of-the-art computer-aided design (CAD) systems installed on the classroom laptop computers.

Bishop O'Connell offers an optional Global Studies Certificate Program. Students select a global focus area, attend core sessions, incorporate their theme into one of their current courses, and attend additional seminars. Upon completion of the program and a successful presentation, students receive a certificate in global studies, which is the equivalent of an additional semester of coursework.

Arts: The arts programs at Bishop O'Connell include orchestra, drama, choir, photography, studio art, video production, and graphic design. With a theater that seats 1,500, the school is able to showcase the artistic expression of its students through music recitals and concerts, theater productions, art and photography exhibitions, and dance performances throughout the school year.

Athletics: A charter member of the Washington Catholic Athletic Conference, Bishop O'Connell fields competitive sports teams for boys and girls. While some sports have a no-cut policy, several have tryouts and cuts. Sports teams include cheerleading, dance, cross-country, sailing, football, soccer, field hockey, tennis, volleyball, swimming, wrestling, basketball, crew, golf, lacrosse, and baseball. Participation is not mandatory.

Student Life: The school has a full-time community service program coordinator to guide students through a four-year service-learning requirement, which focuses on student initiative and interests. In addition, the school has several school-wide, student-organized efforts, including its annual 12-hour dance marathon to support charity.

Campus: Bishop O'Connell's 26-acre campus in Arlington, Virginia, includes athletic fields, science labs, music rooms, a stage, computer labs, a library, and a media center. The school is also home to a new $5 million athletic complex.

Learning Support: Academic support for students with mild learning difficulties is offered through the Muller Academic Services Program. In this program, students are given support to help them succeed in a challenging college prep program. By developing good study skills and habits, students are encouraged to explore their learning styles and be in control of their learning choices.

Schools Attended by Most Graduates in the Past Five Years: James Madison University, Virginia Tech, George Mason University, Virginia Commonwealth University, University of Virginia

Takeaways: Bishop O'Connell combines religious instruction with a rigorous academic program. A student who chooses to take advantage of the dual enrollment program with Marymount University as well as the AP course offerings can easily leave school with a number of college credits under his belt. Additionally, the school's focus on STEM education is a distinctive factor. One standout feature is the athletics program, which is highly respected in the area. Students who attend Bishop O'Connell can expect a heavy workload and high expectations. For a family looking for a traditional Catholic education with a high concentration on college readiness, O'Connell is a solid option.

Bishop Ireton High School

201 Cambridge Road, Alexandria, VA 22314
703.751.7606 | www.bishopireton.org

"In the Catholic tradition and in the spirit of St. Francis de Sales, Bishop Ireton High School is a college preparatory high school that promotes spiritual, intellectual, creative, scientific, technological, social and physical development. As a Salesian community of learning, Bishop Ireton challenges students to recognize and respect the multicultural diversity within our global society. In addition, the school fosters Christian ethics, religious values, and community service. A Bishop Ireton education teaches students to think critically and develops the whole person to meet present and future challenges and opportunities."

Grades 9 – 12 | Co-Ed
Catholic | Diocese of Arlington | Oblates of St. Francis de Sales

Enrollment: 800 | **Average Class Size:** 24
Admissions and Testing: Deadline end of January; HSPT
Tuition and Financial Aid: $12,900 (Catholic, Arlington Diocese), $14,638 (Catholic, Other Diocese), $17,711 (Non-Catholic); financial aid budget over $550,000 serves 15% of students; uses FACTS form.

Curriculum: Bishop Ireton's traditional curriculum combines spiritual instruction with a college prep academic program. There is a focus on core subjects plus computer science, religion, and fine arts. The school offers 17 AP classes and 42 honors classes. All students who take AP courses are required to take the AP exams in May. Theology and religion courses are an integral part of the curriculum. Students have the option to take courses such as Theology of the Body, Salesian Spirituality in Jesus, and Sacraments as Privileged Encounters with Jesus Christ. The school also has a library science department that strives to teach students research techniques and how to use technological resources in an efficient and ethical manner. Ireton offers French, Spanish, Russian, Latin, and German and requires students take at least three years of a foreign language.

Arts: Students are required to take at least one full year of fine arts to fulfill their graduation requirements. Bishop Ireton's wind ensemble is well regarded as is its drama department. Several of Ireton's main stage productions have won Cappie awards. Ireton offers fine arts classes such as theater, choir, and principles of art.

Athletics: Bishop Ireton is a member of the Washington Catholic Athletic Conference and the Virginia Independent Schools Athletic Association. Seventy percent of the student body competes on 48 athletic teams. Offerings include football, soccer, tennis, cross-country, cheerleading, volleyball, field hockey, swimming, basketball, wrestling, ice hockey, track and field, softball, lacrosse, golf, and crew.

Student Life: Bishop Ireton has more than 35 student clubs with options such as the Stage Crew, Cardinals for the Cure, and Anime Club. While some clubs such as the Pro-Life Club and Campus Ministry reflect the school's Catholic background, other clubs such as Civil Air Patrol B-Flight (a club focused on aerospace education) or the Zumba club are solely for student interests.

Campus: Located in Alexandria, Virginia, the campus includes athletic fields, computer labs, science labs, music rooms, a library, a gymnasium, and a media center. The auditorium can seat almost 800 people and is used for both orchestral and theatrical performances.

Learning Support: Bishop Ireton has a program called Academic Enrichment that provides daily academic support through tutoring, organization instruction, and guidance with long-term assignments. The students follow the same curriculum as their peers, but rather than attending study hall, they report to the Academic Advising Enrichment classroom.

Schools Attended by Most Graduates in the Past Five Years: Virginia Tech, James Madison University, University of Virginia, George Mason University, Virginia Commonwealth University

Takeaways: Since 1964, Bishop Ireton has operated as the smallest Catholic archdiocese school in northern Virginia. It offers a number of AP, honors, and unique religious courses. The school is well known for its athletic and fine arts programs but also has a number of student clubs and organizations. Bishop Ireton is a good option for a student who can perform well in a structured setting and for the family looking for a challenging Catholic high school.

Burgundy Farm Country Day School

3700 Burgundy Road, Alexandria, VA 22303
703.960.3431 | www.burgundyfarm.org

"Burgundy Farm Country Day School believes that children learn best in an inclusive, creative, and nurturing environment that engages the whole child. Burgundy's innovative, hands-on approach to education cultivates independent thinking, promotes academic excellence, instills respect for diversity, and teaches responsibility for self, for others, and for the natural world."

Junior Kindergarten – Grade 8 | Co-Ed
No Religious Affiliation

Enrollment: 286 | **Average Class Size:** 15
Admissions and Testing: Deadline February 1; WPPSI /WISC required
Tuition and Financial Aid: \$23,592 (JK), \$24,536 (K), \$25,661 (1-5), \$26,998 (6-8); 20% of students receive aid; uses SSS form.

Curriculum: Located on a 25-acre farm, including a stocked barn, Burgundy gives students the opportunity to study wildlife and environmental studies. This focus on environmentalism and conservation is at the core of the school's culture and curriculum. The lower school utilizes multi-age classrooms for students in the second and third grade, as well as for students in the fourth and fifth grade. Each section has two teachers who provide grade-level instruction in math and language arts. The curriculum links language arts, social studies, math, and science in theme-based units such as the Middle Ages and the Chesapeake Bay. Students receive reading instruction and age-appropriate literature, both fiction and nonfiction.

Burgundy's middle school seeks to develop critical-thinking skills among students with an integrated curriculum. The language arts program is rich in reading, creative expression, and analytical and expository writing. The social studies program provides an understanding of Western social structure and thought, from ancient Greco-Roman society to U.S. history. The science program engages students in firsthand experimentation and teaches the methods of scientific inquiry. All students study Spanish or French.

Arts: Visual art classes begin in junior kindergarten and span the entirety of a child's education at Burgundy. Students work in the school's art studios where they are encouraged to experiment with a range of different art forms, from painting and drawing to pottery. Burgundy hosts a spring arts festival where every child's artwork is displayed. The school's performing arts program culminates in middle school with special grade performances by sixth, seventh, and eighth graders.

Athletics: Burgundy is a member of the ABC Athletic League of Greater Washington. Students from sixth to eighth grade may compete in soccer, softball, cross-country, lacrosse, volleyball, and basketball. Soccer, softball, and cross-country are co-ed. The program is not mandatory.

Student Life: Students are required to work on community service projects regularly. Additionally, the school hosts a number of special events each year that are meant to bring the Burgundy community together, including the Fall Festival, the Festival of Lights, and the Spring Arts Festival.

Campus: The 25-acre campus located in Alexandria, Virginia, hosts a barnyard and garden that students tend with the assistance of the faculty. The Alexandria campus is home to art studios, a performing arts facility, a gymnasium, a 20,000-volume library, and science and computer labs. In addition to Burgundy's main campus, the school also owns a 500-acre campus in West Virginia. Students travel to the West Virginia campus twice a year beginning in second grade for environmental education.

Learning Support: Burgundy has a reading specialist available for students in the lower school, a middle school learning specialist, and a school counselor; however, Burgundy does not identify itself as a school staffed to support students with learning disabilities.

Schools Attended by Most Graduates in the Past Five Years: TC Williams High School, The Field School, St. Stephen's & St. Agnes School, West Potomac High School, Georgetown Day School

Takeaways: Burgundy emphasizes hands-on and collaborative learning, environmental science, and sustainability. With the help of the faculty, students are responsible for taking care of the live animals on Burgundy's campus. In addition, the school offers a diverse community (it was the first racially integrated school in Virginia) and a progressive education model that emphasizes the development of the student as a whole. For a family looking for a progressive education that incorporates hands-on and outdoor activities, Burgundy is worth considering.

Commonwealth Academy

1321 Leslie Avenue, Alexandria, VA 22301
703.548.6912 | www.commonwealthacademy.org

"We empower students in grades 3-12 to reach their highest achievement levels, reflective of their true potential, by teaching personal responsibility for learning and behavior in a comfortable community, conducive to academic risk-taking and social success. We offer a broad-based curriculum, compensatory strategies, and a focus on technology to prepare our students for the challenges of college, career, and life pursuits."

Grades 3 – 12 | Co-Ed
No Religious Affiliation

Enrollment: 150 | **Average Class Size:** 10 or fewer
Admissions and Testing: Deadline February 28, with mid-year rolling admission; no testing required, but most students have ADHD or a specific learning disability; applicants are asked to submit all diagnostic and standardized testing
Tuition and Financial Aid: $32,900; 15% of the students receive financial aid; uses the FAST form.

Curriculum: The program at Commonwealth is structured to serve students who have a specific learning disorder and/or have been diagnosed with ADHD, or will better succeed in a classroom of ten students or fewer. The college prep curriculum is taught with accommodations for each student and a variety of hands-on, interactive, and experiential opportunities to address different learning styles. Writing is integrated into every class in an effort to improve organizational skills, styles, grammar usage, mechanics, and semantics. Writing is also offered as a separate required class in lower, middle, and upper school. Honors classes are available in English, science, history, Spanish, and mathematics. The number of honors classes fluctuates as the need arises for individual students and as faculty become available on a year-to-year basis.

Arts: Computer graphics, web design, fine arts, and performing arts classes are available for students interested in exploring their artistic expression. Examples of unique topics offered include puppetry, mask making, videography, and drums.

Athletics: Commonwealth is a member of the Independent Small Schools Athletic Conference. The school offers basketball, cross-country, soccer, and tennis. All sports are co-ed except for basketball. The athletic program adheres to a no-cut policy. While the program is not mandatory, one-third of the student body is a member of a competitive team. Physical education is taught in a new gym facility adjacent to the main building.

Student Life: Students forge strong relationships with one another and faculty through Commonwealth's advisory program, monthly bagel bashes, and weekly club meetings. Club offerings vary year to year depending on student interest and have included art, bowling, photography, rock climbing, and graphic design. Students also take part in team-building trips to museums, theaters, and outdoor educational adventures around DC at the beginning of the school year. The service learning program starts in the lower school and is required for graduation.

Campus: Current facilities include 21,000 square feet of space: 13 classrooms, four computer labs, two lounges, and labs for chemistry, physics, and biology. Commonwealth Academy has received the NAIS Leading Edge Award for Programmatic Sustainability and was a finalist in the Alexandria Chamber of Commerce Technology Achievement Awards. In 2013, the school will be opening a new gym facility for physical activities.

Learning Support: The entire curriculum has been developed to accommodate students with learning disabilities and/or ADHD. Tutors and learning specialists are available in addition to a full-time social worker. A speech therapist is available for an additional fee.

Schools Attended by Most Graduates in the Past Five Years: Marymount University, McDaniel College, Savannah College of Art and Design, Lynchburg College, George Mason University

Takeaways: Commonwealth offers a significant amount of structure so students always know what to expect, day in and day out. Many students choose to take advantage of the school's after-school homework program, where they complete the bulk of their assignments. Often, students who dislike school in a traditional setting change their mind at Commonwealth. The curriculum is designed to alleviate stress and to work with the student at his or her own pace through an individualized program to build confidence. The incorporation of assistive technology is a main feature of the Commonwealth program, which aids in differentiating learning for all styles. Students with ADHD and/or LDs who need a considerable amount of structure often find Commonwealth to be a great fit.

Congressional Schools of Virginia

3229 Sleepy Hollow Road, Falls Church, VA 22042
703.533.9711 | www.congressionalschools.org

"The mission of the Congressional Schools of Virginia is to prepare children, through an innovative and accelerated curriculum, to embrace the opportunities and responsibilities they will face as global citizens."

Infant – Grade 8 | Co-Ed
No Religious Affiliation

Enrollment: 420 | **Average Class Size:** 18
Admissions and Testing: Rolling admission
Tuition and Financial Aid: $19,020 (Infant), $20,400 (Preschool-K), $21,300 (1-4), $22,200 (5-8)

Curriculum: In recent years, Congressional Schools of Virginia (Congressional) has moved away from a very structured and traditional curriculum to one that places a strong emphasis on critical thinking. In the lower school, students receive ongoing instruction in grammar, spelling, and mechanics. They are also exposed to increasingly challenging literature. Manipulatives are used in mathematics to facilitate concept development and logistical reasoning and to apply mathematics to problem solving. Specialized instructors in art, music, French or Spanish, and physical education supplement instruction by classroom teachers.

Middle school students pursue accelerated programs in math, science, and English. All seventh graders take Algebra I and all eighth graders take Geometry. In language arts, students apply and refine writing, critical thinking, and analytic skills across academic studies. They also write original stories, poems, and essays. Social sciences are studied in year-long themes. In world languages, fifth graders begin a four-year sequence in their choice of French or Spanish.

Arts: The highlight of Congressional's art program is its speech and drama classes, which begin in fifth grade. Congressional believes that public speaking is a skill that must be developed and is necessary for future success. The speech and drama program is designed to advance students' nonverbal and verbal communication, public speaking abilities, dramatic performance, and journalism skills.

Athletics: The Congressional Colts compete in the Capital Athletic Conference. Congressional offers baseball, softball, soccer, basketball, hiking, cross-country, skiing and snowboarding, kayaking, sailing, and whitewater rafting. The program is not centered on winning; instead, the full-time coaching staff encourages commitment, skill, character, and teamwork. The athletic program is not mandatory.

Student Life: Congressional offers its students several extracurricular opportunities at a young age. For example, the school is home to a Model UN club, STEM club, chess club, fencing club, and so on. Students are given the chance to work on the yearbook staff as photographers, layout specialists, fact checkers, or editors.

Campus: Congressional's 40-acre campus includes two libraries, music and art centers, two swimming pools, stables, and three technology centers. The campus includes a challenge course, nature trail, and equestrian stables.

Learning Support: The school is generally capable of working with students with mild learning disabilities or those who are undiagnosed and may simply need extra support. Tutoring is also available by teachers after school.

Schools Attended by Most Graduates in the Past Five Years:
No matriculation information is available.

Takeaways: Congressional implements an academic course load that emphasizes critical thinking. One testament to the school's method of education is its high acceptance rate to Thomas Jefferson High School for Science and Technology. Students at Congressional can take part in accelerated programs if they are looking for an extra challenge. Congressional is a good fit for a family that wants to provide their child with a strong, accelerated educational foundation rooted in critical thinking.

Episcopal High School

1200 North Quaker Lane, Alexandria, VA 22302
703.933.3000 | www.episcopalhighschool.org

"Founded on a tradition of honor and the pursuit of self-discovery, Episcopal High School engages students in a challenging college preparatory education. The school fosters empathy and responsibility for self and others through a commitment to spiritual inquiry and growth in a fully residential community. Students are encouraged to think creatively, work collaboratively, develop individual passions, and celebrate the talents of others. Sharing diverse life experiences, ideas, and values, students learn humility, resilience, and mutual respect. Through access to the educational and cultural resources of the nation's capital, students are inspired to understand and embrace a changing world. Together, faculty and students take initiative as informed citizens and environmental stewards. Episcopal strives to prepare young people to become discerning individuals with the intellectual and moral courage to lead principled lives of leadership and service to others."

Grades 9 – 12 | Co-Ed | Boarding Only
Episcopalian

Enrollment: 435 | **Average Class Size:** 12
Admissions and Testing: Deadline January 15; SSAT (9-10), PSAT, SAT, SSAT, or ISEE (11)
Tuition and Financial Aid: $47,850; over 30% of the student body receives financial aid with a budget of over $4.8 million.

Curriculum: Episcopal High School (Episcopal) offers students a college prep curriculum that includes classes in English, mathematics, foreign language, social studies, science, theology, and the arts. The program boasts more than 40 advanced and honors-level classes, which students must be placed into by means of test scores and grades from previous classes.

Episcopal also offers students an opportunity for independent study. This program allows students to develop a course that covers any topic the student would like to explore in-depth with the assistance of a faculty member. Independent study projects are generally semester-long endeavors and are factored into the student's overall GPA. Some recent examples of independent study projects at Episcopal include Linear Algebra, Hermann Hesse: Life and Works, The Role of Art in Religion, and Number Theory.

Arts: The school has a one-credit art requirement for all incoming ninth graders and a half-credit requirement for all sophomores and juniors. Students have the option to partake in classes in the visual arts (Ceramics, Photography, Drawing, and Studio Art), theater (Acting I and II), music (Concert Choir, Chamber Singers, Guitar, Songwriting, Music Theory, Orchestra, Introduction to Music Recording, and Religious Thought in Music), and dance (Survey of Dance). With the exception of those in choir or orchestra, all ninth graders must take Introduction to the Arts, a multidisciplinary course.

Athletics: The school is home to a competitive athletics program. Episcopal is a member of the Interstate Athletic Conference (IAC) and the Independent School League (ISL). The majority of students take part in all three athletics seasons their freshman year. The school offers cross-country, basketball, crew, field hockey, squash, golf, soccer, lacrosse, track and field, tennis, softball, baseball, football, and wrestling. Additional athletic offerings include kayaking, rock climbing, dance, group fitness, cross training, and strength training.

Student Life: Episcopal is a boarding-only school, meaning that every student who attends boards in the school's dormitories. Students are required to attend chapel three times a week; however, religious affiliation varies among the student population. Episcopal has more than 30 extracurricular activities available for students and these organizations meet after dinner and as a part of the afternoon program. Some examples of student clubs include Young Republicans/Democrats, It's Academic, the French Honors Society, and the Engineering Club.

Campus: Episcopal is located on 130 acres in suburban Alexandria, Virginia. The school is 10 minutes away from Washington, DC. The campus is home to residential dorms for all students, an alumni cottage, numerous athletic buildings, a health center, a learning center, computer and science labs, and a library.

Learning Support: The learning assistance at Episcopal is in place to support students in their areas of weakness, be it with a specific skill or content area. The school is home to a Writing Center and employs two full-time learning specialists.

Schools Attended by Most Graduates in the Past Five Years: University of Virginia, University of North Carolina at Chapel Hill, Washington & Lee University, Sewanee: The University of the South, Wake Forest University

Takeaways: Episcopal is the only exclusively boarding school in the DC area. The school is structured similarly to a traditional boarding school with a number of activities available for students on the weekends. Eighty-five percent of the faculty resides on campus, creating a distinct experience. Though the curriculum is traditional in nature, students are able to explore areas of interest through the independent study program and a number of advanced classes. Students who tend to do well at Episcopal are well rounded, independent, and effective at managing their time.

Flint Hill School

10409 Academic Drive, Oakton, VA 22124 (Lower & Middle School)
3320 Jermantown Road, Oakton, VA 22124 (Upper School)
703.584.2300 | www.flinthill.org

"Our commitment is to develop in a caring community an individual who seeks excellence and embraces the 'Driving Spirit' of Flint Hill School."

Transitional Kindergarten – Grade 12 | Co-Ed
No Religious Affiliation

Enrollment: 1,100 | **Average Class Size:** 16
Admissions and Testing: Deadline January 15; Gesell (Transitional Kindergarten-2), WISC-IV (3-4), SSAT (4-8), SSAT, PSAT, or SAT (9-12)
Tuition and Financial Aid: $29,485 (Transitional Kindergarten-4), $32,465 (5-8), $33,735 (9-12); 16% of the student body receives aid totaling $3.3 million; uses the FAST application.

Curriculum: The lower school encourages students to develop their fullest potential while fostering respect for classmates in a collaborative community. All students in the lower school are issued an iPad2 to support their learning and discovery.

Flint Hill's middle school curriculum is individualized and comprehensive, offering core subjects, arts, athletics, and experiential learning. In seventh and eighth grade, additional electives in media, math, and technology are introduced. Every student in the middle and upper school is given a MacBook Air to support their learning and various academic projects.

The upper school stresses academic excellence within an atmosphere that supports the emotional, moral, spiritual, physical, and social development of each student. In the process, every student is encouraged to assume responsibility through community service, involvement with athletics, and work within clubs and academic groups. With 26 AP courses, online options, and even for-credit after-school classes, all students are able to design programs that suit their needs and will help them realize their goals.

Arts: Across all three divisions, Flint Hill offers visual arts, dance, music, and drama. Nominations and awards include district and state wins. The program uses technology to enhance the learning and application of art, from transitional kindergarten through twelfth grade. In the upper school, students choose from a wide range of offerings including digital art, studio art, ceramics, theater, and 3D animation.

Athletics: The athletic program starts in seventh grade, where every student has the opportunity to choose a team to play on during each season, no matter their particular strengths. This allows for exploration and experimentation, and except for ice hockey and golf, all the upper school offerings are represented in the middle school. In the upper school, Flint Hill is part of the Independent School League and the Mid-Atlantic Athletic Conference. Offerings include cross-country, dance, football, golf, soccer, tennis, volleyball, baseball, basketball, ice hockey, swimming, lacrosse, softball, and track.

Student Life: Students at Flint Hill have the opportunity to develop their leadership skills in all three divisions of the school. Lower school students serve as walkers and lead Town Meeting, middle school students attend leadership conferences and participate in the Student Council, and upper school students can participate in 30 different clubs including the Student Honor Council and Peer Leaders program, among others.

Campus: Flint Hill's two campuses span over 45 acres of land in Oakton, Virginia. The school is home to art, dance, and music studios, two gyms, eight tennis courts, track and athletics fields, computer and science labs, as well as a learning center. Flint Hill recently renovated its 300-seat Olsen Theater, installed a turf field, and made upgrades to its technology infrastructure.

Learning Support: The school is a leader in terms of working with students with learning differences. The learning center employs 13 specialists and 25% of the student body uses some aspect of the learning center. Students are considered for learning support during the admissions process. To be selected, a student must be diagnosed with a learning difference, with testing done in the past three years. Outside of the learning center, all upper school faculty are available from 2:30 - 3:30

every day to meet with students either one-on-one or in groups. This time takes place before afternoon activities begin and is used by the entire student and faculty body.

Schools Attended by Most Graduates in the Past Five Years: Virginia Tech, University of Virginia, James Madison University, The College of William and Mary, University of Colorado at Boulder

Takeaways: Flint Hill is a leader in educating through the use of technology, issuing an iPad or MacBook Air for every student and integrating it into the curriculum beginning in transitional kindergarten. One thing that stands out is Flint Hill's commitment to differentiation. For students who are advanced and looking to take on a heavy course load, they are able to do so with the school's variety of offerings including AP, online, and various non-traditional courses. For students who may need learning assistance, Flint Hill has learning specialists and a nationally recognized program of achievement. Due to its ability to individualize a student's educational experience, the school has a very diverse population.

Foxcroft School

22407 Foxhound Lane, P. O. Box 5555, Middleburg, VA 20118
540.687.5555 | www.foxcroft.org

"Foxcroft provides a residential learning experience for girls in which academic excellence, leadership, responsibility, and integrity are our highest values."

Grades 9 – 12 and Post Graduate | All Girls | Boarding Option
No Religious Affiliation

Enrollment: 165 (70% boarding) | **Average Class Size:** 12
Admissions and Testing: Deadline February 1, then rolling admission; SSAT, and TOEFL if applicable
Tuition and Financial Aid: $49,400 (Boarding), $41,580 (Day); $1.5 million was available in financial aid in 2012 and 30% of students receive financial assistance; uses SSS form.

Curriculum: Foxcroft offers young women a traditional college preparatory program with 17 AP classes. Its program focuses on developing critical-thinking skills, writing, and a liberal arts foundation. Foxcroft's Exceptional Proficiency program enables students to study away from the campus, working on a personal goal or dream, while still keeping up with their class work through online coursework. The school states that girls have taken advantage of this program while training for the Olympics, hiking across South America, or even traveling to Hollywood to take acting classes. In addition, the school has a strong STEM program that allows student teams to provide engineering solutions for local nonprofits.

Arts: Students participate in visual or performing arts ranging from pottery to musical theater. The school hosts two major productions yearly, with past performances including a student-scripted theatrical version of *Mean Girls*, *Chicago*, and *Foxcroft Goes Glee!* Digital Graphic Design and Publishing, Drawing and Design, Voice and Instrumental Lessons, and Theatre Audition Workshop are some of the most popular courses offered.

Athletics: Foxcroft is a member of both the Delaney Athletic Conference and the Independent School League. Each student is required to participate in a structured physical activity each year. Foxcroft offers cross-country, field hockey, tennis, volleyball, basketball, lacrosse, soccer, and softball. Rock climbing, yoga, dance, and dance troupe are also available as physical education options. The school is well known for its equestrian program, which features hunters, jumpers, eventing, and dressage. Lessons are offered at every level from beginner to advanced competition. The facilities include a 60-stall stable, a large outdoor arena, and miles of outdoor trails.

Student Life: Seventy percent of students are boarding students. Students who choose to live in the dorms are cared for by a Housemother and eventually are given the opportunity to become Dean's Prefects. Housemothers are responsible for being in contact with teachers, the Office of Student Life, advisors, the health center, and parents.

Campus: Foxcroft sits on a 500-acre campus north of Middleburg, Virginia. The campus includes numerous athletic fields, tennis courts, a swimming pool, and an athletic/student center. The main building also includes two general computer labs, a language lab, classrooms, and the Goodyear Room, an attractive lounge for meetings.

Learning Support: Foxcroft students have access to a learning center as well as a writing and math center. Learning support and accommodations are determined during the admissions process and reevaluated periodically.

Schools Attended by Most Graduates in the Past Five Years: University of Virginia, Virginia Tech, The College of William and Mary, Sewanee: The University of the South, James Madison University

Takeaways: While Foxcroft does place a lot of value in tradition, from its curriculum to its equestrian program, the school is receptive to new innovative ways to improve learning. An example of this is the STEM and Exceptional Proficiency programs. Started in 1991, the Exceptional Proficiency program has allowed young women to pursue their individual talents and interests while still receiving a strong education. With close to 70% of students choosing to board at the school, there are a number of on-campus activities available. The school hosts weekend trips such as whitewater rafting, visiting Kings Dominion Amusement Park, ski trips to Wintergreen, laser tag, attending college sporting games, and social activities with Woodberry Forest. Foxcroft may be worth considering if you are looking for an all-girls school with a boarding option, a respected STEM program, and a well-regarded equestrian program.

Gesher Jewish Day School

4800 Mattie Moore Court, Fairfax, VA 22030
703.978.9789 | www.gesher-jds.org

"At Gesher Jewish Day School we inspire our students to be passionate about learning, practice justice, kindness, and respect, and aspire to a life guided by Jewish values, Torah, and community."

Grades K – 8 | Co-Ed
Jewish

Enrollment: 163 | **Average Class Size:** 15
Admissions and Testing: Deadline January 31; requires in-house kindergarten readiness screening, and may request additional external educational testing for K-8
Tuition and Financial Aid: $18,025 (K-8); 40% of students receive financial aid.

Curriculum: Gesher offers students a challenging dual curriculum of Jewish and general studies. Beginning in kindergarten, approximately 60% of class time is dedicated to general studies, and 40% is dedicated to Judaic studies and Hebrew.

The kindergarten program uses a phonics-based reading approach and students begin learning Hebrew immediately. In elementary school, the Hebrew language and Judaic studies continue alongside secular subjects (language arts, math, science and social studies). Students take weekly classes in art, music, library, physical education, and computers outside of their homeroom class. Science is taught by science specialists in the lab. The middle school program at Gesher includes advisory groups, community service, and numerous elective options. Jewish history and Israel studies courses provide the context for a capstone experience in Israel prior to graduation. All students leave Gesher with high school credit for Spanish I, Algebra I, and occasionally Geometry.

Arts: Students take one class a week in art and music. The art program at Gesher combines a study of artistic techniques as well as art history. The school produces a Chanukah musical program and an all-school talent show annually. There are opportunities to join choral and instrumental ensembles after school.

Athletics: Gesher is a member of the ABC Athletic League of Greater Washington. Gesher offers basketball, soccer, fencing, mountain biking, softball, and cross-country. The program is not mandatory.

Student Life: Every eighth grader has the opportunity to go to Israel for two weeks. A Head, Heart, and Hands program in every grade connects students to their wider community with organized hands-on community service projects to benefit a number of local and international causes.

Campus: Gesher's new campus is situated on 57 acres and includes a butterfly meadow, soccer fields, a playground, bluebird sanctuaries, an art technology center, and a science center. The school is in the second phase of its expansion to accommodate over 500 students.

Learning Support: Gesher is able to provide specialized reading help through the reading specialist on staff and numerous reading incentive opportunities through its active library programs. Gesher can accommodate some learners with IEPs and will make appropriate accommodations for learners with special needs that access the general curriculum. Study skills classes and after-school support are available.

Schools Attended by Most Graduates in the Past Five Years: Thomas Jefferson High School for Science and Technology, Charles E. Smith Jewish Day School, American Hebrew Academy, The Field School, Commonwealth Academy

Takeaways: Small classes allow students to receive a significant amount of individualized attention. Gesher provides a thorough Judaic education that focuses on the Hebrew language and Jewish history. It's important to note that students at Gesher take nine or ten classes at 40 minutes each. For a student who is prepared and a family that is looking for a dual curricular focus in general and Judaic studies, Gesher can be a great fit.

Green Hedges School

415 Windover Avenue NW, Vienna, VA 22180
703.938.8323 | www.greenhedges.org

"We inspire young people of talent and promise to develop clear values, a desire for wisdom, and an appreciation for all endeavors which broaden the mind and enlighten the spirit."

Preschool – Grade 8 | Co-Ed
No Religious Affiliation

Enrollment: 170 | **Average Class Size:** 15
Admissions and Testing: Deadline February 15; WISC-IV, WISC-IV Integrated, or WPPS I-III (1-8)
Tuition and Financial Aid: $14,230 (3- and 4-year-olds, half day), $24,725 (Montessori full day through grade 3), $24,915 (4-5), $25,435 (6-8); the financial aid budget is 15% of tuition revenue; 20% of the student body receives aid; uses FAST.

Curriculum: The preschool and kindergarten programs (ages 3-5) adopt the Montessori philosophy. Montessori classrooms are comprised of multi-age groups and include a variety of kinesthetic activities. French and an assortment of art, library, and physical education classes are incorporated in the curriculum. The first grade curriculum is distinguished by a unique transitional program, which bridges communal Montessori learning with individual learning as in a traditional classroom structure. First through third grade utilize two full-time teachers in each classroom. The curriculum includes instruction in the core subjects of language arts, math, social studies, and science, with foreign language, art, library, and physical education also embedded within the program. Technology (MacBooks and iPads) is utilized throughout the curriculum.

Middle school (sixth through eighth grade) is departmentalized, with teachers who are experts in their fields. Core subjects, foreign languages (Latin plus French or Spanish), and an assortment of art, library, and physical education are augmented by opportunities for leadership. Students are prepared for the challenges of secondary school and beyond through guidance in developing study habits, sound study skills, independence, self-reliance, and a sense of responsibility. Technology (MacBooks and iPads) is an integral component of the middle school curriculum.

Arts: The arts are built into the curriculum from preschool through eighth grade, including requirements in performing arts, studio art, digital art, band, and music.

Athletics: Competitive athletic teams (soccer, cross-country, basketball, tennis) are offered for middle school students through the ABC Athletic League of Greater Washington. After-school athletic electives include yoga, dance, soccer, and running. Participation is voluntary and extracurricular fees may apply.

Student Life: Green Hedges offers after-school activities that last ten weeks. These activities include Club Yoga, Chess Club, and Weebotics (a robotics club).

Campus: Green Hedges is a neighborhood school located in Vienna, Virginia. The four-acre campus consists of four buildings and two playing fields.

Learning Support: Green Hedges does not consider itself to be a school equipped for students with severe learning or behavioral disabilities.

Schools Attended by Most Graduates in the Past Five Years:
No matriculation information is available.

Takeaways: Green Hedges is known for its multi-age Montessori program for preschool and kindergarten students. The school has a number of field trips that are built into the program and created to supplement education. Though Green Hedges is most known for its primary programs, students who stay at Green Hedges for all 11 years receive a significant amount of personalized time with teachers. The student-teacher ratio in most grade levels is low. Green Hedges is a good option for families looking for a small, nurturing school with a strong academic program.

The GW Community School

9001 Braddock Road, Suite 111, Springfield, VA 22151
703.978.7208 | www.gwcommunityschool.com

"The GW Community School embraces as its mission the development and implementation of a holistic educational program that will develop and optimize the giftedness and intelligence of each student in an in-depth, enriched, and technically advanced college preparatory environment that emphasizes authentic application of knowledge, not merely assimilation of information. Students will experience academic success and the development of social awareness and responsibility in an atmosphere where all are treated with respect and courtesy. The GW Community School recognizes the unique contribution of parents, students, and community members striving for unity of purpose."

Grades 9 – 12 | Co-Ed
No Religious Affiliation

Enrollment: 58 | **Average Class Size:** 8
Admissions and Testing: Rolling admission; interview required
Tuition and Financial Aid: $21,900 (9-12); financial aid available.

Curriculum: The GW Community School (GWCS) offers a college prep curriculum designed to equip students with the skills they will need to succeed at the university level and beyond. Core subjects include science, math, English, history, and foreign language (French or Spanish). Some AP and honors classes are available. Students choose from electives that include basketball, personal fitness, robotics, student publications, and studio art. Flexible instructional options, including independent study, online courses, and cross-enrollment at Northern Virginia Community College, are offered. Teachers lead small classes using interactive approaches and open discussion. Teachers also have a considerable amount of flexibility in molding the curriculum and, as a result, unique classes such as Conspiracy Theories, Political Geography, and Sea Adventures are offered.

Arts: Students can take a course in studio art and theater. The theater program aims to improve students' performance skills, build confidence, and instill the value of teamwork.

Athletics: GWCS competes against schools in the Independent Small Schools Athletic Conference, the Potomac Valley Athletic Conference, and the Maryland Independent School Athletic League. Basketball is offered as a competitive after-school activity.

Student Life: Students at GWCS have the opportunity to learn outside the classroom through internships, college cross-registration, school trips, and community service. Opportunities include the student government, recording studio class, and the annual cardboard boat regatta.

Campus: The school's current facilities are modest due to the school's small size. The school is located in an outfitted office building suite. After-school activities are held at nearby public locations such as the Audrey Moore Recreation Center and King's Park.

Learning Support: Learning assistance is provided on an individualized basis. A period is provided at the end of each day during which students meet with teachers for extra help.

Schools Attended by Most Graduates in the Past Five Years: Virginia Commonwealth University, George Mason University, Goucher College, Longwood University, James Madison University

Takeaways: GWCS is owned and operated by educators who sought to establish a school to better serve a specific population of bright, non-traditional learners. Each student meets with his or her faculty advisor for 20 minutes each day to discuss progress and goals. All students are issued laptops for use at school and at home. Every week parents are emailed a report that details their student's progress as well as their current grades. Many GWCS students struggled in more traditional school environments. GWCS functions as a vehicle for students to become more independent and accountable in a less pressured environment, as the homework load is light.

Highland School

597 Broadview Avenue, Warrenton, VA 20186
540.878.2700 | www.highlandschool.org

"The mission of Highland School is to provide a demanding academic and co-curricular program that develops the skills and character essential for students to meet the challenges of college and leadership in the twenty-first century. To carry out this mission, Highland School has assembled thoroughly modern facilities, a large, diverse, and highly qualified staff, a student body ready to meet the challenges, and an academic philosophy and strategy that makes maximum use of these resources."

Preschool – Grade 12 | Co-Ed
No Religious Affiliation

Enrollment: 460 | **Average Class Size:** 11
Admissions and Testing: Deadline January 30, then rolling admission until April 5; Gesell (Preschool-K), STAR testing (1-5), SSAT (6-12)
Tuition and Financial Aid: $8,590 (Preschool), $12,835 (K), $17,390 (1-2), $19,045 (3-4), $19,770 (5-8), $22,670 (9-12); $1.4 million financial aid budget serves 36% of the student body with an average grant of $9,000.

Curriculum: Within Highland's lower school, students are placed in ability-based groups that change throughout the year based on academic growth. Phonemic awareness is introduced in preschool and continues to be a focus through fourth grade. Students start visiting the science lab weekly in first grade and use technology-based math programs beginning in third grade. Teachers use inquiry-based learning strategies in social studies starting in third grade.

Highland's commitment to "teaching for the 21st century" continues into the middle school. Students begin the day either in homeroom (fifth and sixth grade) or meeting with their advisor (seventh and eighth grade). Beginning in fifth grade, students take classes in the core subjects as well as PE, computer instruction, wellness, library, and science lab. The upper school requires all students to partake in different types of experiential, hands-on learning. Outside of typical science and technology classes,

Highland gives students the opportunity to take Game Development, 3D Architecture 1 and 2, Intro to Programming, Marine Biology, and Robotics, among others. Students leave Highland having completed multiple field studies, a junior internship, a senior project, and a number of community service projects. Students have the option to choose between Latin (seventh through twelfth grade), Spanish (preschool through twelfth grade), and French (eighth through twelfth grade).

Arts: Highland offers guitar classes, jazz band, Advanced Sculpture, Music Theory, 2D Art and Design, 3D Art, Ceramics, Filmmaking, Theater Tech, and acting classes. Highland's art facilities include the 355-seat Rice Theater, a 60-seat black box theater, an art gallery, 2D and 3D art rooms, a music/film tech lab, music rooms, and a theater workshop.

Athletics: Highland is a member of both the Delaney Athletic Conference and the Piedmont Athletic Conference. Highland boasts 138 conference championships and nine state championships. Eighty percent of the student population participates in athletics. There are 20 varsity, four junior varsity, and 19 middle school teams. Highland offers baseball, basketball, cheerleading, cross-country, dance, field hockey, golf, lacrosse, soccer, softball, swimming, tennis, and volleyball.

Student Life: International Week is held annually every February and the school selects a different nation every year. Throughout the week students have access to several presentations, programs, performances, and even Skype sessions that help to enhance their global perspective. The highlight of 2013's International Week was a speech given by author Padma Venkatraman (*Climbing the Stairs*, *Island's End*) on her experience growing up in India and relocating to the United States.

Campus: Highland sits on a 42-acre campus with a complex of approximately 183,300 square feet in Warrenton, Virginia. Highland is less than one hour from both Shenandoah National Park and Washington, DC. Highland's facilities include two gymnasiums, a 355-seat theater, a black box theater, and an art gallery.

Learning Support: Highland's learning center is equipped to work with students who have diverse learning needs and styles. Learning support at Highland is broken down into divisions that correspond with the individual schools (upper, middle, and lower), with each division having different goals appropriate to students' developmental levels.

Schools Attended by Most Graduates in the Past Five Years:
No matriculation information is available.

Takeaways: Students at Highland can participate in a number of service learning, leadership and character development, and college prep options. Highland has a fully-equipped learning center that strives to work with all students, regardless of their learning style. Additionally, the science and technology programs provide significant opportunities for students in these areas. The school can be a match for those who have a penchant for technology and enjoy hands-on learning.

The Hill School

130 South Madison Street, P. O. Box 65, Middleburg, VA 20118
540.687.5897 | www.thehillschool.org

"The goal of a Hill School education is to build character, self-confidence, and scholarship through academic and co-curricular excellence, individualized attention, and a strong sense of community."

Junior Kindergarten – Grade 8 | Co-Ed
No Religious Affiliation

Enrollment: 224 | **Average Class Size:** 12
Admissions and Testing: Deadline February 1, then rolling admission; In-house testing
Tuition and Financial Aid: $9,500 (JK), $16,600 (Kindergarten), $21,800 (1-8); financial aid budget over $700,000 serves about 25% of the student body.

Curriculum: The academic program at The Hill School challenges students at their level of developmental readiness. In language arts, all students read independently and write frequently to master writing skills and develop a voice. In social studies, students explore Middleburg's place and culture and then branch out to a variety of times and places, all while learning geography, note-taking, test preparation, and how to work with textbooks and original sources. The math curriculum focuses on problem solving in small groups, and in science, students conduct labs, observe behavior and life forms, and actively explore nature. Spanish instruction is introduced in the lower grades. In the upper school, Latin is added and most students graduate with credit in Latin.

Arts: The Hill School places a heavy emphasis on the arts. Students are required to take studio art every year and most grades have some type of annual dramatic performance. Students work with metal, clay, and wood to develop their artistic skills. The music program introduces students to singing, musical games, music appreciation, and instruments.

Athletics: The Hill School requires interscholastic competition in field hockey, soccer, cross-country, basketball, and lacrosse. Students also participate in intramural competitions in gymnastics and track and field.

Student Life: The mentoring program pairs all middle school students with a student in kindergarten through third grade. The pairs meet weekly to build their relationship. Another unique program is Team and Teen Saturday for eighth graders. The program is designed to include all eighth-grade students who participate as junior faculty on the last three Saturdays of the school year and help provide the staff with feedback on the academic program. The student publications *Calliope* and *Curves, Angles, Dots* allow children to write for the larger school community.

Campus: The 137-acre Middleburg, Virginia, campus includes athletic fields, an amphitheater, walking and running trails, an arboretum, a science center, ponds and wetlands, and academic facilities separated by small courtyards connected by a central brick walkway.

Learning Support: In the lower grades, homeroom teachers coordinate with the reading specialist and other support personnel so that students receive support both individually and in small groups. In the upper school, Academic Support is a separate class in which students learn study skills while working on core academic classes. In addition, many teachers at Hill tutor students and work with them daily to help with organization or specific assignments. Academic support teachers meet weekly to monitor student progress and make adjustments as necessary.

Schools Attended by Most Graduates in the Past Five Years:
No matriculation information is available.

Takeaways: There are a number of noteworthy aspects to The Hill School, from classroom differentiation to a strong sense of community. The arts program also provides numerous opportunities for creative expression for all students. The school can be a good option for many families, particularly those who may have multiple students working at different ability levels, but who are looking for one central school.

The Howard Gardner School

4913 Franconia Road, Alexandria, VA 22310
703.822.9300 | www.thehowardgardnerschool.org

The school's mission is "to help bright, creative non-traditional learners use their unique strengths to thrive academically, intellectually, and emotionally."

Grades 6 – 12 | Co-Ed
No Religious Affiliation

Enrollment: 48 | **Average Class Size:** 14
Admissions and Testing: February 15, then rolling admission; testing can vary, and different tests are acceptable
Tuition and Financial Aid: $19,950 (6-8), $22,450 (9-12); 40% of the students receive financial aid from the financial aid budget of more than $120,000.

Curriculum: The curriculum at Howard Gardner School (HGS) is progressive and unique. Aside from the core classes, the curriculum heavily stresses environmental studies and the arts. HGS is one of only 40 schools in Virginia to be recognized by Virginia Naturally for excellence in environmental curriculum. Science offerings include Ecology, Environmental Studies and Policy, Zoology and Evolution, and Microbiology and Genetics. Upper school students may take Spanish, Latin, or Russian, while middle school students receive Spanish instruction twice per week. Students can also choose from unique elective offerings such as Engine Repair, Gardening, and Alternative Energy. The school intends to prepare students for college; instruction is active and hands-on, and teachers use multi-sensory methods. Many assignments are completed in groups. Accelerated students can move more quickly through the curriculum and take college courses through distance learning when appropriate. No AP classes are offered.

Arts: Art classes are offered as electives that students take for eight-week sessions. Classes include Painting, Drawing, Studio Art, Graphic Design, Filmmaking, Music Recording, and others upon request.

Athletics: Two physical education credits are required for graduation. Students can fulfill this requirement by participating in rock-climbing, basketball, bowling, skateboarding, golf, dance, or other activities that may be offered. There is no competitive interscholastic sports program.

Student Life: HGS incorporates weekly "field studies" into its program. These field studies include day trips, overnight camping trips, workshops, and an internship program. A few examples of these outside-the-classroom experiences include trips to Jamestown and Williamsburg and to local wetlands to learn about water testing. Upper school students are required to hold internships at which they work at least once per week. HGS works to help students secure internships related to their personal interests.

Campus: HGS uses an old farmhouse to house its administration's facilities. A new 5,000-square-foot classroom building was recently completed, which includes seven high school classrooms and a large, configurable middle school classroom. A scenic on-site pond serves as an outdoor "lab" for the school's ecology program.

Learning Support: One learning specialist is on staff to help students with learning challenges. HGS is not set up to support students with learning disabilities.

Schools Attended by Most Graduates in the Past Five Years: Virginia Commonwealth University, McDaniel College, Guilford College, Hampshire College, Earlham College

Takeaways: HGS is small and non-traditional, and many of the teachers have been with the school since its inception in 2004. The school environment is very student-driven and encourages hands-on activities and multi-sensory teaching methods. Each Wednesday alternates between a field study and a group community service event. Another interesting aspect of the school is that the school day begins at 10 a.m. The middle school was recently established in 2012, and the number of students is very small—12 students are currently enrolled in sixth through eighth grade.

If your child needs a non-traditional, close-knit setting that focuses on the environment, The Howard Garner School may be a match for you.

The Langley School

1411 Balls Hill Road, McLean, VA 22101
703.356.1920 | www.langleyschool.org

"We believe that each child's potential is boundless and every child can act with integrity, generosity, and consideration for others. We reach across multiple disciplines to discover, amplify, and embrace the talents of every child, every day. By nurturing, supporting, and academically challenging our students, our inclusive community builds quietly confident, independent thinkers who flourish as learners and individuals."

Preschool – Grade 8 | Co-Ed
No Religious Affiliation

Enrollment: 500
Admissions and Testing: Deadline Mid-January; WPPSI-III / WISC-IV (JK-5), SSAT (6-8)
Tuition and Financial Aid: $15,090 (Preschool), $20,280 (JK), $29,420 (K-5), $30,730 (6-8); about 13% of students receive aid from a budget over $1 million; financial aid applications are processed using SSS by NAIS.

Curriculum: The Langley School's curriculum is child centered, meaning that students can expect hands-on learning and individualized attention. Spanish is introduced in preschool. Spanish instruction continues to be a daily activity until sixth grade, when students can choose to either continue with Spanish or switch to Mandarin Chinese.

Instruction is differentiated within the homeroom for grades one through five. Beginning in sixth grade, subjects are taught by specialists and students assume the middle-school model by moving from class to class. All children in kindergarten through third grade have iPads in the classroom, students in fourth through fifth grade have laptop carts in the classroom, and students in sixth through eighth grade each have their own iPad. In addition, students begin working with a science specialist in lab in first grade. Langley's teachers attempt to inspire every student to experiment, share, problem solve, create, perform, and think in innovative ways.

Arts: In addition to participating in music classes beginning in preschool, all students learn to play an instrument in the school band program in fourth and fifth grade. Formal drama instruction by a specialist begins in fourth grade, while formal art instruction begins in kindergarten. Middle school students may take part in band, choral, and strings groups, as well as two main-stage dramatic productions.

Athletics: Langley is a founding member of the Capital Athletic Conference. It offers competitive team sports in soccer, cross-country, basketball, lacrosse, baseball, softball, and volleyball for fifth through eighth graders. Co-ed tennis is also available. Students may participate in an annual track and field meet. Participation in interscholastic team sports is not mandatory.

Student Life: The Langley School puts a high value on community. The school hosts annual community events, such as the Fall Fair every October and Field Day each May. Community service is important, and students take part in large, wide-ranging service projects, such as collecting non-perishables for the needy or working with younger students at local public schools.

Campus: The Langley School is located on a nine-acre campus in McLean, Virginia. The school's facilities include an artificial turf athletic field, an arts center featuring a multi-purpose auditorium, a 20,000-volume library, science and computer labs, a creative media studio featuring green-screen technology, and a 23,350-square-foot athletic center with two gyms. The school has plans to open a new middle school building during the 2013-14 school year.

Learning Support: The school does not have a learning center, though it does have a counselor and learning specialists who work in partnership with classroom teachers to help students as needed.

Schools Attended by Most Graduates in the Past Five Years: The Madeira School, Flint Hill School, Georgetown Day School, Bullis School, The Potomac School

Takeaways: The Langley School strikes a balance between progressive and traditional instruction. The school offers students an enriched and challenging curriculum, producing students in eighth grade who are ready for the rigors of high school in the metro DC area. One of

Langley's most valued and unique services is the guidance it provides to eighth grade students and their families during the high school selection process. The school integrates an SSAT prep course and mock interviews into the eighth grade curriculum to prepare students for the application process. Additionally, with the inclusion of foreign language starting in preschool, many students leave Langley with several high school credits already under their belt.

Langley is a good fit for a student and family looking for continuity and rigor from an early age through middle school, combined with a support staff committed to maximizing the potential of each student.

Loudoun Country Day School

20600 Red Cedar Drive, Leesburg, VA 20175
703.777.3841 | www.lcds.org

"Loudoun Country Day School (LCDS), an accredited, independent, co-educational private school, educates students in preschool through eighth grade. We cultivate the intellectual, social, emotional, and physical growth of each child. We pride ourselves on our rigorous core curriculum, nurturing environment, and extensive programs in foreign languages, arts, technology, and athletics. LCDS inspires excellence and builds character, preparing each child for the challenges ahead."

Preschool – Grade 8 | Co-Ed
No Religious Affiliation

Enrollment: 311 | **Average Class Size:** 16
Admissions and Testing: Rolling admission; Dial Developmental Screen Assessment (Preschool), WPPSI-III (K), WISC-IV (1-8), other in-house testing required
Tuition and Financial Aid: $12,800 (Preschool), $21,350 (K-8); financial aid and SMART payment program available.

Curriculum: LCDS has a long tradition of using a blended approach of traditional and progressive instructional methodologies to engage its students. In addition to the core disciplines of language arts/English, math, science, and social studies/history, LCDS offers programs in foreign languages, technology, art, music, library, and physical education/athletics. The school strives to develop well-rounded students through its comprehensive program.

Arts: Art offerings at LCDS include visual, performing, and musical arts. In preschool and kindergarten, art instruction takes place in the homerooms throughout the year. Students create several works of art, modeled after the styles of highly accomplished artists. Art instruction with the art teacher begins in first grade and continues through eighth grade. Vocal music instruction begins in preschool and continues through eighth grade. When students reach the fourth grade, they have the option of continuing in vocal music or moving to either band or orchestra.

Athletics: In preschool through fifth grade, students participate in an active movement and physical skills development program through physical education classes two to three times per week. In fourth and fifth grades, students compete in exhibition games in soccer and basketball. In the middle school, students partake in a comprehensive athletics program, including competing against other schools in field hockey, soccer, basketball, lacrosse, and tennis. LCDS also has an intramural program of various activities (wall climbing and volleyball, to name two examples) for those students who prefer not to play on a team sport. LCSD is a member of the Piedmont Athletic Conference.

Student Life: LCDS has an active Student Council that strives to strengthen community spirit. Students lead a number of community service and social activities for the student body through the year. Fourth through eighth grade students are eligible to serve on the Student Council as representatives, and sixth through eighth grade students are eligible to serve as officers. LCDS offers a number of after-school programs. Lab Rats, Lego Robotics, SSAT prep, mock trial, swim team, chess, and drama are among the activities that have been offered in recent years.

Campus: The 69-acre campus has a media center, a gym, and two computer labs. The lower and middle schools share the same building, but are separated within the building. Each classroom is fitted with interactive whiteboards, projectors, and computers.

Learning Support: Two resource teachers in the lower school serve students who need mild remediation and enrichment. This makes it possible for the school to meet the needs of those who need additional support, particularly in reading and math.

Schools Attended by Most Graduates in the Past Five Years:
No matriculation information is available.

Takeaways: LCDS prides itself on providing a broad and challenging academic program as well as a comprehensive art and athletics program. The school strives to develop critical and creative-thinking skills in its students. Graduating classes frequently include students who go on to attend the Thomas Jefferson School of Science and Technology and the Loudoun Academy of Science. LCDS is a good fit for families located in Loudoun County that are looking for a nurturing yet challenging environment.

Loudoun School for the Gifted

44675 Cape Court, Unit 105, Beaumeade
Technology Campus, Ashburn, VA 20147
703.956.5020 | www.loudoungifted.org

"We are here to offer you a truly educational, challenging, enjoyable, and inspiring school experience so you pursue every opportunity to read and learn deeply and broadly, think honestly, creatively, and critically, and work with optimism and grit to solve complex and meaningful problems."

Grades 6 – 12 | Co-Ed
No Religious Affiliation

Enrollment: 38 | **Average Class Size:** 5-7
Admissions and Testing: Deadline March 1; testing is flexible—will take SSAT, PSAT, or SAT scores, if available
Tuition and Financial Aid: $18,550 (6-8), $20,750 (9-12); no traditional financial aid available.

Curriculum: Classes at Loudoun School for the Gifted (LSG) are discussion-based and non-traditional. They are designed to allow students to pursue their passions and receive individualized help. Students are "colleagues" to their teachers and the atmosphere is casual. LSG is known for its math and science programs, but the humanities are strong as well. Six AP classes are offered. Students can take a wide variety of in-depth college-type courses. Global Financial Economics, Comedic Literature, Optics, Website Design, and Military Conflict in Central Asia are just a few of the unique course offerings. Language offerings include Latin, French, German, and Chinese.

Arts: Students at LSG have the opportunity to take classes in architecture, classical drawing, musical theater, ensemble, and improvisation.

Athletics: LSG offers water polo, jiu-jitsu, yoga, tennis, golf, cross-country, cycling, soccer, ultimate frisbee, and kickboxing as part of its physical education program. Participation is not mandatory, but the school considers it part of a complete education. The program is not competitive and is meant to encourage individual fitness and self-discipline.

Student Life: There is a strong emphasis on experiential learning and students take two to four field trips each month to locations such as Antietam, the National Institutes of Health, the National Weather Service, the West Wing of the White House, and the *Washington Post* production facility. Many students also take one international trip a year to Italy, France, or the UK.

Campus: The main building is brand new and very modern, with most walls made of glass. In the classroom, tables are located in the middle of the room to facilitate discussion-based classes.

Learning Support: LSG caters to gifted students and is not a good fit for students who need accommodation or a great deal of structure.

Schools Attended by Most Graduates in the Past Five Years: University of Virginia, University of California—Berkeley, University of Massachusetts—Amherst, Case Western University, Virginia Tech

Takeaways: Founded by Dr. Deep Sran in 2008, The Ideal School added grades six through eight in 2012 and was renamed Loudoun School for the Gifted to reflect the school's focus and academic program. Classes are very small, with five to seven students per class, and students are given autonomy to drive their own learning. LSG is a good fit for accelerated students who have strong, specific academic interests and require individualized challenges that they may not receive at more mainstream schools.

The Madeira School

8328 Georgetown Pike, McLean, VA 22102
703.556.8200 | www.madeira.org

"Launching women who change the world."

Grades 9 – 12 | All Girls | Boarding Option
No Religious Affiliation

Enrollment: 321 (54% boarding) | **Average Class Size:** 12
Admissions and Testing: Deadline January 31; SSAT required
Tuition and Financial Aid: \$50,437 (Boarding), \$38,297 (Day); financial aid budget over \$2 million serves 21% of the students, with an average grant of \$35,000; uses SSS form.

Curriculum: Students at Madeira receive a rigorous and traditional education. Every girl has a tailored four-year graduation plan unique to her individual interests. Junior and senior classes begin to model college courses, meaning that students regularly receive assignments with long-term due dates. Madeira students have the opportunity to select from a wide variety of courses including Comparative Ethics, Multivariable Calculus, Biotechnology, and even iPad App Development. The school offers 19 AP classes, with 91.3% of students earning a 3 (out of 5) or higher on the AP tests.

A signature of Madeira is the co-curriculum program. All Madeira girls are in internship activities all day, every Wednesday. Freshmen study topics such as public speaking, financial literacy, diversity, and study skills. Sophomores work in collaborative groups at several community service organizations. All juniors are in internships in the office of a U.S. legislator for the full year. Each senior develops her own leadership internship that matches her interests.

Arts: Visual and performing arts learning opportunities are available to all students. The film program instructs girls to plan, write, film, and edit short films, including many documentaries featured on the school's website and entered into the Annual Madeira Film Festival. The school has strong visual, fine, and performing arts departments.

Athletics: Madeira belongs to the Independent School League and also competes in the Interscholastic Equestrian Association (IEA). Madeira offers cross-country, field hockey, soccer, volleyball, tennis, basketball, squash, swimming, diving, softball, and track and field. Pilates and karate are also available. All girls must complete 12 athletic activity credits, eight of which must be through team sports, riding, aquatic sports, or dance and fitness classes. Students must also pass a water safety physical test to graduate.

Student Life: The school includes students from 24 countries and 20 states. Many boarding students are attracted to the school because of its close proximity to Washington, DC and the opportunities and activities the school presents locally and globally through the co-curriculum.

Campus: Madeira is located 15 minutes from Washington, DC on a 376-acre campus in McLean, VA. The campus encompasses a large student center, classroom buildings, art and dance studios, dormitories, faculty housing, athletic fields, riding trails, a natural pond, and a full ropes challenge course. Indoor athletic facilities include a competition swimming pool, horse stables, and an all-season equestrian ring.

Learning Support: Madeira has a full-time learning specialist on staff who oversees The Skills Center. The center helps students to develop foundational study skills such as time management, test-taking strategies, and prioritizing. Madeira is not equipped to work with students with significant learning disabilities.

Schools Attended by Most Graduates in the Past Five Years: The College of William and Mary, University of Virginia, Syracuse University, George Washington University, Carnegie Mellon University

Takeaways: Madeira not only provides students with a rigorous education, but also gives real-world experience through its award-winning experiential learning program. This program consists of four co-curriculums that provide students with internship opportunities similar to those offered at the college level. Though the curriculum is challenging, the faculty is available to help girls succeed. Additionally, the athletics and arts programs are extensive and provide a variety of opportunities for young women to express themselves, both competitively and creatively. For a girl to succeed at Madeira, it's important that she is able to manage her time and organize herself to get her work completed in a timely manner. For a self-starter who values unique internship experiences, Madeira will provide an excellent education.

Merritt Academy

9211 Arlington Boulevard, Fairfax, VA 22031
703.273.8000 | www.merrittacademy.org

"Our school is built upon three pillars: Academic Excellence—we provide a challenging academic program to all our students; Character Education—we emphasize Christian-based values throughout our school to help build character in all our students; Service to Families—we are committed to serving our families, earning their trust by being responsive, flexible, and supportive."

Infant – Grade 6 | Co-Ed
Christian | Independent | Non-Denominational

Enrollment: 400 | **Average Class Size:** 13
Admissions and Testing: Rolling admissions; no testing required
Tuition and Financial Aid: $17,424 (Preschool), $19,000 (K-6); no financial aid available.

Curriculum: Students in Merritt's preschool participate in daily art projects, language development, writing exercises, imaginative play, and cognitive explorations in a small-group setting. Merritt strives to develop student independence, decision making, self-advocacy, and problem-solving skills. Aside from the core focus on developing foundational academic skills, students take classes in library, physical education, computers, music, and French or Spanish.

The Merritt elementary school curriculum is fairly traditional with its inclusion of core classes and specialty classes such as PE, French, Spanish, art, and music. The incorporation of STEM principles is a big component of a Merritt education.

Arts: The arts program at Merritt is similar to the Fairfax County Public Schools model in that students have art class once or twice per week and are introduced to various media and cultures. The emphasis at Merritt is on technology and students are given opportunities to learn design programs and multi-media skills.

Athletics: Merritt is a member of the ABC Athletic League of Greater Washington. The three competitive teams are soccer, basketball, and softball. Students may join other noncompetitive sports through the school such as Girls on the Run, ballet, cheerleading, martial arts, and tennis. The athletic program is not mandatory.

Student Life: Students at each age level study topics such as servant leadership, ethics, etiquette, decision-making, stewardship, determination, teamwork, and service. Students at Merritt take several field trips including visiting the White House, Jamestown, Nationals Park, Arena Stage, and the Smithsonian Institution Museums. The school also hosts a number of school-wide activities throughout the year such as the Halloween Parade, Bat Day, Johnny Appleseed Parade, Pickle Day, Geography Bee, Caroling on Campus, Pi Day, Fairy Tale Ball, Earth Day, and the Spring Fling.

Campus: The campus includes a gymnasium, a playground, a conversation garden, an in-ground swimming pool, two computer labs, an art studio, and a library.

Learning Support: The school counselor handles issues relating to learning support needs, and the school makes as many accommodations as it can; however, Merritt is not structured to provide support for students with learning disabilities.

Schools Attended by Most Graduates in the Past Five Years: Flint Hill School, Fairfax County Public Schools, Loudoun Country Day School, New School of Northern Virginia, St. Leo's Catholic School

Takeaways: Merritt stands out in its ability to differentiate its learning environment for students. The school has a gifted program with four different levels to assist students of diverse abilities. Merritt also has an ESL (English as a Second Language) enrichment program to support students who are not native English speakers. The school focuses on character education and development. Each month, two values, such as caring and patience, are incorporated in lessons school-wide. Merritt Academy has been recognized as a National School of Character by the Character Education Partnership. Merritt is a good option for families looking for a school that values differentiation, technology skills, and hands-on learning. Merritt is also worth considering for families with students who may need a strong ESL program.

Middleburg Academy

35321 Notre Dame Lane, Middleburg, VA 20117
540.687.5581 | www.middleburgacademy.org

"Middleburg Academy inspires students to excellence in academics, the arts, and athletics. We are a dynamic community of students, faculty and staff, parents, and alumni dedicated to lifelong learning, service to others, spiritual growth, and the success of each student. Our school strives to develop young men and women of moral integrity who will be responsible leaders and citizens in a diverse and ever-changing world."

Grades 9 – 12 | Co-Ed
No Religious Affiliation

Enrollment: 160 | **Average Class Size:** 14
Admissions and Testing: Deadline February 1; SSAT required
Tuition and Financial Aid: $20,980; limited aid available; uses FACTS tuition management services.

Curriculum: Middleburg offers students a college prep program with an emphasis on problem solving. Its recent transition from being the Catholic Notre Dame Academy has left some remnants of the traditional program behind. This is most clearly evidenced by the school's seminar program, which focuses on the development of students' spiritual well-being in particular areas each year. The most unique aspect of Middleburg's curriculum is the dual enrollment program. Unlike AP classes, which Middleburg also offers, dual enrollment classes are taken at the college level and do not require an end-of-the-year exam for credit. The courses are taken on campus and accepted by all Virginia public universities. Sixty percent of Middleburg's faculty has been accredited to teach at the college level.

Arts: Middleburg offers classes in drama, music, and visual arts. Classes include Architectural Design, Visual Communications, Music Theory, Photography, Ceramics, Painting, Drawing, AP Studio Art, and College Art. In addition, students have the option to join either the male or female glee club or partake in any of the dramatic performances the school puts on.

Athletics: Middleburg is a member of both the Capital Athletic Conference and the Virginia Independent Schools Athletic Association. There is a no-cut sports policy, and although it is not mandatory, 85% of the student body participates in a sport each year. The school offers basketball, cross-country, field hockey, golf, baseball, swimming, lacrosse, tennis, volleyball, and soccer. Middleburg has won recent championships in basketball, baseball, tennis, and golf.

Student Life: All students at Middleburg Academy partake in the advisory program, which requires students to meet as a group twice a week for 40 minutes with one faculty advisor. The topics covered during these meetings include time management and organization, healthy relationships, college planning, health problems, and many others.

Campus: Located 50 miles outside of DC, the scenic Middleburg campus is located on 90 acres in Middleburg, Virginia. The campus includes a student center, gym, athletic facilities, and a great deal of space for outdoor activities.

Learning Support: The Academic Strategies Program (ASP) provides support for students with mild learning differences. Students must apply for the program by providing the director of the program with documentation and testing as well as parent and teacher input. The director of the ASP then puts together an individualized learning profile for each student. Academic Strategies class is taken in place of an elective in the student's schedule and can either be continued or dropped, depending on how the student's needs change in the future.

Schools Attended by Most Graduates in the Past Five Years:
No matriculation information is available.

Takeaways: Formerly Notre Dame Academy, Middleburg continues to offer an academically rigorous program, the highlight of which is the dual enrollment program. The advisory meetings allow students to create bonds with one another and get to know faculty members on a personal level. Given its small size, the school has developed a strong communal atmosphere for its students. Middleburg is a good option for a family that likes the structure of a Catholic school but would prefer a less religious atmosphere.

The New School of Northern Virginia

9431 Silver King Court, Fairfax, VA 22031
703.691.3040 | www.newschoolva.com

"The mission of the New School of Northern Virginia is to provide a respectful, stimulating environment with small classes where students succeed academically, discover the joy of learning, and experience the rewards of active participation in a community."

Grades 4 – 12 | Co-Ed
No Religious Affiliation

Enrollment: 150 | **Average Class Size:** 8-12
Admissions and Testing: Rolling admission; no standardized testing required, but students are interviewed in depth and asked to attend classes for up to three days
Tuition and Financial Aid: $15,697 (4), $17,424 (5), $19,341 (6), $23,924 (7-8), $26,570 (9-12); limited financial aid is available.

Curriculum: At The New School instruction is engaging and discussion-based, and students have independence in determining their courses of study. The school offers a college prep program that trains its students in the traditional academic disciplines (English, science, social studies, foreign language, mathematics, etc.) and skills essential for success in college and the professional world. These essential skills are a fundamental component of the school's pedagogy and culture, which include a focus on ethics, community, problem solving, creativity, and communication. The curriculum also includes a computer science component and a senior research project requirement in addition to the core subjects.

The school has a strong international student population and offers classes in ESL, reading and writing, and American culture. Between five and eight AP courses are offered each year. French, German, and Spanish are the language offerings.

Arts: In the arts, the theater department offers the Cappies program, which trains students to be critics and allows opportunities for publication in local print media. The art department intends to "awaken, nourish, and encourage the visual and performing arts and the creative processes" in all students. A variety of fine arts, music, and performance courses are offered.

Athletics: The New School is a member of the Independent Small Schools Athletic Conference and offers soccer, basketball, softball, and volleyball as competitive interscholastic sports. Bowling and ultimate frisbee are also available as after-school clubs. The program is not mandatory, but all students are encouraged to participate in athletics outside of their required physical education classes. There are no cuts made on any teams.

Student Life: Many activities are available outside of the classroom; however, students are encouraged to create their own clubs and committees to pursue their interests. The Fairness Committee, for example, puts students in charge of arbitrating community disputes. Current clubs include debate, drama, recycling, video games, Peru club (students raise money to help impoverished communities in Peru), international student club, creative writing club, and more.

Campus: The New School's campus in suburban Fairfax is made up of several buildings built around courtyards and surrounded by trees. The facilities include an art studio with an outdoor sculpture patio, gym, media center, science center, black box theater, and playground.

Learning Support: The New School accepts all students who it believes will benefit from its small class sizes and multi-sensory approach. No special accommodations are given as far as academic requirements, but tutors and learning specialists can privately be arranged as needs arise. The school is not equipped to accommodate behavior problems or learning issues that require significant intervention.

Schools Attended by Most Graduates in the Past Five Years: George Mason University, St. John's College, Goucher College, Virginia Tech, School of the Museum of Fine Arts (SMFA)—Boston

Takeaways: The New School provides a college prep curriculum for students who may learn best in small classes. Although teachers provide some lectures, the majority of learning takes place through projects and small group discussions. Classes are interest-based, such as 20th Century

Social Movements through Music. The main belief of the New School is that students should participate, collaborate, and ultimately "own" their education. One interesting program is the Senior Exhibition, which requires students to write a 15-page research paper and present on it for an hour in front of a faculty panel. This assignment serves as the culminating feat of a New School education.

The New School is a good fit for students who may have struggled in a traditional setting and need a stimulating environment that provides academic challenges, artistic opportunity, and a strong sense of community.

The Newton School

45965 Nokes Boulevard, Suite 120, Sterling VA 20166
703.772.0480 | www.thenewtonschool.org

"The Newton School was created in 2009 to serve children who may not reach their full potential in a traditional academic environment. Newton students require small class sizes, low student/teacher ratios, social facilitation, and an abundance of physical activity built into the curriculum. The Newton School's belief is that integrating movement into the school day helps enhance academic performance, improve physical ability, build self-esteem, and better prepare children to meet life's challenges."

Grades K – 8 | Co-Ed
No Religious Affiliation

Enrollment: 60 | **Average Class Size:** 8
Admissions and Testing: Rolling admission; educational testing and evaluations within the previous two years are requested
Tuition and Financial Aid: $28,600 (K-8); limited aid is available, but varies from year to year; tuition includes all technology, supplies, and field trips.

Curriculum: Newton's academics closely follow the Virginia Standards of Learning, but teachers have access to a variety of supplemental programs to tailor instruction to an individual student's needs. Academics, language, organization, and social skills are all reinforced through kinesthetic activities. Reading, oral language, writing, and math are key priorities and are taught by trained faculty in grade-appropriate, 30-60 minute sessions. Class sizes are kept extremely small with a student/teacher ratio of 4:1.

Technology is integrated into the program, providing the opportunity to learn and develop keyboarding and presentation skills. Self-regulation is practiced and reinforced throughout the day through programs such as yoga. Social skills are integrated into the curriculum through a unique program developed by a speech and language therapist specifically for The Newton School.

Arts: The Newton School employs outside professionals who teach art, music, and drama one to two times per week. Students perform for their peers and parents every quarter. Art and performance are key components of the Newton program to promote self-confidence and self-expression.

Student Life: Students have a number of opportunities for experiences outside of the classroom, such as field trips to local museums, the theater, local landmarks, and more. Recent field trips have included the Air and Space Museum, National Building Museum, Shenandoah Valley Discovery Museum, Loudoun District Court, Mount Vernon, The Kennedy Center, and Adventure Theater. The school also offers after-school clubs for students dealing with topics such as science, painting, basketball, video game design, cooking, and art.

Campus: Newton's campus is located in Sterling, Virginia. The school's 24,000-square-foot facility includes 10,000 square feet of dedicated gym space as its hallmark. The gym facility includes a foam pit, trampolines, an indoor basketball court, sports court, and a ball pit, providing full integration of physical activity into the school day.

Athletics: There are no competitive teams at this time—sports are incorporated in daily physical activities and sport groups are offered as after-school clubs. Movement and physical activity are at the core of Newton's educational philosophy.

Learning Support: Certified professionals from many therapeutic disciplines work closely with teachers to make sure that children's needs are accommodated. As part of its normal operations, the school offers small group services in speech and language and occupational therapy as well as many other accommodations to meet students' needs. Many parents are drawn to The Newton School for the on-site integrated resources.

Schools Attended by Most Graduates in the Past Five Years: The Newton School has not yet had a graduating class. The first eighth grade class will graduate in June 2014.

Takeaways: The most unique aspect of Newton is its gym-play area where students can incorporate movement into their academic routine. The curriculum incorporates extensive physical activity. Students are exposed to bike riding, obstacle courses, and doing math while jumping rope. A daily report is sent home with each student detailing what the student worked on that day as well as how he or she did, focusing on the positives. The school considers self-regulation to be an important aspect of its approach. In addition to yoga and mindfulness, the school has its Social Stars program, which incorporates weekly school-wide lessons that teach concepts such as sportsmanship, working in a group, and flexibility. Many Newton families come from more traditional school environments and they find the positive, flexible environment at The Newton School to be a welcome respite. The school is well suited for students who have a hard time staying still and remaining engaged, students with attention issues, and those who need a lot of physical activity built into the school day.

Nysmith School for the Gifted

13625 Eds Drive, Herndon, VA 20171
703.713.3332 | www.nysmith.com

"The Nysmith School philosophy is to teach the children new information as they are ready for it. Small class sizes and low student-to-teacher ratios facilitate the diversified curriculum. By incorporating daily computers, science, logic, and foreign language, we are able to expand the children's academic opportunities and make school fun."

Preschool – Grade 8 | Co-Ed
No Religious Affiliation

Enrollment: 620 | **Average Class Size:** 16
Admissions and Testing: Rolling admission; IQ test scores (1-8)
Tuition and Financial Aid: $20,200 (Preschool); $26,200 (K-3); $29,700 (4-8); limited financial aid available; awards capped at 25% of tuition.

Curriculum: Classes at Nysmith are taught in a hands-on, interactive manner with two teachers in each classroom. The math curriculum places an emphasis on logic rather than on rote memorization, allowing students to move on to higher-level math at an early age. Beginning in fourth grade, students take part in a "math hour" every school day, which allows them to focus on their particular math level. Students at Nysmith have the opportunity to take math up to pre-calculus. The focus on logical thinking is woven through the entire school curriculum, especially in science classes, which are filled with labs and experiments so students learn through investigation.

While Nysmith has a reputation of catering to students who are mathematically inclined, the school does have a strong language arts program. The reading program, which begins in kindergarten (or preschool for students who are developmentally ready), is based on a combination of phonetic and whole language methods. Language art classes are differentiated similarly to math and science classes. Foreign language instruction begins at age three when students are introduced to

French, and seventh and eighth grade students choose between Spanish, French, and Latin.

Arts: All students have art class once a week, during which they draw, sculpt, paint, and make prints. In music, students learn Orff instruments, music theory, and music history. Several performances are given during the year. The drama program is vibrant, with annual plays and theater tech classes. Students may also play in one of three bands, a string ensemble, or sing in the Nysmith Glee Club.

Athletics: Nysmith's focus is academic, so there are no competitive athletic programs. However, a few optional after-school sports clubs are available, including soccer, lacrosse, basketball, and tennis. Physical education is a big part of the curriculum and includes gymnastics, soccer, T-ball, kickball, dance, and use of the school's rock climbing wall.

Student Life: A staple of a Nysmith education is applying what is learned in class to the outside world. Every field trip that students take at Nysmith reinforces what is being covered in class. For example, each year eighth graders visit Kings Dominion to observe the physical laws that help the rides run. In addition to co-curricular programs, students have the opportunity to choose from many extracurricular clubs and activities, ranging from poetry club to juggling.

Campus: Nysmith's campus is located in Herndon, Virginia. The school building is divided by age group, and each of the four wings has computer and science labs. The campus includes a gym, a stage, a library, a media center, athletic fields, tennis courts, a rock climbing wall, and an outdoor amphitheater.

Learning Support: Nysmith employs one full-time learning specialist for students who are twice exceptional, meaning the student may have a learning disability but is gifted and working above grade level.

Schools Attended by Most Graduates in the Past Five Years: Thomas Jefferson High School for Science and Technology, The Madeira School, Flint Hill School, The Potomac School, Georgetown Day School

Takeaways: Nysmith was founded by Carole Nysmith in 1983 because she felt that instruction in the public school system was lacking for gifted students at an early age. To this day, students are encouraged to explore interests, take academic risks, and apply what is being taught in the classroom to the outside world. It is often assumed that students leave Nysmith slanted towards math and science. Though the school does provide students with a strong math and science foundation, the school has developed a comprehensive liberal arts program as well to ensure that Nysmith produces well-rounded students.

Nysmith may be a good fit for a gifted child who needs additional challenge and opportunity to explore his or her interests. The school aims to accommodate the gifted population, even if students struggle with a mild learning disability.

Oakcrest School

850 Balls Hill Road, McLean, VA 22101
703.790.5450 | www.oakcrest.org

"Oakcrest School in partnership with parents challenges girls in grades 6-12 to develop their intellect, character, faith, and leadership potential to succeed in college and throughout their lives."

Grades 6 – 12 | All Girls
Catholic | Independent

Enrollment: 187 | **Average Class Size:** 16
Admissions and Testing: Deadline February 1; SSAT (6-12), HSPT (9)
Tuition and Financial Aid: $20,660 (6-8), $21,660 (9-12); tuition assistance available; uses FAST form.

Curriculum: In the middle school, students are expected to master core content knowledge while developing their critical-thinking skills. Hands-on projects are the norm and students are engaged in the learning process. Seventh and eighth grade foreign language courses, as well as Algebra I, are taught at the upper school level and credits count towards students' graduation requirements. Oakcrest offers mini-courses to the middle school students, such as Rocketry and Film Editing, which allow the students to explore interests outside of the core curriculum. In the upper school, Oakcrest's college prep, liberal arts curriculum includes courses in the arts, humanities, mathematics, science, and technology. All students in the upper school take either honors or AP classes. The school offers 11 AP classes and Latin and Spanish as foreign languages.

Arts: Oakcrest's art department has required and elective courses in studio art and music. Aside from the requirements, the middle and upper schools put on an annual student-led theater production. Students work on every aspect of the production, from set design to choreography to directing.

Athletics: Oakcrest competes in the Potomac Valley Athletic Conference, the Washington Metropolitan Prep School Swim Dive League, and the Virginia High School League. Oakcrest offers cross-country, soccer, tennis, volleyball, basketball, swimming, lacrosse, softball, and track and field. The program is not mandatory.

Student Life: The school strives to ensure that each student has the opportunity to explore and expand her intellect, will, and spirit. Advisors help the students reach these goals by meeting with them monthly. There are also character workshops and a service program.

Campus: Oakcrest sits on five acres with tennis courts, basketball and softball facilities, a computer lab, a language lab, a science lab, a gym, music and art rooms, and a 900-seat theater in suburban McLean, Virginia. The school is currently located in a church; however, Oakcrest has purchased a plot of land off the Dulles Toll Road in Vienna to build a new facility.

Learning Support: The school employs a part-time learning specialist to support students with learning differences. However, the school is not equipped to remediate students with severe learning disabilities.

Schools Attended by Most Graduates in the Past Five Years: University of Dallas, University of Maryland—College Park, University of Virginia, Virginia Tech, The College of William and Mary

Takeaways: Oakcrest offers girls a traditional education experience in a Catholic environment inside the Beltway, which is a highlight for suburban Virginia families that do not wish to commute to DC. There is a large focus on character formation and students meet with their advisors regularly. The class sizes are smaller than those at many other Catholic schools in the area, enabling students to receive personalized attention. Oakcrest is a good option for a girl who has strong study and organizational skills and who is able to perform well in a traditional atmosphere.

Oakwood School

7210 Braddock Road, Annandale, VA 22003
703.941.5788 | www.oakwoodschool.com

"Oakwood School provides a multi-sensory educational program in which students with learning differences are guided to achieve their unique academic and social potential in a nurturing community environment."

Grades K – 8 | Co-Ed
No Religious Affiliation

Enrollment: 103 | **Average Class Size:** 8-13
Admissions and Testing: Rolling admission; current psychological and educational testing required
Tuition and Financial Aid: $30,350 (K-8); financial aid budget of over $150,000 serves about 10% of students.

Curriculum: The curriculum at Oakwood is specifically designed for students with mild-to-moderate learning differences. The school serves students with dyslexia, ADHD, auditory processing deficits, and executive functioning needs. Each of the ten classrooms serves between eight and thirteen students taught by two teachers, keeping the student-to-teacher ratio quite low. Oakwood uses small skill groups to lay strong foundations in reading, math, and writing. Emphasis is placed on improving executive functioning skills through direct instruction and practice in organization and time management. Instruction is typically multi-sensory and teachers employ research-based approaches, such as the Orton-Gillingham method, to remediate reading disorders. For reading and math, students are grouped by skill levels rather than by grade level and groups are kept very small. Technology is built into the curriculum. Students use laptops and a computer lab to support and enhance their learning.

Arts: An art teacher provides instruction every other week with additional art activities led by the classroom teachers on a regular basis. A music teacher provides weekly instruction to all classes. Interactive assembly programs and field trips reinforce classroom instruction. Private music lessons and art are offered in the extended day program.

Athletics: Daily physical education encourages movement, and the instruction is adaptive. No competitive sports are offered. Oakwood believes movement is an important part of an all-around education.

Student Life: Various school activities such as Student Council, Color Guard, and Reading Buddies offer leadership opportunities for older students. Oakwood also offers an extended day program with club activities in drama, art, music, and fitness.

Campus: Located off Braddock Road and the Beltway, the small, suburban campus includes a gym, computer lab, music room, and outdoor play facility.

Learning Support: An occupational therapist and a speech therapist are available in addition to the highly trained faculty. Faculty members strive to make sure that each student's needs are met.

Schools Attended by Most Graduates in the Past Five Years: Paul VI Catholic High School, Bishop O'Connell Catholic High School, Flint Hill School, The Field School, Commonwealth Academy

Takeaways: The qualifications and ongoing professional development of the staff at Oakwood set the school apart from similar schools that cater to children with learning disabilities. The environment is nurturing—attention is given to each individual student. The staff strives to meet the students where they are in their learning and works to help them build their self-esteem. Through its commitment to staff development and implementation of research-based techniques, Oakwood remediates students' deficits instead of merely accommodating them. Homerooms are grouped by grade level, but subjects are taught by skill level. Oakwood is a good fit for students with learning disabilities who would benefit from the individualization that is offered.

Paul VI Catholic High School

10675 Fairfax Boulevard, Fairfax, VA 22030
703.352.0925 | www.paulvi.net

"To provide an excellent Catholic education to young men and women by affording them the means to achieve spiritual, intellectual, personal, social, and physical development according to the teachings of the Gospel and St. Francis de Sales. Paul VI Catholic High School is committed to graduating responsible, moral, service-oriented young adults who will continue to 'grow in grace and wisdom.'"

Grades 9 – 12 | Co-Ed
Catholic | Diocese of Arlington

Enrollment: 965 | **Average Class Size:** 22
Admissions and Testing: Deadline January 31; HSPT (9)
Tuition and Financial Aid: $12,310 (Catholic), $17,230 (Non-Catholic); financial aid budget over $1.4 million serves 20% of the student body.

Curriculum: Paul VI's (PVI) college prep curriculum is literature-based and emphasizes the development of writing skills at all grades and within all content areas through required research assignments. Twenty-one AP classes and four dual enrollment courses with Northern Virginia Community College are offered. PVI provides students with laptops in order to download textbooks. The school has unique academic departments not often seen at the secondary school. These departments include Business & Economics, which offers five different classes to prepare students for futures in business. Students can also take Family and Consumer Science courses on topics such as nutrition and food preparation, clothing construction, interior design, and fashion marketing.

Arts: PVI offers fine arts classes for students to explore their creative interests and talents. For those students who possess a special talent in band, strings, choir, acting, or art, advanced courses are offered. Students who actively participate in the arts have the opportunity to go on a yearly retreat.

Athletics: PVI is a member of the Washington Catholic Athletic Conference. Students can participate in baseball, basketball, cross-country, cheerleading, dance team, football, golf, ice hockey, lacrosse, soccer, softball, swimming, tennis, track and field, volleyball, and wrestling. The program is not mandatory. PVI is known for its baseball program, but it also went undefeated in basketball in recent years and its soccer program is ranked in the top ten in the region among all private and public schools by the *Washington Post*.

Student Life: Students at PVI have a variety of co-curricular activities from which to choose, from spiritual clubs such as the Catholic Athletes for Christ to clubs for fun such as the Classic Film Club and the Computer Competition Club. Mass is offered in PVI's chapel at 7:10 a.m. every Monday through Friday, if students choose to attend. They also have the option to attend confession during the school day every Friday.

Campus: Located in downtown Fairfax, the 16-acre campus includes a baseball field, a football field, and practice fields, in addition to science and computer labs.

Learning Support: PVI has three distinct programs in place to assist struggling students. The Academic Center for Excellence (ACE) provides support to students who are struggling with the transition to high school or the demands of a college prep program. The De Sales Learning Center provides specialized support during study hall period to average and above average students who have been diagnosed with a learning disability. The Options program offers students with learning disabilities a modified inclusion classroom, allowing them to work at their own pace.

Schools Attended by Most Graduates in the Past Five Years: Virginia Tech, University of Virginia, James Madison University, George Mason University, Georgetown University

Takeaways: PVI is equipped to accommodate students of various abilities and interests. Students are able to take classes in content areas that they find relevant to their lives, such as business or fashion design, along with the traditional core curriculum. PVI employs a number of college and career counselors to help students make the most informed decisions about their futures. The counselors advise juniors and seniors on post high school plans and even consult with parents to review ACT and SAT results. PVI has a lot to offer many different types of students. The classes are offered at several different levels, making PVI a good fit for a family with multiple students who may have different academic strengths and weaknesses.

The Potomac School

1301 Potomac School Road, McLean, VA 22101
703.356.4101 | www.potomacschool.org

"The Potomac School's mission is to foster each student's intellectual development, love of learning, and strength of character within an inclusive community distinguished by a spirit of support and challenge."

Grades K – 12 | Co-Ed
No Religious Affiliation

Enrollment: 1,020 | **Average Class Size:** 16
Admissions and Testing: Deadline January 10; WISC-IV (K-5), SSAT or ISEE (6-10), PSAT (11)
Tuition and Financial Aid: $30,115 (K-3), $32,325 (4-6), $34,625 (7-8), $34,660 (9-12); $4 million financial aid budget serves 19% of the students.

Curriculum: In the lower school, the integrated curriculum weaves all the core subjects together into thematic learning units. Students take part in reading and writing workshops beginning in kindergarten. The middle school aims to expand fourth through sixth grade students' self-confidence and self-advocacy. The main projects students work on in the middle school years all culminate in a final presentation. These projects include an Ancient Egypt Museum (fourth grade), Invention Convention (fifth grade), and an Architectural Designs project (sixth grade). In the intermediate school, seventh and eighth graders: take classes in English, math, history, science, and world language; take electives in music, art, and adolescent brain and body studies; and participate in a variety of athletic offerings.

Upper school students have seven class periods each day. In addition to core requirements, Potomac offers a variety of unique electives. In the English department, for example, students can take classes such as The Harlem Renaissance, Shakespeare's Wise Fools, or The Craft of the Nonfiction Essay. These electives are offered on a semester basis, giving students the opportunity to take several throughout their time at Potomac. The curriculum encourages students to pursue interests and passions at an advanced level, preparing them for opportunities in college and beyond.

Arts: Students begin taking music classes in the lower school. Middle and upper school students have the opportunity to participate in handbells, band, or choir. Instruction in the theatrical arts begins in the lower school where students take part in regular performances. Recent performances have included *Rent*, *Annie*, and *Journey to the West!* Potomac has a comprehensive and in-depth visual arts program that focuses on developing skills including collaboration, identity, observation, focus, design, and craft. The school offers a unique program available to upper school students with a strong interest in the arts: The Visual and Performing Arts Concentration (VPAC).

Athletics: Potomac is a member of both the Independent School League and the Mid-Atlantic Athletic Conference. The school is known for its athletic program, which includes 63 teams in 21 sports. A sample of offerings includes baseball, golf, cross-country, soccer, tennis, squash, lacrosse, swimming, track and field, football, basketball, and wrestling. Potomac requires of its upper school students nine seasons of participation, which can include weight training or yoga in addition to competitive sports. Potomac boasts a large number of state and league championships, and the tennis and lacrosse programs are particularly successful.

Student Life: Potomac has a number of unique extracurricular activities and traditions. One important tradition is the Red and Blue teams. Beginning in the lower school, all students are assigned to either the red or the blue team (siblings are assigned to the same team) on which they remain for their entire time at the school. Students in the upper school can join any of the 35 extracurricular clubs and activities. These options range from traditional clubs such as Debate Team, Mathletes, and Yearbook to more progressive organizations such as the Hip Hop Matters Club, the Young Financiers Organization, and the E-Gaming Club.

Campus: The Potomac School is spread across 90 acres in McLean, Virginia, and is roughly three miles away from Washington, DC. Potomac provides transportation to various areas of Maryland, DC, and Virginia, if it is not possible for a parent to make the daily commute. All of Potomac's students and facilities are located on one central campus.

Facilities include a performing arts center, athletic fields, a library, dedicated music and science labs, and several gyms.

Learning Support: Math and language specialists are available in addition to counselors, but Potomac does not have a robust support structure in place for students with learning needs.

Schools Attended by Most Graduates in the Past Five Years: University of Virginia, The College of William and Mary, Duke University, Georgetown University, Middlebury College

Takeaways: The curriculum at Potomac is comprehensive, and students graduate having received a well-balanced education that has prepared them for the rigors of a top university. Potomac has a strong writing program—beginning in kindergarten with writing workshops—that continues into the upper school with many English electives. The school has a new Science and Engineering Research Center, which partners with universities such as Johns Hopkins and Georgetown. Potomac is a good fit for families looking for a challenging curriculum that encourages students to participate in extracurricular activities and athletics.

St. Stephen's & St. Agnes School

400 Fontaine Street, Alexandria, VA 22302 (Lower School)
4401 W. Braddock Road, Alexandria, VA 22304 (Middle School)
1000 St. Stephen's Road, Alexandria, VA 22304 (Upper School)
703.751.2700 | www.sssas.org

"To help our students succeed in a complex and changing world, we seek to inspire a passion for learning, an enthusiasm for athletic and artistic endeavor, a striving for excellence, a celebration of diversity, and a commitment to service. Our mission is to pursue goodness as well as knowledge and to honor the unique value of each of our members as a child of God in a caring community."

Junior Kindergarten – Grade 12 | Co-Ed
Episcopalian

Enrollment: 1,140 | **Average Class Size:** 15
Admissions and Testing: Deadline January 15; SSAT or ISEE (6-11)
Tuition and Financial Aid: $24,010 (JK), $26,884 (K-2), $27,074 (3-5), $29,640 (6-8), $32,074 (9-12); $4.1 million financial aid budget serves 22% of the student body with an average grant of $16,000; uses the SSS form.

Curriculum: St. Stephen's & St. Agnes School (SSSAS) offers a comprehensive, JK-12 college prep curriculum with rigorous academics and a focus on pursuing "goodness as well as knowledge." A strong emphasis is placed on critical thinking, communication, collaboration, and creative problem solving. SSSAS utilizes project-based learning and design thinking. Cultural competency skills and a global perspective are integrated into academic coursework.

In the lower school, literacy is woven throughout all disciplines, and the math program emphasizes the role of algebra in the early development of mathematical thinking. Teachers differentiate instruction to address the needs of each student. Students participate in projects, fairs, performances, and field trips.

A distinctive research-based feature of the middle school is single-gender math and science classes. An award-winning literary magazine reflects the strength of the writing program. Students use the science labs and a STEM approach to study the Chesapeake Bay. In the upper school, students complete courses in nine areas of study in a challenging program that offers 25 AP classes and 15 honors options. Students take on increasingly significant leadership roles such as hosting the annual Students for Sustainability Conference. Upper school students have recently traveled to Haiti, China, France, Argentina, Romania, and Croatia.

Arts: Art offerings include classes in visual, performing, and studio art. In music, students can select to join the chorus, drama, orchestra, or band. Students can also take classes such as wind or jazz ensemble, Playwriting, and AP Music Theory. The arts are fully integrated into academic courses, interdisciplinary studies, and school events.

Athletics: SSSAS is a member of both the Interstate Athletic Conference (boys) and the Independent School League (girls). It offers baseball, basketball, cross-country, field hockey, football, golf, ice hockey, lacrosse, soccer, softball, swimming, tennis, track and field, volleyball, winter track, and wrestling. Good sportsmanship, health, and fitness are emphasized.

Student Life: SSSAS students have access to a variety of clubs and committees through which they can pursue interests and develop leadership skills. In the lower school, these include mobile learning, a diversity club, public service podcasts, fencing, ceramics, filmmaking, and a science club. Students in the middle school can pursue interests in student government, an environmental club, and the literary magazine. Students in the upper school can take part in different activities such as student council, honor council, multicultural clubs, service organizations, Robotics Club, Debate Club, Model UN, Drama Club, the school newspaper, literary magazine, and yearbook.

Campus: SSSAS's three campuses are all within a 1.5-mile drive of each other, six miles south of DC. The lower school campus sits on 16 acres, the middle school campus sits on seven and the upper school on 35. In total, SSSAS is home to 13 academic buildings, 107 classrooms, eight tennis courts, nine athletic fields, an outdoor six-lane track, a gym for each campus, a batting cage, a weight room, four computer labs, 11 science labs, six art studios, six music studios, a chapel, a performing arts center, and a black box theater.

Learning Support: In small classes, teachers are able to provide individual attention and extra help to their students. However, SSSAS does not identify itself as a school that specializes in learning support.

Schools Attended by Most Graduates in the Past Five Years: University of Virginia, The College of William and Mary

Takeaways: SSSAS develops academic and organizational skills from the time a student is in kindergarten and scaffolds upon them to equip the student for success in college. As a faith-based community, ethical values and service learning are woven into the daily culture. The SSSAS program is grounded in tradition and forward thinking. The school strives to prepare students for the future in a "complex and changing world." While the expectations are high, if students are driven and want to take advantage of all the opportunities around them, they will do well at SSSAS.

Trinity Christian School

11204 Braddock Road, Fairfax, VA 22030
703.273.8787 | www.tcsfairfax.org

"Trinity Christian School exists to educate students to the glory of God by pursuing excellence for mind and heart."

Grades K – 12 | Co-Ed
Christian | Independent

Enrollment: 680 | **Average Class Size:** 15-18
Admissions and Testing: Rolling admission; in-house testing
Tuition and Financial Aid: $10,400 (K-5), $11,250 (6-8), $12,850 (9-12); financial aid is available ($625,000); all financial aid is needs based; uses the FAST application.

Curriculum: Trinity offers a traditional academic curriculum and subject matter is presented in a biblical framework. In addition to the core curriculum, the lower school program includes use of the science center for hands-on learning and the implementation of technology. The middle school curriculum is designed to encourage students to be independent thinkers, strengthen their writing skills, and accelerate math studies. The upper school program includes oral presentations, drama, papers, speeches, debates, worldview discussion, and research in major areas. Nine AP and 12 honors classes are offered. Senior year culminates in a senior seminar and a senior thesis project that students must defend before a panel of teachers and administrators. Every student in the upper school is required to complete 40 hours of community service each year.

Arts: All kindergarten through fifth grade students study music and art weekly and perform at least twice per school year. Once students enter the middle school, they may choose band, string ensemble, chorus, or drama as an elective. In the upper school, classes in graphic arts add to the already strong arts program. Theater and art classes are open to all students, but auditions are required for band, string ensemble, and chorus.

Athletics: Trinity competes in the Delaney Athletic Conference. The school offers cross-country, soccer, volleyball, basketball, cheerleading, baseball, and lacrosse. Participation is not mandatory, but upper school students may earn credit towards their physical education graduation requirement by participating in varsity sports. Students may also earn physical education credit through verified independent fitness activities.

Student Life: Clubs offered at Trinity include Chess, Math Help, Study Skills, Ballroom Dancing, Photography, Improv, and Bible Study.

Campus: The 25-acre campus off Braddock Road includes a lake, a gym, science labs, two computer labs, a library, a media center, athletic fields, and two separate academic buildings.

Learning Support: Trinity is not equipped to meet the needs of children with significant diagnosed learning differences, but does offer some differentiated instruction, as well as a writing lab with a dedicated teacher available to students in the middle and upper schools. A reading specialist and math specialist support the teachers in the lower school.

Schools Attended by Most Graduates in the Past Five Years: Virginia Tech, Christopher Newport University, James Madison University, University of Virginia, George Mason University

Takeaways: Christianity is central to every academic program and students attend chapel weekly. Trinity strives to provide students with a biblical worldview and believes that, "no idea, concept, or subject matter can be fully grasped unless it is related to the God who created it." The school offers a challenging academic experience with a strong foundation in critical thinking and language-based skills, especially writing. Trinity is a good option for families that are looking to have Christian studies play an integral part in their child's school experience.

Virginia Academy

19790 Ashburn Road, Ashburn, VA 20147
571.209.5500 | www.virginia-academy.com

"We at the Virginia Academy, fully trusting the power of God, have set ourselves to the task of teaching children that in life we must seek a proper relationship with God. This teaching is concerned not only with the counsels of God revealed in His Word, but also in the counsels revealed in His World. We desire to teach that all truth is God's truth, and Jesus Christ is central to all truth; again not simply in the Word, but in history, in geography, in music, in the arts, and also in the universe."

Preschool – Grade 9 | Co-Ed
Christian | Non-Denominational

Enrollment: 730 | **Average Class Size:** Depends on grade and number enrolled, 15-24 (max)
Admissions and Testing: Rolling admission; no testing required
Tuition and Financial Aid: $8,000 (K-5); $8,500 (6-8)

Curriculum: Virginia Academy follows the ABeka curriculum from preschool through fifth grade. A combination of ABeka and Bob Jones University Press is used in sixth through ninth grade, which focuses on an accelerated curriculum, spiritual and physical development, and an appreciation for the arts and sciences. In the lower school, students receive daily lessons in Bible, reading, math, science, and language skills—all taught from a Biblical worldview. Students begin studying French in preschool and all students participate in an international testing program called the National French Exam. By the eighth grade, students will take either Algebra I or Geometry as well as a class in Western Civilization. In the 2013-14 academic year, the Virginia Academy will begin its high school program with a ninth grade class and add a grade each year until the school has a full high school program.

Arts: Students take classes in music and drama and there is an art club for interested students. There is a drama program for the middle school and ninth grade students.

Athletics: Elementary school students can participate in flag football and soccer. In the middle school, Virginia Academy offers basketball, flag football, soccer, cheerleading, cross-country, and volleyball. High school sports include boys' football, basketball, and lacrosse and girls' volleyball, basketball, soccer, and cheerleading. The school also now offers on-site equestrian training, gymnastics, and martial arts.

Student Life: Both the lower and upper schools offer leadership positions to students in the form of a student council. Additionally, the school offers a variety of clubs dedicated to various topics, including chess, international culture, guitar, and environmental issues.

Campus: Virginia Academy has a theatrical performance auditorium, athletic fields, a new gymnasium, a computer lab, and a science lab.

Learning Support: Virginia Academy has a learning lab with a learning needs specialist who is qualified to work with students with special needs.

Schools Attended by Most Graduates in the Past Five Years: There has not been a graduating class yet.

Takeaways: Virginia Academy is a fast-growing school that provides a thorough academic course load through a Christian world view. The recent addition of a high school class means that students have the option to attend the Virginia Academy during their entire pre-college educational career. The Virginia Academy is a good option for parents and students looking for a Christian education that will be challenging and traditional.

Wakefield School

4439 Old Tavern Road, P. O. Box 107, The Plains, VA 20198
540.253.7600 | www.wakefieldschool.org

"The mission of Wakefield School is to provide a rigorous liberal arts education through a challenging, content-rich curriculum and extracurricular activities that are delivered by skilled, supportive, and creative teachers, coaches, and advisers. We believe in broad knowledge, the equal importance of character and intellect, the benefits of hard work, and the unique potential of our students. We foster self-discipline, independence, creativity, and curiosity. We provide students with the fundamental knowledge and the critical-thinking skills to distinguish that which is true from that which is not, and the strength of character to use that wisdom. We welcome families who will embrace our ambitious vision: to develop capable, ethical, and articulate citizens who will seek the challenge, make a difference, and live extraordinary lives . . . each in his or her own way."

Preschool – Grade 12 | Co-Ed
No Religious Affiliation

Enrollment: 432 | **Average Class Size:** 16
Admissions and Testing: Deadline February 1, then rolling; SSAT (4-12)
Tuition and Financial Aid: Ranges from $13,540 (JK), $17,870 (K), $20,180 (1-3), $21,600 (4-5), $22,750 (6-8), $23,950 (9-12); $1 million aid budget serves 25% of the students.

Curriculum: Wakefield offers students a traditional education with a progressive twist. There is a strong commitment to critical thinking that spans the curriculum. The most distinctive aspect of the curriculum is the emphasis on composition. The school breaks up the study of English so that students take classes in both literature and composition separately every year. The composition program culminates in a year-long, research-intensive, 30-page senior thesis. Though Wakefield is rooted in a liberal arts foundation, the school does not ignore science or math and believes that composition and critical thinking are just as crucial for success in the scientific fields as they are in liberal arts. Students are encouraged to analyze information and to think critically in all of their classes.

Arts: Wakefield serves as the Virginian host to the UK-based Alexander Talbot Rice Foundation's program to identify excellence in the visual arts. Wakefield students have the opportunity to stay after school for private art and music lessons. One of Wakefield's most unique art offerings is its all-school play that includes students of all ages.

Student Life: Students at Wakefield are separated into teams—Athenian or Spartan—at the time of their acceptance. The teams compete for points throughout the year, culminating in the spring semester with an all-day field day. Because the school has students at all different developmental stages, there are many extracurricular activities, some of which are geared towards specific ages and interests and others which are open to all students.

Campus: The campus includes separate buildings for the lower and upper schools, an art and music building, a science and technology building, two gyms, and an administration building.

Athletics: Wakefield is a member of the Delaney Athletic Conference but also competes in the Cavalier Athletic Conference depending on the sport. Wakefield offers lacrosse, soccer, volleyball, tennis, swimming, cross-country, squash, and basketball. The school will also debut its equestrian program in the 2013-2014 school year. Lower grades are required to participate in physical education and the opportunities for competitive sports begin in the middle school.

Learning Support: Wakefield has a learning support department in place with a learning specialist for each school division (upper, middle, lower). The department's goal is to work with students' strengths and to employ accommodations when necessary to ensure academic success. The school requires a full psycho-educational evaluation from fourth grade up to be granted learning support, which must be updated every three to four years.

Schools Attended by Most Graduates in the Past Five Years: University of Virginia, University of Mary Washington, Virginia Tech, James Madison University, Elon University

Takeaways: The primary goal of Wakefield is to develop articulate citizens who are capable of expressing themselves through both written and oral communication. This emphasis on composition and the requirement of research projects enable students to develop strong study habits and promote prioritizing skills in a very unique way. Additionally, the school offers extensive learning support to students with learning differences. Wakefield is a good fit for families looking for a school to emphasize written and oral communication alongside a solid foundation in core curriculum. Many types of students can attend Wakefield because of the strength of its learning support department.

Westminster School

3819 Gallows Road, Annandale, VA 22003
703.256.3620 | www.westminsterschool.com

"Westminster School is dedicated to providing a superior elementary and middle school education whose fundamental goals for each child are a disciplined and well-informed mind, strength of character, dedication to learning, generosity of spirit, and joy in the possibilities of life. The Westminster program is founded on a traditional curriculum, rigorous academic standards, and an atmosphere that promotes respect, integrity, kindness, and a sense of excellence. Westminster's academic program provides thorough training in basic subjects within a broad humanities curriculum. The classical tradition, great books, and exposure to the arts are emphasized and integrated throughout an accelerated, thoroughly rounded program."

Preschool – Grade 8 | Co-Ed
No Religious Affiliation

Enrollment: 280 | **Average Class Size:** 16
Admissions and Testing: Deadline February 15; in-house testing (Preschool-4) and SSAT or ISEE (5-7)
Tuition and Financial Aid: $8,400-$10,800 (Preschool), $14,828 (K), $16,268 (1), $17,700 (2), $19,152 (3-8); $350,000 financial aid budget; accepts the SSS application.

Curriculum: Westminster offers a classical education in the traditional style. One of the goals of the Westminster elementary education is to provide a solid foundation in the core subjects of English, math, science, and social studies. The entire curriculum is integrated; therefore, there are no electives. The history program at Westminster is centered on Western civilization with an exposure to classic works of literature. Writing is a primary focus across the curriculum. Students have the ability to complete Geometry in eighth grade. All students take French from kindergarten through eighth grade and Latin in seventh and eighth grade. Students complete high school French 2 and Latin 1 by the end of eighth grade. An emphasis is placed on the derivation of the English language from Latin and French. All classes are taught by specialists and the students move from class to class throughout the day.

Arts: Students in kindergarten through eighth grade take music and art classes. Orchestra is offered from third through eighth grade. Westminster's drama program places a strong emphasis on public speaking. Every student has a speaking role in a class play each year they are enrolled. All seventh-grade students participate in a Shakespeare play and all eighth-grade students participate in a Broadway musical.

Athletics: All Westminster students participate in a physical education class every day. Westminster is a member of the Capital Athletic Conference. Westminster's no-cut sports program starts in fifth grade. Five major sports are available for both genders: basketball, soccer, softball, track, and cross-country. Athletics are not required but are highly encouraged for all students in fifth through eighth grade.

Student Life: Each year, every grade goes on at least one field trip relating to every subject, as well as field trips to the theater and other local attractions. Many clubs that meet after school and on the weekends are available, including Chess Club, Chorus, MathCounts, Science Olympiad, French Club, and Odyssey of the Mind.

Campus: Westminster School is located in a residential neighborhood. Current facilities include 23 classrooms, a library, a computer center, a theater, an art studio, a music classroom, an orchestra rehearsal room, a playground, a grass field, and a gym. The Griffin Academy preschool is located in a rented space at St. Alban's Church, approximately a mile from the main campus.

Learning Support: All Westminster teachers remain after school for 45 minutes for the purpose of providing small-group help sessions. The Resource Center provides students with additional remediation or enrichment in math and language arts. Additional online programs are licensed to many students through the Resource Center to facilitate enrichment and remediation. All of these services are included in the tuition. Westminster will accept students with mild learning disabilities or ADHD; however, students are expected to keep up with the curriculum and the school only allows for minor special accommodations.

Schools Attended by Most Graduates in the Past Five Years: Flint Hill School, Bishop Ireton High School, St. Stephen's & St. Agnes School, Thomas Jefferson High School for Science and Technology, The Madeira School

Takeaways: Westminster offers a traditional curriculum, which allows students to become familiar with the classics at an early age. There is an emphasis on good organization and study habits and students are expected to remain organized. The school trains students on how to keep an assignment notebook and an organized binder, and how to properly take notes. The school building itself is worth noting: it's decorated with stained glass and accurately reflects the traditional nature of the school. For a family who values traditional education, Westminster should be considered. Students leave with a very strong foundation in reading, writing, and public speaking, and the school reports that its students are working up to one-and-a-half years ahead of their public school counterparts.

CHAPTER 17

Washington, DC Schools

Beauvoir, The National Cathedral Elementary School

3500 Woodley Road NW, Washington, DC 20016
202.537.6485 | www.beauvoirschool.org

"Beauvoir, the National Cathedral Elementary School, founded in 1933, is a primary school dedicated to educating a diverse student body in a caring and creative environment. Our program is designed to nurture the spiritual, ethical, intellectual, emotional, physical, and social development of our children. We seek to foster a spirit of inquiry and a joy in learning."

Preschool – Grade 3 | Co-Ed
Episcopalian | Protestant Episcopal Cathedral Foundation

Enrollment: 393 | **Average Class Size:** 20, with two teachers
Admissions and Testing: Deadline January 4; WPPSI-III/WISC-IV
Tuition and Financial Aid: $31,250; more than $1 million financial aid budget; awards range from 18%-98% of tuition; uses TADS (Tuition Aid Data Services) form.

Curriculum: Beauvoir is unique in that it is focused solely on early childhood and early elementary years. The curriculum is designed to integrate different themes and subjects so that topics overlap and students understand the interconnectedness of the core academic subjects from an early age. The aim of Beauvoir is to engage students with arts, play, and academics to instill a "beautiful view" of learning. Learning is hands-on, active, and experiential. Students at Beauvoir take classes in art, science, social studies, global studies, technology, mathematics, language arts, Spanish, and library. In addition to academics, Beauvoir aims to build the character of its students through regular chapel programs and the incorporation of the school's Life Rules of respect, responsibility, honesty, and kindness in all school events.

Arts: In the visual arts, students discover various forms of media, gain problem-solving skills, and learn to appreciate artistic expression at a young age. They experiment with drawing, painting, collage, and sculpture. Students are also exposed to the performing arts of music and drama, which overlap with what students are learning in other classes. For example, students in second grade use folk songs and relate them to their social studies class and school-wide global studies class. Further, students can participate in the chorus and perform during select chapel services.

Athletics: There is plenty of room for play and movement, and students take advantage of the pool, playgrounds, gardens, and gymnasium. Beauvoir recently completed the expansion of its outdoor play spaces and children's garden. The school believes physical activity is essential to a well-rounded elementary education.

Student Life: The After Beauvoir Center (ABC) offers extended daycare services to all families. There are also a variety of after-school enrichment classes available including jewelry making, cooking, robotics, piano, yoga, and lacrosse. The school also hosts Beauvoir's Foreign Language Institute, which offers classes in Mandarin, Spanish, and French to students from ages four to ten.

Campus: Beauvoir is located on the grounds of the Washington National Cathedral. The campus includes a main academic building, outdoor pool, art studio, science lab, library, gymnasium, performance hall, music studio, playgrounds, dining room, and gardens.

Learning Support: Beauvoir employs a full team of learning specialists. Three instructors focus on reading, and each specialist is assigned to a grade level, beginning with first grade. The learning specialists work with classroom teachers to identify students who need additional support. They assist students one-on-one or in small groups. Beauvoir has four math specialists who spend their time working with each class in all grade levels.

Schools Attended by Most Graduates in the Past Five Years:
No matriculation information is available.

Takeaways: Boasting a hands-on, experiential curriculum, Beauvoir is a well-respected early elementary school. Graduates often feed into some of the most competitive private schools in the area with a large portion moving on to St. Albans and National Cathedral School. A unique aspect of Beauvoir is its Voices for Learning program, which is an institute that provides research-based, year-round professional development to educators from across the country. The program also offers seminars to parents on current parenting and educational topics as well as opportunities for parents and children to participate in specialty classes together in the arts and sciences. Beauvoir is a good fit for families looking for an academic program to prepare their students to enter competitive private schools in fourth grade and a commitment to developing character, ethics, and community.

British School of Washington

2001 Wisconsin Avenue NW, Washington, DC 20007
202.829.3700 | www.britishschoolofwashington.org

"The British School of Washington is a thriving international school in the heart of Washington, DC, championing the learning of languages and the visual and performing arts. With over 400 students representing more than 40 nationalities, we are a through school for ages 2 years 9 months through 18 years. With an exceptional Early Years provision, we offer a unique combination of best practice curriculums from the International Primary Curriculum through to the International Baccalaureate Diploma Program. Our highly trained British teachers use differentiated learning strategies to enable success for every student. Inspired, our students are accepted to leading universities."

---

2 Years, 9 Months – Grade 12 | Co-Ed
No Religious Affiliation

Enrollment: 450 | **Average Class Size:** 12 for secondary, 17 for primary
Admissions and Testing: Rolling admission; testing is recommended but not required
Tuition and Financial Aid: $21,540 (Nursery and Preschool), $23,520 (K-5), $25,660 (6-10), $26,210 (11-12); $2,200 new student fee.

Curriculum: At the British School of Washington (BSW), students progress through five academic levels. In the nursery and reception level (ages three to five), students learn through play. The classroom is arranged into stations as the students move from one activity to the next. Activities include role playing, writing, cooking, and investigation. Students in kindergarten through fifth grade follow the International Primary Curriculum (IPC). IPC is a comprehensive, thematic curriculum that has specific learning goals for each subject and takes a global approach.

Students in sixth through eighth grade follow the International Middle Years Curriculum (IMYC), which provides academic challenge and fosters international mindedness. In the upper secondary school (ages 14-16), the curriculum is based on the International General

Certificate of Secondary Education (IGCSE). IGCSE offers a flexible course of study that allows students to choose subjects that most interest them. The curriculum culminates with the International Baccalaureate (ages 16-18) program, which requires students to fulfill three core requirements and take an additional six classes. The three core requirements include an extended essay, a Theory of Knowledge class, and a Creativity, Action, and Service project.

Arts: Students begin taking art classes at the nursery level and continue exploring the arts from all over the world as they move through the curriculum. Arts clubs available at the school include the Junior Shakespeare Club, school choirs, the Music Theory Club, Musical Appreciation Club, Cinema François, and Arts and Crafts.

Athletics: BSW competes in the Sixteenth Street Interscholastic Athletic Conference in soccer, basketball, track and field, cross-country, volleyball, swimming, and kickball. BSW also competes in the Independent School Athletic Conference. Outside of these leagues, the school offers table tennis, dance, volleyball, cricket, fitness, yoga, gymnastics, karate, skiing, and kayaking. Students have an athletic activity requirement that can be fulfilled through competitive or noncompetitive after-school sports.

Student Life: The school is divided into houses to provide students a sense of team unity and pride. Each house has captains and deputies to serve as representatives and organize house events. The houses compete against each other in planned events throughout the year. These events can range from chess to table tennis. Students can contribute to the school newspaper, join Model UN, and participate in any of the other clubs and activities the school has to offer.

Campus: The campus includes science labs, graphic art and computer labs, music and technology labs, a music room, playing fields, and a fitness center. BSW is located by Georgetown University and students have access to some of Georgetown's facilities.

Learning Support: BSW does not have special provisions in place for students with learning disabilities, but states that it is able to support those with minor learning difficulties. For English as an Additional Language (EAL) students, BSW has a support system run by a specialist teacher. Additional assistance includes an intensive two-week English course prior to the start of school. This is a requirement for any student, three years old or older, who does not have an appropriate level of English to access the curriculum. Students can receive support in place of studying a modern foreign language.

Schools Attended by Most Graduates in the Past Five Years:
No matriculation information is available.

Takeaways: The British School of Washington offers families a unique experience among schools in the DC metro area. One of the major draws to the school is the challenging International Baccalaureate program. For international families or students who may plan to study abroad in the future, BSW is a solid option.

Capitol Hill Day School

210 South Carolina Avenue SE, Washington, DC 20003
202.547.2244 | www.chds.org

"The mission of Capitol Hill Day School is to deeply engage a diverse community of students in connecting the classroom to the larger world, and supporting each child in developing the confidence, compassion, and intellectual capacity to live a life of purpose and value."

Preschool – Grade 8 | Co-Ed
No Religious Affiliation

Enrollment: 224 | **Average Class Size:** 16-24 (two teachers per class in Preschool-5)
Admissions and Testing: Deadline January 11; WPPSI-III/WISC-IV (Preschool-8)
Tuition and Financial Aid: $25,810 (Preschool-5), $27,120 (6-8); $450,000 financial aid budget serves 25% of students; grants range from $3,000 to $23,000, with an average award of $12,500.

Curriculum: Capitol Hill Day School (CHDS) implements a project-based learning approach in all of its classes. Teachers act as facilitators helping students navigate through their learning. In the elementary grades, the curriculum is centered on problem solving and critical thinking. Students learn language-based skills in grades one through three as they work on fluency, decoding, and reading comprehension. The fourth and fifth graders begin to analyze elements in literature such as plot, theme, and character development.

In the upper grades, students must set goals and analyze their progress twice a year in student-led conferences with parents and teachers. Each grade incorporates a major theme into the curriculum. For example, fifth graders spend an entire year focusing on Chinese writing, history, and social issues.

Arts: Art, music, drama, and poetry are all part of the integrated curriculum. Students take weekly art classes to explore their creativity.

Athletics: CHDS competes in the ABC Athletic League of Greater Washington. It offers basketball, soccer, softball, and track. Participation is not mandatory.

Student Life: The school has a unique Field Education program and offers a total of 300 field trips annually, which directly relate to classroom studies. CHDS uses the resources of the Washington, DC metro area and beyond to support and enrich the classroom experience. While the early childhood grades take weekly trips, all grades participate in at least twenty trips per school year, and fourth through eighth graders take part in overnight trips. This program seeks to enable children to make connections between their classroom learning and the real world.

Campus: The historic campus includes a four-story schoolhouse and a neighboring townhouse. In February of 2013 the main school building was reopened after a yearlong renovation project was completed. The renovations focused primarily on creating a safer atmosphere and updating the classroom technology.

Learning Support: CHDS accommodates students with mild-to-moderate learning differences. It has a full-time school counselor and learning specialist who support a variety of student needs. The specialist visits each classroom and monitors students. Tutors for math, languages, reading, and writing can be arranged on a case-by-case basis and tutoring sessions are held after school hours.

Schools Attended by Most Graduates in the Past Five Years: Georgetown Day School, The Field School, St. Stephen's & St. Agnes School, School Without Walls, Sidwell Friends School

Takeaways: CHDS offers students a hands-on learning experience. The use of project-based learning attempts to develop students' critical-thinking and problem-solving skills by allowing them to work on topics that are of interest to them. CHDS's Field Education program offers a different field trip every week, with the goal of immersing students in the culture around them and providing linkages between the students' education and the real world. Capitol Hill Day School is a good fit for a student who is bright and can handle a challenging curriculum but may learn best in an experiential way.

Edmund Burke School

4101 Connecticut Avenue NW, Washington, DC 20008
202.362.8882 | www.burkeschool.org

"Edmund Burke School consciously brings together students who are different from one another in many ways, actively engages them in their own education, has high expectations for them, gives them power and responsibility, and supports and advances their growth as skilled and independent thinkers who step forward to make positive contributions to the world in which they live."

Grades 6 – 12 | Co-Ed
No Religious Affiliation

Enrollment: 300 | **Average Class Size:** 14
Admissions and Testing: Deadline January 6; SSAT or ISEE (6-12)
Tuition and Financial Aid: $32,140 (6-8), $34,085 (9-12); financial aid is need based and 30% of the students receive it.

Curriculum: Edmund Burke has a progressive curriculum that focuses on analytical thinking and project-based learning. The sixth grade classes are taught in thematic units, meaning that students study relatable topics across all subjects. Instruction is primarily in a discussion-based format. High school students in eleventh and twelfth grades are offered a wide variety of electives from an English class that focuses on The Roaring Twenties to a science and history hybrid course that covers the scientific revolution. Burke offers 12 different AP classes.

Arts: The school has a very comprehensive performing and visual arts program. Beginning in sixth grade, students can participate in chorus, drama, and instrumental music. There are three theatrical productions each year, as well as an all-school art show. The school bands perform regularly, both in and out of school.

Athletics: The Edmund Burke Bengals compete in the Potomac Valley Athletic Conference. Offerings include soccer, volleyball, cross-country, basketball, swimming, wrestling, ultimate frisbee, golf, and track and field. There is a no-cut policy in place to encourage students to play any sport that interests them.

Student Life: Community service plays an important role at Burke. The Community Service and Service Learning Program (CSSL) aims to teach responsibility and compassion. Each grade has a service project, and every student in the high school has to perform 15 hours of community service each school year.

Campus: The campus building includes 60,000 square feet in Northwest Washington, DC. It houses two art studios, a library, a gym, a ceramics studio, five science labs, two computer labs, a digital media suite, a photography lab, and a theater. The campus is right off the red line, with the closest metro stop being Van Ness-UDC.

Learning Support: Edmund Burke is equipped to accommodate mild-to-moderate learning differences. The curriculum is engaging and can cater to students with learning differences and ADHD. A significant amount of group work and hands-on instruction is incorporated into the classroom regularly. There are two learning specialists on staff to assist the student body; they offer support inside and outside of the classroom.

Schools Attended by Most Graduates in the Past Five Years: Wesleyan University, George Washington University, University of Wisconsin, University of Pittsburg, St. Mary's College of Maryland

Takeaways: Two things that stand out about Edmund Burke School are its commitment to diversity and its expansive arts program. The school highly values diversity and encourages students to be active members of their community. Furthermore, their arts offerings are deep and varied. You will find that the Burke community is informal and committed to a progressive philosophy of teaching. Instructors aim to make learning interactive and interesting while producing strong critical thinkers and problem solvers. Edmund Burke is a great fit for families looking for an urban school that emphasizes the arts alongside a challenging academic curriculum.

Emerson Preparatory School

1324 18th Street NW, Washington, DC 20036
202.785.2877 | www.emersonprep.net

"Emerson is dedicated to principles rather than rules as a means of guiding our students' endeavors in school and in life. We see behavior as being motivated by a desire to find one's place in a larger accepting community. To that end, we work to instill a sense of personal and communal responsibility in our students through a collegial atmosphere of mutual respect, accountability, and commitment to the school community as a whole."

Grades 9 – 12 | Co-Ed
No Religious Affiliation

Enrollment: 75 | **Average Class Size:** 7
Admissions and Testing: Rolling admission; no testing is required, but SSAT, PSAT, and psycho-educational reports are useful if available
Tuition and Financial Aid: $25,500 full-time; part-time available at $22,000 (1-2 subjects); Emerson devotes substantial funds to help with aid; uses the SSS form.

Curriculum: Courses at Emerson are divided into three tiers: core skills and knowledge courses; college prep courses; and college-level elective courses. In order to graduate, students must complete 24 units of credit, 20 of which must be in core academic subjects (English, math, social studies, science, and foreign languages). To fulfill their elective requirements, students can take classes such as Emerging Technologies, Cognition and Ethics, or a faculty-supervised independent study. Emerson offers instruction in the Romance languages and in Arabic, Japanese, German, Russian, and Mandarin for students who already have some level of proficiency. Qualified students have the option of taking honors classes, which Emerson offers instead of AP courses. AP exams, however, are available upon request.

Arts: Emerson does not offer courses in visual or performing arts. Currently, the only courses directly related to the arts are those in art history.

Athletics: Emerson's program is solely academic. No athletic activities are offered.

Student Life: Emerson's offerings are purely academic and do not include school-sponsored extracurricular activities.

Campus: Emerson's campus in Dupont Circle in Washington, DC includes nine classrooms, a computer lab, a conference room, a courtyard, a reading room, and a science laboratory.

Learning Support: Emerson is not specifically structured for students with learning disabilities; however, many students come to Emerson from larger schools due to academic and/or social struggles and find that the intimate, casual environment is better suited to them.

Schools Attended by Most Graduates in the Past Five Years:
No matriculation information is available.

Takeaways: Each course at Emerson is one semester in length, meets for 90 minutes five days per week, and is equivalent to a yearlong course at other high schools. This structure prepares students for semester course loads in college and builds greater focus and enthusiasm than the typical seven-class schedule that most high schools adopt. Course instructors have a great deal of flexibility in designing their courses and selecting texts. Examples of unconventional class offerings have included Comparative Mythology, a seminar on Walt Whitman, and Introduction to Neuroscience. The college counseling program includes weekly college counseling, family meetings, ongoing follow-up, and admission test practice and prep.

Emerson is non-traditional and a good fit for students who don't like a "four walls" approach to academics. Many students choose Emerson because the flexible program allows them to pursue their outside passions independently in a casual atmosphere while accumulating several college credits.

The Field School

2301 Foxhall Road NW, Washington, DC 20007
202.295.5800 | www.fieldschool.org

"Self-discovery, skills of mind, and generosity of heart . . . Its three elements are, to us, inseparable. To achieve self-discovery, students need to develop the essential skills of critical thinking, writing, problem solving, and discussion. Self-understanding without generosity of heart in the community is not truly meaningful. But, together, these elements are what The Field School considers the goals of a great education."

Grades 6 – 12 | Co-Ed
No Religious Affiliation

Enrollment: 320 | **Average Class Size:** 11
Admissions and Testing: Deadline January 15; SSAT or WISC-IV (7-12)
Tuition and Financial Aid: $37,500; 10% of Field's annual operating budget goes to financial aid; 20% of the student body receives aid; uses the SSS form.

Curriculum: The Field School implements a progressive curriculum that focuses on inquiry, analysis, and creativity. In the middle school, the curriculum is integrated between disciplines, and there is an emphasis on study skills such as note-taking, interpersonal communication skills, and academic skills such as writing and analysis. At the upper school level, English students read a variety of classics and the math program offers courses beyond calculus. Every student at Field takes a studio art class every day of every school year. There are no AP classes offered at Field because they are counter to the school's educational beliefs. At The Field School, teachers do not stress memorization of facts for an exam, but rather critical thinking, analysis, and advanced verbal skills.

Arts: One period every day is dedicated to studio art. These classes include ceramics, photography, drama, music, 2D art, digital art, and publications. Students can also take part in an extensive theater program, studio band, audio engineering, and a cappella music.

Athletics: Field competes in the Potomac Valley Athletic Conference. Field offers wrestling, basketball, track, yoga, racquetball, swimming, baseball, softball, tennis, lacrosse, and ultimate frisbee. Students are required to participate in at least two of three sport seasons a year. Field employs a no-cut sports policy.

Student Life: Students take part in a special winter internship for two weeks each year, through which they can gain experience at museums, television studios, sports arenas, congressional offices, and more. Students have used their internships to explore options at the CBS Nightly News, a working farm, a local radio station, Google, The World Bank, and the Justice Department. Aside from the winter internship, students are able to join a number of clubs such as Model UN, the Zombie Club, the Anime Club, the Asian Pop Culture Club, the West Wing Club, and the Improv Club.

Campus: The current campus was built in 2002 on 10.5 acres. Facilities include a dark room, a music room and recording studio, five science labs, a pottery studio with a kiln, a media center, two computer labs, a batting cage, a gym, and a turf football field.

Learning Support: Field offers psychiatric counseling but is not structured for students with significant learning disabilities who need remediation or extensive accommodations.

Schools Attended by Most Graduates in the Past Five Years:
No matriculation information is available.

Takeaways: One of Field's biggest strengths is its ability to differentiate instruction for every child. The environment is carefully crafted to be welcoming and encouraging. Teachers spend time getting to know each student and his or her unique learning style. All of this is possible due to the small average class sizes of 11 students. Field has a high rate of students entering their top-choice colleges; two college counselors work with each student through the entire college application process. The school excels at improving students' executive functioning skills and is a great fit for a student who can handle the content and challenge of the curriculum, but may need support with organization and time management.

Georgetown Day School

4530 MacArthur Boulevard NW, Washington,
DC 20007 (Lower School)
4200 Davenport Street NW, Washington, DC 20016 (Upper School)
202.295.6200 | www.gds.org

"Georgetown Day School (GDS) honors the integrity and worth of each individual within a diverse school community. GDS is dedicated to providing a supportive educational atmosphere in which teachers challenge the intellectual, creative, and physical abilities of our students and foster strength of character and concern for others. From the earliest grades, we encourage our students to wonder, to inquire, and to be self-reliant, laying the foundation for a lifelong love of learning."

Preschool – Grade 12 | Co-Ed
No Religious Affiliation

Enrollment: 1,075 | **Average Class Size:** 16
Admissions and Testing: Deadline January 7; WPPSI-III/WISC-IV (Pre-K-5), SSAT or ISEE (6-12)
Tuition and Financial Aid: $29,990 (Preschool-K), $32,050 (1-5), $33,335 (6-8), $34,325 (9-11), $34,550 (12); financial aid budget of over $5 million serves about 20% of the student body.

Curriculum: GDS is a progressive school that provides a challenging and innovative curriculum. Science classes start in preschool and children take their first foreign language class in third grade. In the middle school, teachers seek to instill a sense of responsibility and community in students. Students conduct on-site studies at locations such as the Chesapeake Bay, and complete a two-month study of Constitutional issues for which they gather information by interviewing national experts.

In the upper school, college prep coursework challenges students in subjects such as humanities, sciences, math, and the arts. Twenty AP classes are offered in almost every discipline. The upper school math curriculum is accelerated so that students have the opportunity to surpass AP Calculus BC with classes such as Differential Equations, Multivariable Calculus, and Linear Algebra.

Arts: In the lower school, students participate in studio arts and acting. Middle school offerings include an in-depth study of drama, music, and the visual arts. The upper school offers more advanced visual arts classes as well as an award-winning dance program. Graduation requirements include one year of studio arts. Students can choose to take classes such as fashion photography, digital imagery, portraiture, and advanced digital design to fulfill this requirement.

Athletics: GDS is a member of both the Mid-Atlantic Athletic Conference for boys and the Independent School League for girls. GDS offers 63 interscholastic teams across 18 sports, including golf, baseball, volleyball, lacrosse, basketball, crew, track, soccer, cross-country, softball, tennis, and wrestling. Recent championships include track and field, cross-country, and soccer. Participation is optional, and the goal of the program is to foster character, compassion, and teamwork.

Student Life: Students at GDS are expected to be well rounded and involved in extracurricular activities such as the trivia club *It's Academic.* All students must complete 60 hours of community service.

Campus: GDS has two five-acre metropolitan campuses that feature libraries, gyms and athletic fields, black box theaters, fully equipped science labs, art studios, technology/multimedia labs, and student lounges and activity areas.

Learning Support: GDS employs numerous learning specialists and has created a structured learning support program that aims to identify any issues at an early age and remediate it so that by the time the student is in the upper school, they are self-sufficient.

Schools Attended by Most Graduates in the Past Five Years:
No matriculation information is available.

Takeaways: Georgetown Day is a sought-after school and admission is competitive. The atmosphere is very liberal—teachers are called by their first names and older students may leave campus for lunch and errands. The academics are challenging and students tend to matriculate to some of the top universities in the country, including a number of Ivy League schools. The athletics program offers a vast array of options for students with various areas of interest and GDS is well known for its robust arts program. Consider GDS if your child would thrive in a challenging academic environment with a significant variety of art options, all within an urban setting.

Georgetown Visitation Preparatory School

1524 35th Street NW, Washington, DC 20007
202.337.3350 | www.visi.org

"Our mission is to empower our students to meet the demands and challenges of today's rapidly changing and morally complex world. We guide our students to become self-reliant, intellectually mature, and morally responsible women of faith, vision, and purpose."

Grades 9 – 12 | All Girls
Catholic | Independent

Enrollment: 490 | **Average Class Size:** 13
Admissions and Testing: Deadline January 4, then rolling; HSPT (9-12)
Tuition and Financial Aid: $24,500 (9-12); the financial aid budget of $1.75 million serves 25% of students; uses SSS form.

Curriculum: The curriculum and course offerings at Georgetown Visitation (Visi) are traditional. In addition to the standard core subjects, girls take a personal development and wellness class their first two years, religion each year, and one-year accelerated math classes. Seniors are able to take four electives and are given more freedom in their schedule. Religious classes culminate in a bioethics/moral decision-making course taught in twelfth grade. Ten honors and 17 AP courses are offered for those students who are working above grade level or looking for a challenge. Students can choose between French, Spanish, and Latin to fulfill their foreign language requirement.

Arts: Visi conducts a dance ensemble that performs several times a year, as well as an instrumental music program. Visual arts at Visi are prevalent and the theater program is strong. The chorus is the largest group on campus and the select Madrigal Singers, the vocal ambassadors of the school, is an award-winning group of singers that performs on and off campus. The drama department puts on two major productions each year with young men from local schools.

Athletics: Visi is a member of the Independent School League and hosts 21 teams in 13 different sports. There have been 30 league championships over the past two decades, and the soccer, basketball, field hockey, and lacrosse teams have been recently listed in the top five in the region among all private and public schools by the *Washington Post*. The athletics program is not mandatory but is a valued part of the school's culture.

Student Life: Tradition is important at Visi. One ongoing tradition is the Gold and White games. Students are assigned to either the Gold Team or the White Team when they enroll in the school. Throughout the year, the two teams compete in athletic, academic, and community service activities such as a canned food drive. Visi has a number of clubs and organizations including the Irish Dancing Club, the Black Women's Society, the Organic Gardening Club, and the Christian Action Service.

Campus: The 23-acre campus in Georgetown includes a gymnasium, a full performing arts center, a chapel, and a bell tower. There are also four state-of-the-art technology centers on campus.

Learning Support: There is no particular learning support in place, but students at each grade level have a personal counselor who helps each girl with time management, social adjustment, and study skills.

Schools Attended by Most Graduates in the Past Five Years: University of Notre Dame, Georgetown University, Boston College, University of Maryland, University of Virginia

Takeaways: Visi is the second oldest, continuously running all-girls school in the country. The school combines rigorous academics with religious instruction. Students can expect heavy workloads. Visi stands out because of its unique traditions including Father/Daughter Mass and Brunch, the Marshmallow Roast, Founders Day, Class Retreat, and Gold and White games. Additionally, the athletics program offers a wide variety of options. Visi is a good fit for young women looking for a challenging academic experience combined with many extracurricular outlets for pursuing their interests.

Gonzaga College High School

19 Eye Street NW, Washington, DC 20001
202.336.7100 | www.gonzaga.org

"Gonzaga College High School is a Catholic College Preparatory School for boys operated by the Society of Jesus and its colleagues under the governance of an independent Board of Trustees. Drawing its inspiration from the spiritual vision of St. Ignatius Loyola and the apostolic and educational tradition of the Jesuits, Gonzaga offers a values-oriented and academically challenging curriculum to young men of diverse backgrounds from all over the Washington metropolitan area. Gonzaga views its urban setting in the heart of the nation's capital as a significant advantage in fulfilling its goals, allowing its students to interact with the larger Washington community and to learn leadership skills and civic responsibility as part of their overall development. Moreover, Gonzaga strives to create a dynamic and caring learning environment, which it unites with its academic, extracurricular, and athletic programs, to help form men with and for others—that is, graduates who are open to growth, intellectually competent, religious, loving, and committed to doing justice."

Grades 9 – 12 | All Boys
Catholic | Archdiocese of Washington | Jesuit

Enrollment: 960 | **Average Class Size:** 26
Admissions and Testing: Deadline December 10; HSPT (9 only)
Tuition and Financial Aid: $19,275 (9-12); financial aid budget of $2.3 million serves 33% of students; uses SSS form.

Curriculum: The curriculum at Gonzaga is traditional and challenging. The school offers 36 honors and AP classes in total. Religious studies are an integral component of a Gonzaga education. Throughout the curriculum students receive spiritual and ethical instruction. Some of the religious courses offered are Systematic Theology, Social Justice, and Ignatian Studies. Consistent with a Jesuit education, the school focuses on the classics. Latin and Greek are offered, as well as Spanish, French, and Chinese.

Arts: Visual art studies extend to film study, photography, and communications design. The music department includes a symphonic band, wind ensemble, choral arts, and chamber choir. The drama program at Gonzaga is strong and students from other schools participate.

Athletics: Gonzaga competes in the Washington Catholic Athletic Conference. Gonzaga's athletics are top tier, with offerings in baseball, golf, swimming, basketball, soccer, crew, football, squash, track and field, lacrosse, rugby, tennis, ice hockey, water polo, cross-country, and wrestling. Participation is not mandatory, but athletics are a major part of school culture.

Student Life: The Office of Campus Ministry on Gonzaga's campus seeks to provide guidance to students both personally and spiritually. The office provides community service activities, individual and personal retreats, and pastoral counseling. The school hosts a number of co-curricular activities. Some examples include Crossfit, Speech and Debate, Sons of Italy, The Phoenix Club, and National Honors Society.

Campus: The urban campus is made up of eight buildings on one city block, six blocks away from the Capitol Building. The school is only a few blocks away from the Union Station Metro stop on the red line. The campus includes St. Aloysius Church, science and computer labs, a gym, and a turf field.

Learning Support: Gonzaga's academic curriculum is very demanding, and although a full library staff and part-time tutoring options are available, Gonzaga is not a special needs school.

Schools Attended by Most Graduates in the Past Five Years:
Fordham University, James Madison University, University of Maryland—College Park, University of Virginia, Virginia Polytechnic Institute

Takeaways: Gonzaga is a good option for a young man who is self-motivated and can flourish in a traditional setting. For some families, the metro accessibility of the campus is a plus. The school has a number of honors and AP classes in which students can expect a heavy workload. A highlight of the school is its Georgetown University Bridge Program, which allows seniors to take classes at Georgetown University for college credit. Gonzaga is highly regarded for its competitive athletics program, both on the regional and national level.

The Jewish Primary Day School of the Nation's Capital

6045 16th Street NW, Washington, DC 20011
202.291.5737 | www.jpds.org

"The mission of the Jewish Primary Day School of the Nation's Capital (JPDS) is to provide a strong foundation in Jewish and secular learning, laying the groundwork for our students to become knowledgeable, responsible Jews and citizens, deeply committed to the community at large, to Jewish living and values, and to the people and state of Israel. Our school strives to create an environment filled with warmth, joy, and intellectual excitement that celebrates the unique qualities of each student, respects varied approaches to Judaism, fosters a strong sense of ethics and of self, embraces diversity, and builds a community of lifelong learners."

Preschool – Grade 6 | Co-Ed
Jewish

Enrollment: 315 | **Average Class Size:** 16-18
Admissions and Testing: Deadline January 10; no testing required
Tuition and Financial Aid: $21,250 (Pre-K-6); about 30% of the students receive financial aid; uses the PSAS student aid form.

Curriculum: At JPDS, the preschool through first grade program is inspired by the Reggio Emilia philosophy, which focuses on children's inherent abilities, widely ranging modes of expression, and capacity to direct their own learning. The Hebrew and Judaic Studies programs in preschool through first grade complement the Reggio Emilia philosophy. Students are exposed to intensive oral Hebrew language on a daily basis. Vocabulary is introduced and strengthened through Hebrew songs, games, stories, and dramatic enactment of stories. The curriculum teaches about the holidays, the Sabbath, morning prayers, and several stories from the bible. Judaic Studies instruction is conducted exclusively in Hebrew. Vocabulary is taught using songs, stories, and games. Students in second through sixth grade begin to move away from the Reggio Emilia philosophy to a more structured approach to learning. Students have opportunities to express themselves creatively throughout the day. Creative writing, critical thinking, and strong academics are highlights of the school's curriculum.

Arts: Students are exposed to a wide sampling of artists and produce works imitating those samplings. Through their exploration, students develop an understanding of various art concepts. A strong emphasis is placed on music, especially that of Jewish origin. By the end of second grade, students are able to read basic music. Older students are encouraged to explore a wide variety of musical genres. Instruction in art history, cooking, choir, drama, Israeli dancing, musical theater, podcasting, and singing are also available.

Athletics: JPDS competes with some schools in the Potomac Valley Athletic Conference. JPDS offers baseball, softball, basketball, football, soccer, cross-country, and track. Participation in interscholastic sports is not mandatory. The school also offers karate, yoga, obstacle courses, kickball, dodgeball, and capture the flag as part of its physical fitness program.

Campus: JPDS is located in Northwest Washington, DC. The facilities include an art room, computer lab, gym, library, science lab, multi-purpose room, and playground. JPDS will be expanding in September 2013 and opening an early childhood facility for students in preschool through first grade. This early childhood facility will be modeled after the Reggio Emilia schools in Italy. It will have a state-of-the-art playground, a piazza, and science and art studios.

Learning Support: JPDS employs two learning specialists to support students with learning differences. The two guidance counselors are also involved in the learning assistance program. The administration meets twice per week to discuss academic issues pertaining to individual students and then touches base with teachers to ensure that a specific plan of action is in place.

Schools Attended by Most Graduates in the Past Five Years: Charles E. Smith Jewish Day School, Edmund Burke School, The Field School, Georgetown Day School, Holton-Arms School

Takeaways: JPDS places a strong emphasis on Hebrew instruction and the study of the Torah. The school instills Jewish values in its students and strives to individually meet the needs of each student. The third grade, for instance, includes three classes but five different math groups, all of which are tailored to the level and learning styles of the students. Further, teachers often combine several subjects in their instruction. For example, art and music are heavily incorporated into math classes. Finally, in the early childhood program, students do have a strong hand in the direction of their education. Once they begin an assignment or project, their level of interest determines how far they will take it. JPDS can be a match for families looking for strong academics with an emphasis on Hebrew and Judaic studies, an initiative to build students' autonomy through self-directed projects, and a strong sense of Jewish pride.

The Kingsbury Day School

5000 14th Street, NW, Washington, DC 20011
202.722.5555 | www.kingsbury.org

"The Kingsbury Center provides a transformative educational and social experience for children and adults with learning differences. The Kingsbury Center includes a day school for students with learning differences and ADHD; and both tutoring, and diagnostic and psychological service divisions, which support the Center and the general community."

Preschool – Grade 12 | Co-Ed
No Religious Affiliation

Enrollment: 210 | **Average Class Size:** 8-10, with two teachers
Admissions and Testing: Deadline February 1, then rolling admission; IEP/ILP, psycho-educational or neuropsychological evaluation, speech/language, occupational therapy or physical therapy evaluations when applicable
Tuition and Financial Aid: $18,500 (Preschool), $38,960 (K-12); financial aid available.

Curriculum: The Kingsbury Day School (KDS) believes that creativity, personal expression, and athletic performance are as critical to a young person's development as academic achievement. KDS is a special education school with an enrichment model approach. By incorporating best practices, technology, student interests, and individual learning styles into every lesson, the school seeks to provide students with a highly differentiated learning environment that will build confidence and a passion for learning. KDS offers a variety of enrichment courses for all students. From Enrichment Clusters to AP Psychology, students can challenge themselves in their specific areas of interest. For students identified as Gifted and Talented/Learning Disabled, the school offers specialized courses. In upper school, students can participate in Entrepreneurial Studies and Innovation.

Arts: KDS offers a variety of art classes including graphic art, photography, and yearbook. In music, KDS offers music and technology, music appreciation, chorus, and instrumental instruction. Students in the lower and middle school engage in visual arts to explore their creativity and boost self-esteem. The study of art is taken to a much deeper level in the upper school where students can explore specialized topics such as computer graphic imaging.

Athletics: Kingsbury competes with schools in the Maryland Independent School Athletic League and the Independent Small Schools Athletic Conference. Students can participate in team sports starting in second grade. KDS offers soccer, cheerleading, kickball, flag football, basketball, tennis, lacrosse, and track and field.

Student Life: KDS's calendar is filled with activities including Grandparents' Day, a Spring Festival, Field Days, music and art shows, student government, and drama.

Campus: KDS's campus consists of a 57,000-square-foot building in the Carter Barron neighborhood of DC. The facilities have designated areas for the center's professional services, which are available to KDS students as well as children and adults in the community.

Learning Support: KDS is a special education school that is equipped to support students with mild-to-moderate learning differences and attention issues. The school is a part of The Kingsbury Center, which provides services in the areas of speech and language, tutoring, occupational and physical therapy, and psycho-educational assessment and therapy.

Schools Attended by Most Graduates in the Past Five Years: Montgomery College, Mitchell College, University of the District of Colombia, Radford University, Florida A&M University

Takeaways: KDS is the oldest special needs school in DC. The school offers advanced courses and an assortment of specialized classes to appeal to students' interests. For example, the school has added a class in the upper school that studies entrepreneurship. KDS has many DC Public School students whose needs could not be met by the public school system. Currently, 75% of KDS students are DC funded. Apart from the day school, KDS houses a diagnostic and psychological testing service and a tutoring program. The psychological testing service employs a team of licensed psychologists who are able to diagnose learning disabilities, social-emotional and behavioral problems, and ADHD. KDS is a good fit for students with mild-to-moderate learning differences and/or ADHD who require a remedial curriculum, an environment that encourages creativity, and a staff experienced in remediating learning disabilities.

The Lab School of Washington

4759 Reservoir Road NW, Washington, DC 20007
202.965.6600 | www.labschool.org

"The Lab School of Washington is different from other schools in extraordinary ways. Lab transforms the lives of students with dyslexia, ADHD, and other learning differences. We recognize our students' exceptional talents, capitalize on their strengths, and use our innovative, arts-infused curriculum to prepare them for 21st century successes. Our non-traditional approach to rigorous, college preparatory academics and strategic problem solving is uniquely effective, earning us worldwide recognition as the leader in learning differences education."

Grades 1 – 12 | Co-Ed
No Religious Affiliation

Enrollment: 340 | **Average Class Size:** 8-12
Admissions and Testing: Deadline February 1; WPPSI-III/WISC-IV/WAIS, WJ-III (1-12)
Tuition and Financial Aid: $37,500 (Elementary), $37,500 (Intermediate), $38,250 (Junior High), $39,900 (Upper School); aid is limited, but available; uses the FAST application.

Curriculum: The Lab School (Lab) pioneered the concept of using art as a gateway to learning and as a springboard to help students manage their learning disabilities and master challenging academics. Elementary and intermediate students explore history, social studies, literature, science, geography, and other subjects through Lab's academic club method. Academic clubs, such as the Industrialists Club, the Knights and Ladies Club, the American Revolution Club, the Renaissance Club, and others, use a tactile, hands-on approach, following one theme throughout the year. The curriculum is rigorous and aims to prepare each student for college and career. It relies heavily on multi-sensory and experiential learning methods and is continually expanding to include the most recent research in the field of education. There is a strong emphasis on ensuring that each student develops his or her executive functioning skills by the start of high school.

Arts: Arts offerings include visual and media arts such as advanced drawing, architectural design, portfolio development, stagecraft, digital photography, documentary filmmaking, film studio and movie making. Lab offers performing arts courses including drama, rehearsal and performance, scene study, Shakespeare, music performance, and music perspectives. Younger students study musical theater, woodworking, computer graphics, and photography.

Athletics: Lab is a member of both the Maryland Independent School Athletic League and the Independent Small Schools Athletic Conference. Lab offers basketball, soccer, swimming, lacrosse, tennis, track, and volleyball. The program is not mandatory and is available to students starting in the intermediate division for basketball and swimming and students continue through junior high and high school. Two-thirds of the student body participates. The girls' varsity volleyball team and the boys' varsity soccer team are both reigning league champions.

Student Life: High school students have opportunities for travel. Recent international destinations have included Costa Rica, England, France, the Galapagos Islands, and China. Students have taken a civil rights tour of Alabama and studied whales in Maine and Canada and endangered sea turtles on the South Carolina coast. Other activities include Model UN, an award-winning debate team, student council, theater productions, and a wide range of clubs. Junior high and intermediate students also participate in a variety of clubs and after-school opportunities.

Campus: Lab includes two campuses. First through fourth grade are located at a campus on Foxhall Road, in a quiet residential neighborhood in Northwest Washington, DC. Fifth through twelfth grade students attend school about a half mile away on Reservoir Road. Among the structures on the Reservoir campus are a building known as the "castle" and an athletic building housing a gym, pool, and weight room.

Learning Support: Lab's teachers are experienced in educating students with learning differences and in integrating innovative teaching strategies and cutting-edge technology into their classes. Occupational therapy, psychological services, and speech and language services are integrated into the program, as appropriate.

Schools Attended by Most Graduates in the Past Five Years: University of Arizona, East Carolina University, Guilford College, Roanoke College, Savannah College of Art and Design

Takeaways: The Lab School was established more than 45 years ago by Sally Smith, who believed in the power of art-infused coursework to engage students with learning differences. The school continues to serve students in Sally's tradition. For children who learn differently, Lab aims to remediate, not just accommodate. At Lab, students are taught how they learn best and how to become advocates for themselves. In addition to the day school, Lab offers a variety of other support services including occupational therapy, speech-language therapy, psychological services, and a lecture series. It is a good fit for students with learning disabilities and/or attention issues who are underserved in more mainstream environments and who require instruction specifically catered to their individual learning styles.

Lowell School

1640 Kalmia Road NW, Washington, DC 20012
202.577.2000 | www.lowellschool.org

"Lowell's mission is to create an inclusive community of lifelong learners in which each individual is valued and respected. Our charge, then, is to strengthen minds, ensure equity, and honor individuality."

---

2 Years 6 Months – Grade 8 | Co-Ed
No Religious Affiliation

Enrollment: 320; **Average Class Size:** 16
Admissions and Testing: Deadline January 10; WPPSI-IV (K); WISC-VI (2-5); SSAT (6-8)
Tuition and Financial Aid: $16,748 (Preschool, Half Day), $26,339 (Preschool, Full Day), $30,498 (K-8); financial aid serves more than 25% of students and requires a financial assistance application.

Curriculum: In the preschool, Lowell employs its Emergent Curriculum: teachers act as facilitators and guides, maximizing children's opportunities for learning and helping them acquire strong foundational skills at a developmentally appropriate pace. In the primary school, language art classes are geared toward developing critical thinking. Math courses up through basic algebra and geometry are taught with a hands-on approach. In the middle school, group work is frequently used to cover advanced topics such as conflict resolution and debate. The humanities program is particularly challenging in the middle school as students study literary works such as *Beowulf*, *The Iliad*, and *The Odyssey*. Spanish instruction begins in the preschool and continues through middle school up to Spanish II.

Arts: The campus includes three studios that are operated by four art educators who are also active practicing artists. Students experiment with printmaking, weaving, drawing, painting, woodworking, sculpture, and hand-built projects. Students also take classes in music, which are supplemented by after-school music programs.

Student Life: The school offers "mini-courses" after school for students. These mini-courses change based on the season. Previous mini-courses have included Markers & Microscopes, Spanish Clubhouse, Woodworking, and Yoga.

Athletics: Athletes can begin as early as kindergarten with the junior track and field and swim teams, and continue all the way through eighth grade. Available sports include cross-country, soccer, kickball, basketball, swimming, track and field, lacrosse, and ultimate frisbee.

Campus: Lowell is home to an eight-acre campus that borders Rock Creek Park. The campus has one main building and two supporting buildings. The facilities include a gym, a pool, fields, a technology lab, two libraries, a woodshop, three art workshops, and a dance studio.

Learning Support: Five learning specialists are available for learning support, but Lowell is only equipped to handle minor learning differences. When necessary, Lowell works with the family to facilitate any additional support and classroom accommodation.

Schools Attended by Most Graduates in the Past Five Years: Maret School, Edmund Burke School, Georgetown Day School, The Field School, St. Andrew's Episcopal School

Takeaways: One standout feature of Lowell is its integrated, thematic curriculum. Lowell strives to develop its students' multicultural understanding, collaboration skills, and sense of commitment to community. Lowell offers students the opportunity to take part in unique opportunities such as the STEM program, which engages students in problem-based units. Lowell is a good fit for families looking for a progressive education with a wide variety of options for extracurricular and after-school activities.

Maret School

3000 Cathedral Avenue NW, Washington, DC 20008
202.939.8800 | www.maret.org

"Maret School galvanizes the intellectual, analytical, creative, and physical capabilities of our students and equips them to excel in future academic endeavors. We join with our parents to instill in each student the self-reliance and moral awareness to develop healthy personal relationships, work through challenges, and enjoy life. In a community that embraces different cultures, interests, perspectives, and talents, we prepare our students to become responsible, thoughtful, and well-informed adults who are able to play an active role in improving the world."

Grades K – 12 | Co-Ed
No Religious Affiliation

Enrollment: 635 | **Average Class Size:** 18
Admissions and Testing: Deadline December 28 (4), January 7 (all other grades); WISC-IV (K-5), SSAT or ISEE (6-11) or PSAT (11)
Tuition and Financial Aid: $28,450 (K-4), $30,850 (5-8), $32,745 (9-12); financial budget over $2 million serves about 20% of the students.

Curriculum: The lower school consists of kindergarten through fourth grade. The program is centered on exploration and students are encouraged to take risks. Students are introduced to mathematical and scientific concepts in kindergarten. The lower school aims to foster a lifelong love of reading and writing in every child and introduces Spanish instruction in kindergarten.

Maret's middle school curriculum helps students to become independent learners and exposes them to a broad yet rich variety of material. One crucial aspect of Maret's middle school program is its social curriculum, which incorporates Maret's core values of integrity, respect, creativity, excellence, connectedness, and joy. The social curriculum includes weekly small and large group meetings, end-of-the-year citizen awards, and a general focus on human development.

The upper school curriculum is rigorous and builds upon the foundation laid in the lower and middle school programs. Students are expected to think critically and analytically. While students begin taking the same general classes in early upper school, they are offered a wide variety of elective options throughout their upper school experience, including Aesthetics of History and Film, Comedy and Satire, Bioethics, as well as many others.

Arts: Students at Maret are required to take visual and performing arts from kindergarten through ninth grade. Maret offers drawing, painting, sculpting, and photography, to name a few. There is a middle school variety show, several upper school performances and musicals, and art shows at all levels. Children take part in vocal ensembles starting in kindergarten.

Athletics: Maret is a member of both the Mid-Atlantic Athletic Conference and the Independent School League. Maret offers golf, cross-country, football, soccer, tennis, volleyball, and ultimate frisbee. Participation is mandatory, but upper school students may also choose martial arts, dance, weight training, or craft a special independent study athletic course. Additional physical education classes meet four times a week and are required for all students.

Student Life: Service learning is an important part of everyday life at Maret. It is integrated into classes at every level, which means that students will embark on service-oriented field trips to enrich almost every subject. Each grade has its own service learning project.

Campus: The seven-and-a-half-acre campus includes two gyms, two libraries, athletic fields, a theater, and three technology labs. All three schools are on the same campus; this is unique in the District.

Learning Support: Two learning specialists are on staff, and Maret offers several enrichment programs for students with learning needs.

Schools Attended by Most Graduates in the Past Five Years: Washington University in St. Louis, Tulane University, Stanford University, Brown University, University of Pennsylvania

Takeaways: Maret offers students an innovative and rigorous college prep program with a school-wide emphasis on critical thinking and creative problem solving. Students can expect heavy homework loads. The teachers are highly trained and participate in the Case Institute for Curricular Innovation and Excellence, offered only at Maret. The Service Learning Program incorporates community service projects into every grade. Further, upper school students receive extensive college counseling that focuses on finding each individual student's ideal school. A major draw for many families is that Maret is the only DC school with its lower, middle, and upper schools located on one campus—a huge convenience factor. Maret is a good fit for a family that is looking for a strong kindergarten through twelfth grade curriculum and a range of extracurricular opportunities.

National Cathedral School

3612 Woodley Road NW, Washington, DC 20016
202.537.6300 | www.ncs.cathedral.org

"We believe in the power of young women and educate them to embrace our core values of excellence, service, courage, and conscience."

Grades 4 – 12 | All Girls
Episcopalian | Protestant Episcopal Cathedral Foundation

Enrollment: 585 | **Average Class Size:** 15
Admissions and Testing: Deadline January 15; EL-SSAT or Primary ISEE (4), WISC IV (4-6), ISEE or SSAT (5-11)
Tuition and Financial Aid: $36,255 (4-12); $2,742,216 in financial aid awarded to 20% of the student population with an average grant of $23,369; accepts either TADS or SSS application.

Curriculum: The curriculum at National Cathedral School (NCS) is rigorous and offers intensive preparation for college. Both the curriculum and instruction are traditional, which, for some families, is a major highlight of the school. Course offerings are diverse, especially for upper school students who have many AP and post-AP classes from which to choose. There is also a wide selection of unconventional classes that focus on specialized subjects and that one would expect to come across in a college course catalog. Foreign language choices include French, Spanish, Chinese, and Japanese, as well as Latin and classical Greek. Religion classes and chapel services are required of students. Lower and middle school students study the origins and history of Christianity and world religions. Upper school students must take a minimum of two semesters of religion classes, which do not necessarily focus on Christianity.

Arts: A variety of arts courses in music, dance, drama, and the visual arts are available to students. There are opportunities to take part in art shows, concerts, theatrical productions, and singing groups.

Athletics: NCS belongs to the Independent School League. NCS offers basketball, softball, crew, cross-country, soccer, swimming, tennis, dance, field hockey, lacrosse, track and field, climbing, and volleyball.

Participation is not mandatory, and students may fulfill their athletic requirements through the school's strength and conditioning program if desired. The soccer team is ranked in the top ten in the area among all public and private schools by the *Washington Post*. NCS has also won recent championships in cross-country, crew, soccer, softball, and basketball.

Student Life: NCS's identity as an Episcopal school and its historic affiliation with the Washington National Cathedral provide an opportunity for students to learn and grow in a spiritual community that honors people of all faiths and values service to others. Weekly chapel services and religion are integral parts of the NCS experience. There are over 30 student-organized clubs, several student publications, an advisory program, a student government, various international study opportunities, and community service initiatives. Student groups have traveled to various locations across the globe, including China, Cambodia, Costa Rica, France, Chile, Argentina, and Japan.

Campus: NCS is part of the 59-acre Cathedral Close, which is shared with St. Albans and Beauvoir. The campus is located on the grounds of the Washington National Cathedral. Facilities include four interconnected academic buildings, an auditorium, a state-of-the-art athletic and fitness center, turf fields, and the historic Hearst Hall.

Learning Support: The NCS Teaching and Learning Center is designed to help both students and teachers succeed in the classroom. At the center, learning specialists work with students to find ways of becoming more effective learners. The center's resources allow students to understand how they learn best in a particular academic setting, and they provide teachers with the resources and training needed to support different learning styles. While the learning support staff is present, the curriculum is rigorous and not intended for students who may need more than minor accommodations.

Schools Attended by Most Graduates in the Past Five Years: Columbia University, Harvard University, University of Virginia, University of Pennsylvania, Yale University

Takeaways: The curriculum at NCS is highly challenging. One of the highlights of NCS is the Coordinate Program with its brother school, St. Albans School: all visual and performing arts classes are coordinated with the all-boys school, which is right next door. Girls in upper grades may also take co-ed classes with boys from St. Albans. The school environment at NCS is a fit for the type of girl who is autonomous, highly motivated, and a self-starter. Families looking for a very strong academic program and the opportunity for a well-rounded education might consider NCS for their daughters.

National Presbyterian School

4121 Nebraska Avenue NW, Washington, DC 20016
202.537.7500 | www.nps-dc.org

"Founded in 1969 as an educational mission of The National Presbyterian Church, National Presbyterian School is a traditional, co-educational elementary school dedicated to educational excellence in an ecumenical Christian environment. A loving and inclusive community, NPS strives to help children develop intellectual, spiritual, and personal foundations that will serve them throughout their lives."

Three Years Old – Grade 6 | Co-Ed
Presbyterian | National Presbyterian Church

Enrollment: 290 | **Average Class Size:** 14
Admissions and Testing: Early January; WPPSI-IV/WISC-IV (K-6)
Tuition and Financial Aid: $15,990 - $23,415 (Nursery), $21,725 - $25,200 (Preschool), $25,425 (K-6); financial aid budget of over $1 million serves about 20% of students; uses TADS form.

Curriculum: National Presbyterian School's (NPS) curriculum emphasizes secondary school preparation and the development of crucial 21st century skills such as collaboration, effective communication, problem solving and leadership. Reading instruction focuses on phonemic awareness in the primary grades and evolves into guided reading groups and group literature discussions. Math is taught with the goal of developing creative and flexible problem solvers who are comfortable taking risks. NPS uses several mathematics curriculums including Everyday Math, Investigations, and Singapore Math. Social studies classes teach students about their responsibilities as citizens and the foundations of our country and other world cultures. Science classes are modeled after the Full Option Science System (FOSS) curriculum, a research-based curriculum that incorporates hands-on and active investigation. Students take Spanish starting in kindergarten. Finally, all students attend chapel each week and second through sixth graders receive religious instruction, which reinforces the school's belief in a Judeo-Christian system of values.

Arts: Students explore various eras in history as well as numerous media and techniques. Music instruction at NPS relies on hands-on experiences and frequent listening activities. Students are exposed to a sampling of musical styles over their academic careers, from Christmas carols and traditional hymns to jazz and opera. The drama curriculum includes performance skills, playwriting, readers' theater, and improvisation.

Athletics: NPS is a member of the Capital Athletic Conference. NPS offers basketball, softball, lacrosse, soccer, and track. The school also offers a mile-run club and summer lacrosse clinics. Participation in competitive sports is not mandatory.

Student Life: Students have access to after-school instruction in art, music, writing, cooking, sports clinics, and even martial arts. Students in fourth through sixth grade can join the NPS chorus and students in fifth and sixth grade may join the handbell choir. Both groups have many performances throughout the year.

Campus: The NPS campus is located in Washington, DC near American University. The facility includes a gymnasium, science lab, playground, and athletic field.

Learning Support: The school employs two reading specialists, one learning specialist, and a math specialist to offer support where needed.

Schools Attended by Most Graduates in the Past Five Years:
No matriculation information is available.

Takeaways*:* NPS aims to provide students with a challenging, enriching education in a warm, positive environment. Unlike many of its private school counterparts which end in eighth grade, NPS ends at sixth grade. The school is committed to making the "decade of childhood" (ages 2-12) positive and memorable. The sixth graders, being the oldest, learn leadership skills that equip them to succeed at their next school. NPS is full of traditions from the morning handshake to the value of the month. The buddy program allows older students to mentor younger children, and the mentor program enables faculty and staff to advise students. NPS is a good fit for families looking for a challenging curriculum, low student-teacher ratios, a strong sense of community, and an emphasis on the development of students' character and emotional skills.

Parkmont School

16th Street NW, Washington, DC 20011
202.726.0740 | www.parkmont.org

"At Parkmont we build a community where students ally themselves with creative adults whose driving concern is their success and well-being. We challenge them with an academic program that fuses adolescent interests with traditional disciplines and respects the variety of their talents and motivations. We provide them with substantial experience in the world beyond school that invites them to see more clearly the possibilities ahead. Our students get ready to chart their own course, and we make sure they're prepared for the journey."

Grades 6 – 12 | Co-Ed
No Religious Affiliation

Enrollment: 65 | **Average Class Size:** 10
Admissions and Testing: Rolling admission; no testing required
Tuition and Financial Aid: $29,800 (6-12); needs-based financial aid is available, and about 50% of students receive aid.

Curriculum: The curriculum at Parkmont is college prep and aims to teach students how to think critically, write complicated essays, and engage in debate. The schedule is broken up into five seven-week sessions per school year. Within each session, students have a daily two-hour Main Lesson that allows students to receive in-depth instruction in a core content area. The Main Lesson topic changes every session. Middle school students have English and math classes every day, and upper school students have math class every day and reading group three times per week, all of which run for the duration of the school year. At the end of the school day, students participate in an afternoon class that may be a sport such as tennis, basketball, or softball, or in creative endeavors such as art, photography, or yearbook. Upper school students are required to complete 180 hours in an internship each year. Spanish is the only foreign language offered.

Arts: Art course offerings include ceramics, photography, visual arts, dance, and drama.

Athletics: Parkmont is a member of the Washington Small Schools Association Athletic League. The school offers soccer and occasionally other club sports. A variety of sports are also part of the afternoon class program, the goal of which is to encourage teamwork, sportsmanship, confidence, respect, and a positive self-image.

Student Life: Students take local and international field trips throughout the year. Recent trips have included visits to Niagara Falls, the National Gallery of Art, Everglades National Park, Chichen Itza, Alaska, Panama, the Grand Canyon, and the Supreme Court. Upper school students spend three hours, twice a week, participating in internships and learning about career opportunities. Recent internships have been at the National Zoo, Tenley Sport and Health, the Washington Humane Society, and Easter Seals Child Care.

Campus: The campus is a large house in the residential community of Northwest DC. The non-traditional school building adds to the school's sense of community.

Learning Support: Parkmont staffs learning specialists who are experienced with students with learning disabilities, ADHD and executive functioning issues, anxiety, depression, emotional instability, and autism. Students have study skills classes, study hall, and tutoring available to them if they need help with homework or organization.

Schools Attended by Most Graduates in the Past Five Years: Montgomery College, Washington College, Trinity Washington University, Towson University, West Virginia University

Takeaways: Parkmont offers a Montessori-inspired environment for students who may have "fallen through the cracks" at a more mainstream school or who are not achieving their full potential. Parkmont is very small and draws most of its students from DC and Maryland. Instruction is individualized, and teachers aim to alter teaching methods on a case-by-case basis to help each child. The three core class model takes a lot of stress out of the school day for students; it is simple and repetitive, yet includes variable and stimulating activities. Students never have homework in more than three classes, which makes developing organization and focus more attainable. Parkmont is a good option for students with learning disabilities or high anxiety who feel overwhelmed in the traditional school system and would thrive in a small environment with simple, solid academics.

Sheridan School

4400 36th Street NW, Washington, DC 20008
202.362.7900 | www.sheridanschool.org

"Sheridan School's mission is to create an inclusive, vibrant learning community. We take joy in learning, show kindness and empathy towards others, embrace new experiences and ideas, and continually seek a deeper and fuller understanding of the world. We seek to inspire self-knowledge, intellectual discipline, and personal integrity in our community members. At both our city and mountain campuses, the Sheridan community challenges itself to live the ideal of respect for oneself, others, and the environment."

Grades K – 8 | Co-Ed
No Religious Affiliation

Enrollment: 226 | **Average Class Size:** 24 (one class per grade) with three full-time teachers in Kindergarten and two full-time teachers in Grades 1-8
Admissions and Testing: Deadline January 18; WPPSI-IV/WISC-IV (K-5), SSAT or ISEE (6-8)
Tuition and Financial Aid: $28,780 (K-3), $31,330 (4-8); 20% of students receive aid from a $500,000 budget; grants range from $2,500 to full tuition; uses TADS application.

Curriculum: Sheridan's curriculum is progressive and focuses on hands-on learning, creativity, and problem-solving skills. The school employs a constructivist approach, meaning that learning is an active, social task and that students are challenged slightly above their current level of development. In language arts, teachers work to develop students' reading, writing, speaking, and listening skills through read-alouds, mini-lessons, small-group instruction, one-on-one teacher conferences, peer editing, partner discussion, and small book clubs. Math instruction centers on Math In Focus and stresses teaching to mastery. In science, students work in laboratories to conduct experiments. The science teachers also coordinate with the school's mountain campus to allow for outside learning. Students are exposed to French and Spanish in kindergarten, after which they choose one language to study.

Arts: Music lessons in violin, brass, percussion, guitar, and woodwinds are free after school. There are monthly art and drama weekend workshops. Sheridan offers a spring musical among other performances. Students in fourth through eighth grade have the opportunity to join the Sheridan art group—Sheridan Illustrators.

Athletics: Sheridan competes in the Capital Athletic Conference. Baseball, cross-country, soccer, basketball, softball, and track are offered for fifth through eighth graders. There are no cuts or tryouts, and all students are guaranteed equal playing time. Most sports have a varsity and JV team for both boys and girls. The program is not mandatory.

Student Life: The school offers an outdoor education program that promotes responsibility, cooperation, awareness, and appreciation of nature. Aside from Sheridan's outdoor education program, students have the opportunity to join different student groups, including student council, literary magazine, and yearbook.

Campus: Sheridan has two campuses—a main campus in the residential part of DC with a gymnasium and a full stage and a mountain campus on 130 acres bordering Shenandoah National Park and Luray Caverns. The mountain campus serves as a location for experiential learning and outdoor activities.

Learning Support: One learning specialist is available to assist with learning needs and tutors are available for an additional fee.

Schools Attended by Most Graduates in the Past Five Years:
No matriculation information is available.

Takeaways: Sheridan's curriculum is rigorous and progressive, and students often move on to competitive schools. The co-teacher model at Sheridan is noteworthy. All homerooms from kindergarten through eighth grade are taught by two lead teachers. In addition, math, science, and art classes are taught by two teachers. The school believes that this model allows for greater differentiation. Sheridan's two campuses offer a number of unique opportunities for hands-on learning, with the mountain campus offering special access to the Blue Ridge Mountains. Sheridan is a good option for a family looking for a progressive school. The curriculum follows the Core State Standards, while still allowing students to both explore in the classroom and participate in outside learning.

Sidwell Friends School

100 Edgemoor Lane, Bethesda, MD 20814 (Lower School)
825 Wisconsin Avenue NW, Washington, DC
20016 (Middle and Upper Schools)
202.537.8100 | www.sidwell.edu

"Sidwell Friends School is an educational community inspired by the values of the Religious Society of Friends and guided by the Quaker belief in 'That of God' in each person. We seek academically talented students of diverse cultural, racial, religious, and economic backgrounds. We offer these students a rich and rigorous interdisciplinary curriculum designed to stimulate creative inquiry, intellectual achievement, and independent thinking in a world increasingly without borders."

Preschool – Grade 12 | Co-Ed
Quaker | Society of Friends

Enrollment: 1,101 | **Average Class Size:** 14
Admissions and Testing: Deadline December 15; WPPSI-III/ WISC-IV (Preschool-5), SSAT (6-11)
Tuition and Financial Aid: \$33,268 (Lower School), \$34,268 (Middle and Upper School); \$6.1 million aid budget serves about 23% of the students with an average grant of just below \$22,000; uses SSS application.

Curriculum: The goal of stimulating intellectual curiosity begins in the lower school where every class is team taught. Students are grouped into teams that include six or more faculty members who act as advisors to roughly ten students. The curriculum at this level focuses on critical thinking, creativity, and good study and research skills.

The upper school liberal arts curriculum urges students to look deeper into content areas that interest them by implementing inquiry-based learning strategies. Students develop their oral and written communication skills through round table discussions, research papers and presentations, and other hands-on learning projects. Students leave Sidwell with a broad foundation in the science and humanities, strong critical-thinking skills, and communication skills.

Arts: Students are introduced to the visual arts and music early in the lower school. At the middle school level, students add drama to their studies, as well as more specialized music courses. All fifth and sixth graders participate in chorus. Upper school students can concentrate on their specific interests in music, visual arts, theater, or dance. A sampling of courses offered includes music theory, acting, and playwriting.

Athletics: Sidwell competes in the Independent School League and the Mid-Atlantic Athletic Conference. Seventeen sports teams are offered. The school has been recognized in its respective leagues for best overall performance in sports. Starting in seventh grade, students must participate in at least one sport season each year. Athletic credit may be gained through other channels, but 75% of the student body takes part in an interscholastic sport.

Student Life: Sidwell offers students various extracurricular opportunities. Clubs at Sidwell are organized around themes such as community service, politics, languages, ethnicity, drama, computers, chess, and debate. Students also produce two school newspapers, a yearbook, and a literary magazine.

Campus: The lower school's campus is spread across five acres in Bethesda, Maryland. The middle and upper schools' campus in Northwest Washington, DC is newly renovated and includes a gym, an arts center with a professionally equipped theater and art gallery, three athletic fields, a tennis court, technology and science labs, and a Quaker meeting room.

Learning Support: The school employs a team of learning specialists and professionally trained counselors. In the lower school, one learning specialist works with students and their families on identifying learning difficulties that may be hindering a student's academic performance. In the middle school, students may work with a learning specialist on areas such as study skills and organization. In the upper school, students are able to work with personal, academic, or college counselors for any assistance they may need. The school also employs a full-time writing specialist.

Schools Attended by Most Graduates in the Past Five Years:
No matriculation information is available.

Takeaways: The curriculum at Sidwell encourages students to explore academic areas that interest them in hopes of instilling a lifelong love of learning. One example of how the school accomplishes this is with the middle school's "minimesters" program: a four-day experience that allows students to work outside of the classroom. The school's Quaker values are evidenced by regular meetings during which students are able to speak freely and openly about a variety of topics. Students call teachers by their first names.

Sidwell has put a lot into developing its global studies program, which includes one of the most well-recognized Chinese studies programs in the nation. Sidwell Friends is a good fit for a family looking for a progressive independent school that emphasizes critical thinking, written and oral communication skills, and intellectual curiosity.

St. Albans School

3001 Wisconsin Ave NW, Washington, DC 20016
202.537.6435 | www.stalbansschool.org

"We set high standards for our boys in all that we ask of them. We believe that classes should be small enough to promote vigorous inquiry, critical thinking, and spirited discourse; that our core curriculum of arts, sciences, and humanities, along with our extracurricular offerings and opportunities for international experience, develops an aesthetic appreciation for and understanding of the world, teaching boys to express themselves clearly, independently, and confidently; that our coordinate classes with National Cathedral School for Girls enhance opportunities and growth for both schools; that required sports teach teamwork, discipline, and lifelong habits of physical fitness; and that a rigorous college preparatory curriculum paired with a creative and inspiring faculty can challenge every boy to realize his potential."

Grades 4 – 12 | All Boys (Boarding option for 9-12)
Episcopalian

Enrollment: 575 | **Average Class Size:** 13
Admissions and Testing: Deadline January 4; in-house testing (4-5), SSAT or ISEE (6-11)
Tuition and Financial Aid: $38,082 (Day), $53,870 (Boarding); $3.8 million financial aid budget serves 28% of students with an average award of $25,000; uses TADS form.

Curriculum: Academics at St. Albans are rigorous in order to prepare students for top-flight colleges. The lower school is a combined elementary and middle school, where each year students take increased responsibility for their own learning. They work independently and cooperatively on a wide range of core programs, with heavy homework loads and long-term projects. The lower and upper schools combine core academic instruction with religious and fine arts instruction and sports. Students receive traditional instruction in the typical classroom setting, using textbooks and handwriting notes; however, teachers incorporate technology in a thoughtful and deliberate way, especially in the sciences, math, and select humanities courses.

Chinese, French, Latin, Spanish, and Greek are all offered. St. Albans has 13 AP classes in all, but many classes offer the AP exam, even though they are not labeled as AP. Co-ed opportunities begin in the performing arts in seventh grade, or Form II, with girls from NCS (St. Albans follows the British "form" style for naming its grade levels). All upper school elective classes are co-ed, as are all junior and senior year (Forms V and VI) English courses.

Arts: St. Albans was founded as a school for boy choristers at Washington National Cathedral; each year 16-20 lower school boys are selected to sing with this world-renowned group. Other opportunities for performance include dance, choral music, instrumental music, and drama. The music program records and publishes CDs of its performers and the theater program is highly regarded. In the visual arts, St. Albans offers classes in painting, sculpture, photography, and ceramics, to name a few.

Athletics: St. Albans is a member of the Interstate Athletic Conference and offers cross-country, football, soccer, rock climbing, aquatics, basketball, ice hockey, wrestling, baseball, crew, golf, lacrosse, tennis, and track and field. Every student is required to take part in the athletics program. Upper school students must participate in 11 seasons of athletics. The program is considered highly competitive, boasting a top-five soccer team in the region among all private and public schools, as ranked by the *Washington Post*.

Student Life: Twice-weekly chapel services are required of all students. While St. Albans espouses an Episcopal identity, students of all faiths are welcomed as part of the diverse community. There are various student-run publications and many extracurricular activities and clubs, including an assortment of political clubs. Several academic teams allow students to compete with rival schools. There are also a number of domestic and international travel opportunities.

Campus: St. Albans is located on the grounds of the Washington National Cathedral. The oldest building, the chapel, dates to 1902; the main upper school academic building opened in 2009. The school has seven buildings, two gyms, an indoor pool, tennis courts, two libraries, athletic fields, and a theater.

Learning Support: To support students in their academic growth, the school has implemented its STAySmart program, which is specifically geared toward helping students improve their study skills.

Schools Attended by Most Graduates in the Past Five Years: Yale University, Harvard University, University of Virginia, Georgetown University, University of Michigan

Takeaways: St. Albans provides students with strong academics and a wide array of extracurricular opportunities. The sense of community at St. Albans is strong. Every day, teachers and students from different grades sit down together in the dining hall, or refectory, for a family-style lunch. Throughout the year, students rotate to different teachers' tables so that each boy can get to know—and be known by—the faculty. Though the majority of students do not board, most students are on campus from early morning until about 6 p.m. Therefore, boys spend the majority of their time during the week together.

St. Albans intends to employ instructors with advanced degrees who are experts in their respective fields. Most classes follow roundtable discussion, and boys quickly learn and develop their critical-thinking skills. The school is a good fit for the student who is self-motivated, academically advanced, and appreciative of the arts and athletics.

St. Anselm's Abbey School

4501 South Dakota Avenue NE, Washington, DC 20017
202.269.2350 | www.saintanselms.org

"St. Anselm's Abbey School seeks to promote the spiritual, personal, and intellectual development of young men with demonstrated academic achievement. Our school, serving grades six through twelve, with its roots in the values of the Christian gospel and Catholic tradition, strives to create a community built on respect for truth, love of learning, regard for human dignity, and tolerance. We pursue this goal by leading our students through a challenging and balanced program of study in the arts, sciences, and theology that gives them a solid preparation for the demands of college. By living and promoting the Benedictine spirit, we strive within our school to create an atmosphere of peace, a sense of service to community, and a willingness within our students to work toward a balance in mind, body, and spirit."

Grades 6 – 12 | All Boys
Catholic | Independent

Enrollment: 240 | **Teacher-to-Student Ratio:** 7:1
Admissions and Testing: Rolling admission; in-house entrance exam required
Tuition and Financial Aid: $23,300 (6-8), $24,300 (9-12); $925,000 financial aid budget serves 40% of students; uses SSS form.

Curriculum: St. Anselm's Abbey implements a classical liberal arts curriculum. All students study Latin through seventh grade and choose to take courses in either Spanish or French beginning in eighth grade. Middle school students take classes in music, art, religion, world cultures and geography, and algebra. A computer class is taken at each grade level and intramural sports are required for one double period per week.

In the upper school, students use college textbooks for most subjects. Juniors and seniors choose from 22 AP classes in all academic areas. Upper school students study Latin, one modern language, and religion at each grade level. In eleventh and twelfth grades, students may choose to study Greek or Arabic. All eleventh graders must take an AP Language and Composition course. Other unique course offerings include: AP

Comparative Politics; Masterpieces of Sacred Music; and Heroes, Rebels, and Exiles in Literature.

Arts: In both the middle and upper schools, the art program forms an integral part of the curriculum. By focusing on the fundamentals of art and drawing in middle school, students are guided in form and technique, while in the upper school, skills are developed further and students are able to move on to advanced studio art, including AP courses. The performing arts program at St. Anselm's encompasses all aspects of music and theater. There are several major concerts each year that showcase the school's performance groups as well as individual students. An all-school musical is presented each year, as well as an upper school play in the fall and a middle school play in the spring.

Athletics: St. Anselm's belongs to the Potomac Valley Athletic Conference and offers 24 teams in ten sports, including soccer, cross-country, basketball, wrestling, fencing, baseball, track and field, tennis, golf, and lacrosse. Juniors and seniors are required to participate in one varsity sport or a suitable equivalent each year. Recent championships include cross-country, wrestling, baseball, and track and field.

Student Life: St. Anselm's offers a house system, with which they organize House Days, weekly intramural sports, and charity drives. Optional clubs are built into the school day; the students have a half-hour period they can use for study hall, free time, or to participate in one of the various clubs offered each year. Club offerings change yearly, but standards include Latin Club, Model UN, It's Academic/Quizbowl, Cultural Student Organization, Jazz Band, Orchestra, A Cappella, and Math Counts. The retreat program is an integral part of a student's time at St. Anselm's Abbey. Every fall, each student in eighth through tenth grade (Forms A through IV) participates in a daylong retreat. Twelfth graders (Form VI) and faculty lead the eleventh graders (Form V) on a spiritual three-night retreat during which they reflect on their spiritual and personal development thus far in life.

Campus: The 40-acre urban campus is located on the north side of the historic Brookland neighborhood in DC. It includes a new gym, a cafeteria, a performing arts complex, four science labs, an art studio, a library, a lecture hall, and a computer lab. The campus was recently renovated in 2008 with new technologies incorporated in many classrooms.

Learning Support: Whenever possible, St. Anselm's offers accommodations to students who need them. A professional counselor is on staff to handle students who need learning support on a case-by-case basis.

Schools Attended by Most Graduates in the Past Five Years: University of Maryland—College Park, University of Pennsylvania, Washington University in St. Louis, University of Chicago

Takeaways: St. Anselm's Abbey is well regarded for its rigorous academic curriculum and successful athletics program. One highlight of the school is its college counseling program. The college counseling staff works with students and families beginning in ninth grade to prepare them for the college admissions process. Due to the challenging nature of the school, students who tend to do best have strong organizational and executive-functioning skills and are often self-motivated. However, for a boy who is looking to challenge himself athletically, artistically, and academically, and a family that is seeking a Catholic education environment, St. Anselm's Abbey is worthy of consideration.

St. John's College High School

2607 Military Road NW, Chevy Chase, DC 20015
202.363.2316 | www.stjohnschs.org

"Faithful to the charisma of St. John Baptist de La Salle, St. John's College High School is an independent, Catholic preparatory school whose mission is to provide a quality education to young men and women from diverse socioeconomic and cultural backgrounds. St. John's is a community of faith and zeal, which seeks to respond to the needs of youth through Christian education. At the core of the St. John's community are dedicated Lasallian educators who are committed to the academic, spiritual, cultural, and physical development of the students. Rooted in Christian values, the Lasallian experience prepares young men and women for a life dedicated to leadership, achievement, and service to the community."

Grades 9 – 12 | Co-Ed
Catholic | Lasallian

Enrollment: 1,060 | **Average Class Size:** 22
Admissions and Testing: Deadline December 13; HSPT (9)
Tuition and Financial Aid: $16,625 (9-12), $19,525 (Benilde Program); financial aid deadline of February 1; application is available on website, must apply to the Archdiocese of Washington.

Curriculum: St. John's offers 17 AP and honors courses. Students take a religion course each year. St. John's English department works with the other content areas to develop students' writing skills across the curriculum. Unique course offerings include Honors Anatomy and Physiology and 3D Design and Gaming Platform. Students who excel academically are invited to join the De La Salle Scholars program. The program encourages students to engage in critical thinking beyond the normal curriculum in subjects such as religion, literature, philosophy, ethics, and the sciences. St. John's offers Spanish, French, and Latin.

Arts: There are eight levels of band that perform and compete throughout the year, including options such as Jazz and Percussion Ensembles. Students interested in chorus have three options from which to choose. St. John's offers three AP art classes as well as electives such as Design, Drawing & Painting, and Ceramics & Sculpture.

Athletics: St. John's is a member of the Washington Catholic Athletic Conference. Offerings include baseball, basketball, tennis, track and field, football, lacrosse, rugby, soccer, golf, ice hockey, softball, swimming and diving, crew, cross-country, and wrestling. The program is not mandatory.

Student Life: Ninety hours of community service are required of every student over their four years at St. John's. Students can participate in many after-school programs such as the school newspaper and the digital media club. In addition, students have the option of participating in the JROTC program.

Campus: The campus consists of 30 acres adjacent to Rock Creek Park. The facilities include a science and technology center, soccer fields, and turf fields for baseball, football, lacrosse, and field hockey. There are two gymnasiums on campus and an art studio.

Learning Support: The Benilde program offers a college prep program for highly motivated students with mild learning differences. The program provides each student one daily period of resource instruction in order to develop skills such as time management, note-taking, and use of study guides.

Schools Attended by Most Graduates in the Past Five Years:
No matriculation information is available.

Takeaways: St. John's can accommodate many types of students, from those who need a little extra academic support to those who excel and need advanced coursework. The Benilde program and the De La Salle Scholars program are both evidence of this. Class sizes remain relatively small despite the school's enrollment of over 1,000 students. St. John's also offers a vast selection of AP, honors, and elective options. For the student looking for a challenging and diverse educational experience combined with a commitment to athletic excellence, St. John's should certainly be considered.

St. Patrick's Episcopal Day School

4700 Whitehaven Parkway, NW, Washington, DC 20007
202.342.2805 | www.stpatsdc.org

"St. Patrick's Episcopal Day School strives to create a diverse learning community of students, teachers, and parents who recognize the infinite value of every participant as a child of God. We are committed to developing character, advancing human understanding, and promoting academic excellence in our students in order to prepare them to live with integrity, compassion, and purpose."

Nursery – Grade 8 | Co-Ed
Episcopalian

Enrollment: 525 | **Average Class Size:** 16
Admissions and Testing: Deadline January 17; WPPSI-IV/WISC-IV (K-5), ISEE or SSAT (6-8)
Tuition and Financial Aid: $25,639 (Nursery – full day, mornings only also available), $29,920 (K-3), $31,401 (4-8); $1.8 million financial aid budget serves 18% of the student body with an average grant of $19,800; uses the TADS form.

Curriculum: Instruction in reading and writing is a cornerstone of the curriculum. The nursery school program includes home visits to each child by the teacher before the school year starts, hands-on science learning, and the promotion of exceptional literacy in the context of a play-based curriculum. The lower school curriculum focuses on the core academics of language arts, social studies, math, science, and Spanish. Lower school children work with a range of specialized teachers in science, religion, art, music, physical education, and technology.

The upper school continues to explore the core academic program. Fifth and sixth grade teachers specialize in an academic subject, so students have different teachers for their core subjects. Accelerated classes are offered in math and language arts. Special classes include Spanish, science, religion, art, music, PE, and technology. The signature program in seventh and eighth grade is an integrated two-year humanities sequence in American history and literature, which comprises the academic core along with Spanish, science, and math. Students in seventh and eighth grade are assigned to advisory groups of eight to ten students that meet regularly during the week.

Arts: Vocal and instrumental music and studio art are important components of the St. Patrick's program. Students experiment with various musical instruments and styles in the music classroom and a wide range of media (prints, oils and watercolors, collage, sculpture, and ceramics) in the art studio. They can also participate in choral and instrumental ensembles. Singing is an essential part of the culture at St. Patrick's—students participate in chapel services, various ensembles, and regular performance opportunities.

Student Life: St. Patrick's provides students with a variety of learning experiences outside the classroom. The selection includes Handbell Choir, Chamber Singers, Reading Buddies, Student Leadership Counsel, and Community Service Club. After-school activities include chess, cooking, dance, art, and fencing classes. Students take program-based field trips beginning in kindergarten, including overnight trips starting in fourth grade.

Campus: Resources include academic facilities on two campuses (Whitehaven and MacArthur) featuring three science labs, three libraries, three art studios, four music rooms, a gymnasium and performance center, a mini-gym for early childhood classes, three playgrounds, and a playing field. Development recently began on the Foxhall Campus. Thus far, a regulation-size turf athletic field has been completed.

Athletics: St. Patrick's is a member of the Capital Athletic Conference and offers interscholastic programs beginning in fifth grade in soccer, cross-country, lacrosse, basketball, and track and field, and intramural programs beginning in third grade in soccer, basketball, and lacrosse. Participation in team sports or conditioning is required in seventh and eighth grade. Students in fifth and sixth grade can choose to participate at the junior varsity level, while seventh and eighth graders compete at the varsity level.

Learning Support: A team of learning specialists assigned by grade level is available to help students who need additional academic support.

Schools Attended by Most Graduates in the Past Five Years: Maret School, The Potomac School, National Cathedral School, St. Albans School, St. Andrew's Episcopal School

Takeaways: The Episcopal school tradition is essential to the St. Patrick's experience, including its emphasis on strong academics and ethical and moral development. Students, families, and faculty and staff are welcome regardless of their faith backgrounds. Another noteworthy aspect of St. Patrick's is its emphasis on the arts and the range of opportunities available to students to explore their artistic expression. Finally, the curriculum is designed to promote advanced literacy and critical-thinking skills—the emphasis on humanities, reading, and writing, and the integration of these elements into the core subjects, is central to a St. Patrick's education.

The school strives to appeal to a broad range of learners, from those who are excelling to those who need some level of additional academic support. St. Patrick's is a good fit for a family looking for a diverse community and a curriculum that emphasizes critical-thinking skills.

Washington International School

1690 36th Street NW, Washington, DC 20007 (Pre-K-5)
3100 Macomb Street NW, Washington, DC 20008 (6-12)
202.243.1700 (Pre-K-5) | 202.243.1800 (6-12) | www.wis.edu

"The mission of Washington International School is to provide a demanding international education that will challenge students to become responsible and effective world citizens."

Pre-K – Grade 12 | Co-Ed
No Religious Affiliation

Enrollment: 920 | **Average Class Size:** 16
Admissions and Testing: Deadline December 20; WPPSI-III (Pre-K-1), WISC-IV, or alternate tests (Gesell, etc.) (2-5), in-house testing (6-11)
Tuition and Financial Aid: $30,160 (Pre-K-5), $33,620 (6-12); $3.1 million financial aid budget serves 14% of the students with an average grant of $18,000.

Curriculum: Washington International School (WIS) prepares students for a global society by teaching through language immersion. Beginning in the lower school, every student is on the IB track. Students take language immersion classes in pre-k and kindergarten in Spanish or French. In first through fifth grade, students may study Dutch, and in sixth grade students can add Chinese.

Beginning in sixth grade and continuing through tenth grade, classes are taught in an inquiry-based approach that requires students to conduct research and dive deep into a subject or particular question. This approach feeds directly into the IB program. Half of all classes are taught in one language (English), and the other half are taught in another language of the student's choice. All teachers are native speakers of the language they teach, and all students leave the school bilingual. There is a heavy emphasis throughout the curriculum on written and oral communication.

Arts: In the lower school, students participate in an art exhibit. In the middle and upper schools, students have the opportunity to act, dance, sing, and play an instrument, in either the jazz ensemble or the band. WIS also has a unique Global Issues Film Festival. This festival is an annual competition where a winner is chosen at the screening.

Athletics: WIS competes in the Potomac Valley Athletic Conference. Baseball, tennis, basketball, track, golf, swimming, soccer, cross-country, and volleyball are offered. The program is not mandatory but highly encouraged as a supplement to daily physical education.

Student Life: In the lower school, students can participate in clubs and after-school activities such as band, choir, student council, and service learning activities. Middle school students have an extensive list of activities to choose from, including the drama club and writing for the school's literary magazine. Upper school students can join clubs such as Amnesty International, the Conservation Club, and the student government, which sponsors dances and fund raisers.

Campus: The lower school (pre-kindergarten through fifth grade) is located in Georgetown and occupies a full city block. The campus offers an information technology center, an art room, a library, a music room, and a gymnasium. There is an outdoor field, both paved and sand-filled playing surfaces, and playground equipment. The middle and upper schools are located on six wooded acres in Cleveland Park. This campus includes seven science laboratories, an auditorium, a theater, music and art rooms, a soccer field, a basketball court, and a library with books in multiple languages.

Learning Support: WIS has a learning resources center with one learning specialist, one reading specialist, and one Spanish specialist. In addition to these individual specialists, there are learning labs and after-school supervised study opportunities. WIS may not be right for a student with language-based learning disabilities because of the strong emphasis on written and oral communication.

Schools Attended by Most Graduates in the Past Five Years: University of Michigan, University of Virginia, McGill University, University of St. Andrews, University of Toronto

Takeaways: The emphasis on language and internationalism is what sets WIS apart. WIS students represent 97 different countries and more than 60% of the students speak a different language at home than the two they speak at school. The faculty teaches the curriculum from a global perspective, which is sensitive to the varied history and cultures around the world. WIS is a good fit for a family that is hoping to instill a global perspective or for a student who hopes to attend university or work outside of the United States.

6843572R00217

Made in the USA
San Bernardino, CA
16 December 2013